DEFIANT
SUPERPOWER

Also by Donald E. Nuechterlein

Iceland Reluctant Ally
Thailand and the Struggle for Southeast Asia
United States National Interests in a Changing World
National Interests and Presidential Leadership: Setting of Priorities
America Overcommitted: U.S. National Interests in the 1980s
America Recommitted: A Superpower Assesses Its Role in a Turbulent World
A Cold War Odyssey

DEFIANT
SUPERPOWER

The New American Hegemony

DONALD E. NUECHTERLEIN

Potomac Books, Inc.
Washington, D.C.

Library of Congress Cataloging-in-Publication Data

Nuechterlein, Donald Edwin, 1925–
   Defiant superpower : the new American hegemony / Donald E. Nuechterlein.—1st ed.
      p. cm.
   Includes bibliographical references and index.
   ISBN 1-57488-948-6 (acid-free paper)
   1. United States—Foreign relations—1945–1989. 2. United States—Foreign relations—1989– 3. September 11 Terrorist Attacks, 2001—Influence. 4. United States—Foreign relations—2001– 5. Great powers. 6. Hegemony. 7. World politics—1945–1989. 8. World politics—1989– I. Title.
   E744.N825 2005
   327.73′009′0511—dc22   2005043115

Printed in the United States of America on acid-free paper that meets the American National Standards Institute Z39-48 Standard.

Potomac Books, Inc.
22841 Quicksilver Drive
Dulles, Virginia 20166

First Edition

10 9 8 7 6 5 4 3 2 1

CONTENTS

FIGURES

PREFACE

In 2001 the United States came face-to-face with the realities of exercising hegemonic influence in a world where no other power currently threatened the country but where a new international entity, the Al Qaeda terrorist organization, was able to launch the first massive attack on American territory since Japan's attack on Pearl Harbor in 1941. September 11 acted as a catalyst for a fundamental reevaluation of U.S. security interests, and the Bush administration put the world on notice that it would confront potential enemies rather than allow security risks to grow. By 2003, however, important European allies rejected what they viewed as America's unilateralism and arrogance in the conduct of its foreign policy. As a consequence, many of them refused to support the U.S. invasion of Iraq, which obliged the United States to pay most of the costs of pacification and reconstruction in postwar Iraq. It was a time when the future of the Atlantic Alliance came into serious question.

This book opens with a discussion of what distinguishes the terms "empire" and "hegemony" in the conduct of foreign policy. It concludes that although the United States exhibits many of the attributes of empire, its actual exercise of political, economic, and military power since World War II resembles the exercise of hegemonic influence rather than imperial control over other countries. Two chapters review the historic changes in American foreign policy that resulted from the attacks of September 11, 2001, and from the Bush administration's decisions to invade Afghanistan in 2001 and Iraq in 2003. Another chapter analyzes President George W. Bush's 2002 *National Security Strategy for the United States,* a document that spelled out in great detail his vision for implementing a more expansive use of American hegemonic power than any previous president had enunciated. Also included are four chapters that examine four basic U.S. national interests: defense of the U.S. homeland, economic well-being of the American people, establishment of a favorable world order, and promotion of freedom and American values abroad. The rising costs of implementing President Bush's vision of America's world hegemony is the subject of one chapter, and two alternative strategies for conducting future policy—collaborative or unilateral internationalism—are analyzed in another. A final chapter, "Limits to the Exercise of Hegemonic Power," examines lessons that may be learned from the Bush administration's conduct of foreign policy since 9/11.

I am indebted to three friends for their valuable help in the preparation of this book: Professor Inis Claude, former British Ambassador Adam Watson, and retired Senior/Foreign Service Officer Eddie Schodt, all residents of Charlottesville. The project could not have been completed without the efforts of my wife, Mil, who once again spent many hours reading and critiquing the manuscript. The final product, of course, remains my responsibility.

Donald Nuechterlein
Charlottesville, Virginia

CHAPTER 1

THE EVOLUTION OF AMERICAN HEGEMONY

Americans have been fascinated with the idea of empire since the country's founding. In 1812 they favored war with Great Britain in order to add Canada to the Union. But British troops invaded Maryland, burned the Capitol and White House in Washington, and put an end for the moment to the congressional war hawks' dreams of a North American empire. Thomas Jefferson had contributed earlier to expansionist sentiment by purchasing the Louisiana Territory from France and thereby opening the West to American settlement and exploitation. By midcentury, after the country had annexed California and Texas as a result of the Mexican War, those dreaming of empire precipitated another confrontation with Great Britain, this time over the Oregon Territory. War was averted through negotiations that resulted in roughly the current border between the United States and Canada. Following the Civil War, the vast Pacific Ocean emerged as the new focus of American expansion, fueled by commercial interests desiring to increase trade in the Far East. By the century's end, the United States had established a protectorate over the Hawaiian Islands, and after a war with Spain in the Caribbean, it annexed the Philippines. That war in 1898–99 resulted in the acquisition of Puerto Rico and in special commercial and military rights in the newly independent Cuba. The new imperialists, led by President Theodore Roosevelt, decided to build a canal across the Isthmus of Panama in order to facilitate world commerce. Congress then approved a canal treaty with Panama in 1903, giving the United States control over a ten-mile-wide strip of territory across that country, to be held "in perpetuity." Completion of the canal in 1914 greatly stimulated world commerce and facilitated the Navy's movement of ships between the Atlantic and Pacific on the eve of war.[1]

ASCENT TO SUPERPOWER STATUS

With America firmly established as a major power in the Pacific and the Caribbean, Theodore Roosevelt persuaded Congress to build a modern navy to uphold the nation's new international status. But Roosevelt's thrust of the United States into the world of great-power politics and his drive for empire produced public opposition in the decade before World War I. An isolationist movement gathered strength in the country, especially among large numbers of immigrants who wanted the government to concentrate on the problems at home. The anti-imperialist mood became more vocal following America's participation in the European war and contributed to the Senate's rejection of President Woodrow Wilson's plan for a League of Nations that would have obliged the United States to help keep the peace. In 1920 Republicans gained control of the White House, and Congress enacted a policy of protectionism and isolationism in international relations that lasted until World War II. Japan's attack on Pearl Harbor ended the isolationists' dominance in foreign policy, and the war thrust the United States into a major role in world politics to an extent far greater than had seemed possible just a few years earlier.

America emerged from the wars in Europe and the Pacific in 1945 as the preponderant world power, militarily and economically. It had exclusive possession of an awesome new weapon, the atomic bomb, the use of which had quickly ended the war with Japan. Europe was ravaged and exhausted by the war. Even Great Britain, which had escaped defeat and occupation by Nazi Germany, found its economy so severely damaged that it was obliged to begin dismantling some of its colonial empire, notably in Palestine and India. President Harry Truman understood the power vacuum that the war created in Europe. But he faced a huge task in persuading the public and Congress that America needed to abandon isolationism and take on a heavy responsibility for creating a new world order that was compatible with U.S. national interests. The Soviet Union, under Josef Stalin's brutal leadership, was the principal challenger for hegemony in postwar Europe, and he used the position of Soviet armies in Eastern Europe and in East Germany to impose Soviet-style communism on governments of that region. Stalin intended to use his power base in Eastern Europe to promote communism and support for Moscow in the war-ravaged states of Western Europe, notably in France and Italy, where the local communist parties were exceptionally strong. In the spring of 1948, Stalin imposed the Berlin Blockade on Western transportation into Berlin in a bold attempt to force the United States, Britain, and France to abandon their occupation zones in West Berlin. The Cold War had started.

A major debate in Congress and the country over the direction of postwar American foreign policy took place in 1947 and early 1948, after Truman proposed what came to be known as the Marshall Plan. This program was designed to provide massive economic assistance to Western European governments to rebuild their economies and prevent local communist efforts to achieve political power through the ballot box. This was an unprecedented aid program that eventually would cost the United States $13 billion over four years, a huge amount at that time. After prolonged debate, Congress enacted the Marshall Plan over strong opposition from isolationist Republicans, in part because Democrats and enough moderate Republicans voted for the legislation. Most had been persuaded by World War II that the United States must not return to isolationism but instead should use its vast economic and military power to ensure that Europe remained noncommunist and in strong partnership with U.S. political objectives in the postwar world. Truman's election victory in 1948 (he had succeeded Franklin Roosevelt, who died in 1945) seemed to confirm that the American public accepted his view that the United States should prevent the spread of Soviet communism in Western Europe. The Republican Party took four more years to abandon formally its isolationist attitude, doing so when it nominated and elected Gen. Dwight D. Eisenhower, a war hero, to the presidency in 1952. American scholar Andrew Bacevich argues in his book *American Empire* that a general consensus formed between Republican and Democratic leaders in the late 1940s around the goal of exercising American dominance in international affairs and that once the Republicans were in the White House, this bipartisan view persisted even into the post–Cold War period.[2]

THE GROWTH OF AMERICAN HEGEMONY

It was one thing to decide that the United States should take a major role in international politics, but it was another to define the nature of that role in policy terms. Both the imperialist policies of the early twentieth century and the isolationism and protectionism of the interwar period were abandoned. Although President Roosevelt believed that Britain, France, and the Netherlands should not resume their control over colonial possessions in Asia, where strong nationalist movements had arisen during the war, President Truman decided not to oppose France's return to Indochina in exchange for its cooperation in permitting a democratic West German government to emerge from Allied occupation and to participate in the Marshall Plan.[3] He also did not object to Britain's return to its colonies in Malaya, Singapore, and Burma. Unlike the imperial roles exercised by Britain and France, however, "hegemony" was a more appropriate term for America's exercise of its power in the postwar period. With the exception of its military occupations of Germany and Japan, Washington did not administer the governments of other sovereign states, preferring instead to exert indirect influence over their policies. This was accomplished through political, economic, and military aid, supported by the presence of U.S. military bases established after 1948 in many parts of the world. This included Britain, France, Italy, Spain, Turkey, the occupied countries of Japan and Germany, and the Philippines, which received their independence from the United States in 1946.

Conclusion in 1949 of the North Atlantic Treaty, which brought together ten European countries plus the United States and Canada into a mutual defense alliance, was the next step on America's road to hegemonic power. This was followed in 1951, after the outbreak of war in Korea, by a series of bilateral defense treaties with countries in East Asia that obligated the United States to come to their aid in case of a communist attack. In the same year, Western European governments, under U.S. pressure, agreed to pool their military resources into a new joint military command that was known as NATO (North Atlantic Treaty Organization). The first commander was General Eisenhower, who had led Allied Armies to victory over Germany in 1945. Thereafter, the United States sent large ground forces to Western Europe, especially to frontline West Germany, and bolstered U.S. naval and air power in the European-Mediterranean region, including highly strategic Turkey, which later joined NATO. This decision to create NATO was prompted by fears in Washington that Stalin might take advantage of military weakness in Western Europe following the outbreak of war in Korea to use the Soviet military presence in East Germany to force the United States, Britain, and France out of Berlin and threaten West Germany unless the allies accepted Moscow's terms for administering that country. The threat of a Soviet attack provided the United States with a basis from which to exert great influence on European governments to accept the presence of U.S. forces in Europe. This included a reluctant France, which later decided (in 1967) to withdraw from NATO's military structure and ask that American forces leave France.

DEFINING HEGEMONY

Numerous writers have discussed the concept of hegemony in international relations. One of the best known is the British historian and former diplomat Adam Watson, who describes in *The Limits of Independence* two different kinds of hegemony. One is "collective hegemony" of the great powers, which impose their will on lesser states that threaten the balance of power among them. This type of hegemony, he says, was the rationale for both the League of Nations and the United Nations and is a type of international pressure that requires a high degree of cooperation among the great powers seeking to uphold agreed standards of international behavior. When relations among the five permanent members in the UN Security Council broke down in the late 1940s, collective action in dealing with the Berlin crisis became impossible. The United States and Britain were then obliged to take unilateral steps to counter the Soviet blockade.

The second form of hegemony cited by Watson relates to a single great power with an economic and military power so superior to others that it is able to exert preeminent influence in international affairs. In a chapter titled "Restraints on Hegemonial Powers," Watson writes: "The United States is much the most influential state in the world today. Its global reach is so great that some Americans and others see it as exercising a 'unipolar hegemony.'" Describing complaints from allies and other powers on how the United States exercises its power, he suggests that this criticism has a restraining influence on U.S. policy makers: "The criticism and resentment acts as a check and balance. It helps to restrain American freedom of action, and makes the United States more willing to act in concert with other great powers." Watson further observes that every hegemony in history has had a negative side and that "only on balance and in comparison with others can we say that American hegemony is more beneficial than most."[4]

Another British scholar, historian Paul Kennedy, sounded a similar warning regarding preeminent power in his widely discussed 1987 book, *The Rise and Fall of the Great Powers*. He argued that all great powers in history rose and declined over time because of the relationship between their strategy in international affairs and their economic capability to sustain an empire. Kennedy's account of the rise and fall of European empires from A.D. 1500 was acclaimed by scholars for its extensive research and excellent writing. But the book generated strong criticism from some Americans who disagreed fundamentally with Kennedy's analysis of America's role as a great power. They rejected his prediction in the final chapter that the United States had reached the zenith of its power, would gradually decline, and then be replaced by another great power, such as Japan or an integrated Europe. Kennedy used the term "strategic overstretch" to describe what occurs when the "political ambitions" of great powers are threatened by a steady decline in their economic strength.[5]

An American political scientist, Joseph S. Nye, Jr., writing before the collapse of the Soviet Union, observes in his book *Bound to Lead* that even though "hegemony" refers to the domination of one state over others, it has been used in "confused ways." Part of the problem, he says, is an unequal distribution of power in the world and the absence of a general agreement on what types of power constitute hegemony: "All too often hegemony is used to refer to different behaviors and degrees of control," he observes, "which obscures rather than clarifies the analysis." Nye concludes that "no modern state has been able to develop sufficient military power to transform the balance of power into a long-lived hegemony in which one state could dominate the world militarily."[6]

These commentaries on American hegemony recall the 1960s and 1970s, when books and articles strongly challenged the wisdom of the United States pursuing a policy of empire. The skeptics reflected the public's disillusionment over the failure of U.S. policy in Vietnam and warned of the dangers of military interventions and strategic overreach. Ronald Steele's provocative 1967 book *Pax Americana* warned of the dangers of taking on security responsibilities around the world for essentially "idealistic reasons" instead of realistically addressing the requirements of the "U.S. national interest." He cited as an example an address of President John Kennedy's in 1963 describing America's international goals: "What kind of peace do we seek? Not a Pax Americana enforced on the world by American weapons of war . . . not merely peace for Americans, but peace for all men and women—not merely peace in our time but peace in all time." Steele warned that "in the eyes of much of the world, America is a nation possessed of an empire of nominally independent client states and pursuing ambitions consistent with those of a great imperial power."[7] A prominent Democrat who expressed strong opposition to America's intervention in Vietnam was Senator William Fulbright, chairman of the Senate Foreign Relations Committee in the 1960s. His widely cited book *The Arrogance of Power* presented a critical analysis of America's hegemonic role in Asia. He deplored the claims of two presidents, John Kennedy and Lyndon Johnson, that U.S. interests in Vietnam were vital and required the use of American forces. "What I do question," he wrote, "is the ability of the United States or any other Western nation to go into a small, alien, underdeveloped Asian nation and create stability where there is chaos, the will to fight where there is defeatism, democracy where there is no tradition of it, and honest government where corruption is almost a way of life."[8]

The failure of the U.S. effort in Vietnam led to a proliferation of books highly critical of the interventionist policies of the Johnson administration, and of President Richard Nixon for not withdrawing U.S. troops more quickly after he became president in 1969. In a 1985 book titled *America Overcommitted,* I argued that the United States was seriously overextended militarily abroad because it had taken on more international security responsibilites than it was prepared to sustain. But I opposed large reductions in U.S. forces and defense spending in Europe as long as the Cold War persisted. Cuts in Asia were feasible, I believed, especially in Korea, once U.S. relations with China had been normalized in the 1970s.[9]

Since the beginning of George W. Bush's presidency in 2001, the term "empire" has resurfaced as a theme in scholarly writing and in the press. One journal, *The National Interest,* highlighted the subject in its spring 2003 issue with a section titled "Empire?" In September 2002 the widely read journal *Foreign Affairs* ran an article by John Ikenberry titled "America's Imperial Ambition," in which he called President Bush's 2002 National Security Strategy document "Imperial Dangers." Arguing that the president's "neoimperial grand strategy" posed a serious danger for American power, he worried that it opened "the oldest trap of powerful imperial states, self-encirclement." Another *Foreign Affairs* article, in November 2003, by Dimitri Simes, was "America's Imperial Dilemma." Simes observed, "Whether or not the United States now views itself as an empire, for many foreigners it increasingly looks, walks, and talks like one, and they respond to Washington accordingly." On the other side, a strong advocate of empire, Robert Kaplan, wrote in a commentary in the July 2003 issue of *The Atlantic* that "it is a cliché these days to observe that the United States now possesses a global empire—different from Britain's and Rome's, but an empire nevertheless." In Kaplan's view, the United States needed to employ its imperial power fully while it remained unchallenged in the world, "because its empire will last for only a few decades."

Three scholars who published books strongly critical of America's drive for empire were Zbigniew Brzezinski, Andrew Bacevich, and Chalmers Johnson. Brzezinski, national security adviser to President Jimmy Carter, argued in *The Choice: Global Domination or Global Leadership* that the United States faced a series of fundamental dilemmas over how it should manage American hegemony and global security—what he called the "Dilemmas of Hegemonic Democracy." He contended that collaboration with its European allies was essential if the United States expected to achieve its large foreign policy objectives.[10] Brzezinski had observed earlier in an article in *The National Interest* that "America may be preponderant, but it is not omnipotent. It will need a broadly cooperative strategy for coping with the region's [Middle East] explosive potential." He argued: "Only by fashioning a comprehensive strategy with its principal partners can America avoid becoming mired, alone, in hegemonic quicksand."[11]

Andrew Bacevich, author of *American Empire*, criticized the cost of America's bipartisan drive for empire, which he argued had inspired American policy makers after World War II, regardless of their party. Even when the Cold War ended, he wrote, the administrations of George H. W. Bush and Bill Clinton continued to pursue the goal of empire in the 1990s. "These policies," he claimed, "reflect a single-minded determination to extend and perpetuate American political, economic and cultural hegemony—usually referred to as 'leadership'—on a global scale."[12]

Chalmers Johnson, in a 2004 book entitled *The Sorrows of Empire: Militarism, Secrecy, and the End of the Republic*, analyzed the dangers of empire for American democracy. He was more pessimistic than most critics of the U.S. policy after World War II, warning that the huge budgets appropriated by Congress over many years for the Pentagon and Central Intelligence Agency, plus creation of numerous U.S. military bases and deployment of military personnel in over one hundred countries, had transformed attitudes in the United States. This was not unlike the situation that arose in the ancient Roman Republic, he argued. Johnson warned that the steady trend toward empire since 1945 had serious implications for America's democratic institutions.[13]

The issue of America's role as an imperial—or, as I prefer, *hegemonic*—superpower was hotly debated in 2002 and 2003 between two principal groups of foreign-policy experts. One, known as "neoconservatives," bunched around Vice President Dick Cheney and Secretary of Defense Donald Rumsfeld. Neoconservatives argued that the United States should employ powerful leadership—unilateral hegemony—in order to reshape the world to suit its own national interests. A second group, known as "conservative realists," believed that the United States should act with allies in pursuing most international security interests and carefully assess the costs and risks of engaging in foreign wars. The realists, among them Henry Kissinger, Brent Scowcroft, and James Baker, who had served previous Republican presidents, worried about the price the United States would have to pay to reshape the entire world to conform with the idealistic international goals promoted by those who influenced the writing of George W. Bush's National Security Strategy document in 2002 (see chapter 4). Colin Powell, Bush's secretary of state in his first term, belonged to this latter group, but his influence on decision making, particularly on the Iraq war, was limited.

THE EXERCISE OF U.S. HEGEMONIC POWER

If one accepts the view, as I do, that empire—the administrative control by one major power over a nonsovereign nation—was not the method by which U.S. foreign policy was conducted after World War II, the focus here becomes the nature and degree of hegemonic influence that the United States exerted over other sovereign countries during the latter half of the twentieth century and into the twenty-first. Figure 1 utilizes a one-to-ten scale to suggest how sixteen crucial foreign policy decisions taken by the U.S. government were viewed by America's European allies. It suggests the *degree of hegemonic influence* that they perceived U.S. officials exerted on them to support American policies. The numeral 1 signifies "benign hegemony," while 10 represents "coercive" power. These scores represent my subjective judgments based on extensive research on how America's major allies viewed the exercise of Washington's hegemony in the years from the end of World War II to the invasion of Iraq in 2003.

Varying degrees of U.S. hegemony were practiced after World War II as a result of America's overwhelming economic and military power and the relative weakness of the major European countries, including Great Britain and France. All the major powers except the United States emerged from that war as defeated states or with severe economic damage, as was the case with Great Britain, the Soviet Union, and China. France had been liberated from German occupation in 1944 and thereafter participated with Britain, the United States, and the Soviet Union in occupying Germany after the war. All European countries needed massive

FIGURE 1
ALLIES' PERCEPTION OF U.S. EXERCISE OF HEGEMONIC POWER: 1948–2003

U.S. Policy	benign 1	2	3	4	5	6	7	8	9	10 coercive
Marshall Plan (1948)				x						
North Atlantic Alliance (1949)				x						
Korean War (1950–53)					x					
Southeast Asia Defense Treaty (1954)					x					
Suez Crisis (1956)								x		
Cuban Missile Crisis (1962)					x					
Vietnam War (1965–73)							x			
Egypt-Israel Peace Accord (1979)					x					
Iran Hostage Crisis (1979–80)		x								
Lebanon Intervention (1982–83)						x				
Cruise Missile Crisis Europe (1983)					x					
Persian Gulf War (1991)			x							
Bosnia Intervention (1995–96)			x							
Kosovo Intervention (1999)					x					
War in Afghanistan (2001)			x							
War in Iraq (2003)									x	

economic assistance; the Marshall Plan represented a major U.S. decision to help rebuild the economies in Western Europe in order to lessen the appeal of local communist parties. Washington brought much pressure—hegemonic influence—to bear on individual governments to collaborate in drawing up a joint economic-assistance plan. This was the first of sixteen cases where Washington exerted its political, economic, and occasionally military influence to shape the decisions of allied governments. The Marshall Plan launched the United States on the path to becoming a world hegemonic superpower.

America's influence was exercised successfully in the 1950s and 1960s through the conclusion of alliances in Europe, East Asia, and the Middle East, all designed to prevent the spread of international communism and to contain the expansionist policies of the Soviet Union and China. The Rio Pact in 1946 between the United States and Latin American states was the forerunner of subsequent defense agreements. Both the Truman and Eisenhower administrations worked closely with NATO governments between 1951 and 1960 to strengthen Europe's defenses and integrate West Germany into a European economic and security system. Both presidents obtained agreement from the United Nations Security Council to defend South Korea and restore its pre-1950 border. President Eisenhower and Secretary of State John Foster Dulles took the lead in 1954 in forming the Southeast Asia Collective Defense Treaty (SEATO), the members of which were Thailand, the Philippines, Pakistan, Australia, New Zealand, Britain, France, and the United States. Dulles was also instrumental in setting up the Baghdad Pact in 1955; it included Turkey, Iraq, Iran, Pakistan, Britain, and the United States. However, America was not a full member of this organization because the Senate was unwilling to agree to a defense pact in the Middle East. Washington participated, however, as an associate member and provided large amounts of economic and military assistance to its members. In 1958, when Iraq withdrew from the pact, it was renamed the Central Treaty Organization (CENTO).

Until 1956 the United States exercised hegemonic influence in a way that was viewed as compatible with the national interests of its major European allies. But 1956 was the year that President Eisenhower forcefully exercised U.S. hegemonic power over Britain and France during the Suez Crisis, forcing them to withdraw their forces from Egypt, where they had deployed troops to prevent Egypt from seizing the Suez Canal. They had kept their plans secret from the Eisenhower administration and thereby contributed to the president's anger and blunt threat to use economic measures against them unless they withdrew. Washington's tough action underscored the reality that neither Britain nor France was any longer a first-class power. The United States thereafter dealt for the most part unilaterally with Moscow and merely kept the allies informed of the negotiations. By forcing two key allies to withdraw from Egypt, the United States demonstrated that it would use its enormous economic power to prevent independent military action by the NATO allies, even when they viewed their interests as vital. During the Cuban Missile Crisis in 1962, however, President Kennedy consulted extensively with Britain and

France on how to deal with this Soviet threat to North America, and he received their full cooperation.

The Vietnam War, which lasted from 1965 to 1973, demonstrated clearly the limits of America's hegemonic power. First France and then Britain declined to participate in that military intervention. In fact, Prime Minister Harold Wilson's government decided in 1967 to withdraw all its forces from bases in Singapore and Malaysia, thus depriving the Johnson administration of the presence of British forces in the strategic southern sector of Southeast Asia while it was fully engaged with the war in Vietnam. America's neighbor and NATO ally Canada also refused to be involved in Vietnam and accepted thousands of young Americans who fled there to avoid being drafted. Australia and New Zealand contributed modest forces to Vietnam and paid their full cost. Contributions of forces from Thailand, the Philippines, and South Korea were largely paid for by the U.S. government through increased economic and military aid.

The dismal failure of American policy in Vietnam demonstrated that even a superpower cannot persuade reluctant allies to support it in war when they do not share its view that vital national interests are at stake. Only a decade earlier the situation had been reversed: in the Suez Crisis, the United States did not share the view of Paris and London that vital interests were at stake in the canal. In the 1970s, because of its failure in Vietnam, the United States found itself in a weakened position internationally. As a result, Richard Nixon and his national security adviser, Henry Kissinger, concluded that an accommodation with Beijing was necessary following twenty years of U.S. hostility toward its communist government. Official relations were opened, and the United States recognized one China with its government in Beijing. This was a reversal of policy toward the Nationalist government in Taiwan, which the United States had recognized as China's legitimate regime following the Red Army's takeover of the mainland in 1949. As a result of this change in U.S. policy, Beijing replaced Taiwan as China's representative on the UN Security Council. Nixon's visit to China in 1972 began a process of opening relations with the People's Republic and culminated in establishment of full diplomatic relations in 1979.

The withdrawal of American troops from Vietnam and the humiliating exodus of all U.S. personnel from Saigon in 1975 weakened U.S. diplo-

macy with the Soviet Union. In 1972 Nixon signed a Strategic Arms Limi-
tation Agreement (SALT I) with President Leonid Brezhnev, but the
treaty failed to diminish Moscow's nuclear missile threat to the United
States. Jimmy Carter concluded a second SALT agreement with Brezhnev
in 1979, but it was so controversial at home that the Senate failed to ratify
it. Meanwhile, Moscow expanded its influence in West Africa (Angola)
and in Central America (Nicaragua and El Salvador) through the supply
of arms to friendly governments. It also concluded a mutual assistance
agreement with Iraq in order to expand Soviet influence in the Persian
Gulf. The reality was that Moscow took advantage of U.S. political weakness in the 1970s to expand its influence into areas where the United
States had previously been the principal power, particularly Central
America. Moscow also strengthened its political influence in neighboring
Afghanistan and in 1979 invaded that country in order to install a puppet
regime. However, the most striking evidence of the decline in America's
hegemonic influence occurred in 1979 when its staunch ally, the shah of
Iran, was overthrown by a revolutionary Islamic movement. It then insti-
tuted a virulent anti-American foreign policy, and later that year Iranian
militants took fifty-two American diplomats hostage and held them
under harsh conditions for fourteen months. President Carter was unsuccessful in mounting an international effort to stop Iran's blatant violation
of international law and its consequent challenge to America's strategic
position in the Persian Gulf. The year 1980 was the low point in America's postwar drive for world hegemonic influence.

President Carter did achieve a notable foreign policy success in 1978–
79, however, when he persuaded the leaders of Israel and Egypt to end
their state of war and agree to a peace treaty based on Israel's withdrawal
from the Sinai Peninsula and from a strip of territory on the Mediterranean. The president agreed to large economic and military assistance to
both countries for an undetermined period. Egypt's decision to make
peace with Israel removed the largest and most influential Arab country
from the coalition that had opposed the creation of the Jewish state in
1948. This was a significant strategic gain for Washington.

When he entered the White House in 1981, Ronald Reagan was determined to restore American influence in the world and force the Soviet
Union to withdraw from Eastern Europe and abandon the Cold War. His

decision in 1983 to install medium-range cruise missiles in Germany, Britain, and Italy to counter similar Soviet missiles in Eastern Europe produced widespread opposition among peace groups across Europe. On the other hand, when Reagan met with the new Soviet leader, Mikhail Gorbachev, in Switzerland in 1985 to begin the process of ending the Cold War, Europeans gave him full support. By the end of his presidency in 1989, Reagan was being applauded by European leaders for a notable success in his determination to end the West's thirty-five-year confrontation with Moscow. When the Soviet Union disintegrated in 1991, America emerged as the world's hegemonic superpower.

In 1990, with the Cold War over, George H. W. Bush took the leadership in organizing a large coalition of European and Arab countries to force Iraq to withdraw its troops from Kuwait, an action that had UN Security Council approval. In the late 1990s Bill Clinton's willingness to lead coalitions to intervene in Bosnia and Kosovo was viewed favorably by European allies, although some, notably France, were critical of America's allegedly arrogant behavior. When in 2001 George W. Bush decided to go to war in Afghanistan, European governments agreed with U.S. objectives and viewed his policy as collaborative. That attitude changed dramatically in 2003, however, when the United States was about to invade Iraq. France and Germany, both of which were on the UN Security Council, refused to participate. France even threatened to veto a UN resolution, effectively killing its support for the U.S.-British plan (see chapter 9).

ALLIED REACTION TO U.S. HEGEMONY

The assessment above of the NATO allies' reaction to major U.S. decisions taken between 1948 and 2003 suggests that for the most part, America's exercise of hegemony was viewed as acceptable because it supported European interests. However, in a number of important cases the European governments, reflecting the views of their publics, were more critical of American policy when it was exercised outside Europe. In the Korean War, Suez Crisis, Cuban Missile Crisis, Vietnam War, and Iran hostage crisis, some European governments, as well as Canada, viewed Washington as aggressive in pressing its policies. Also, Egyptian President Anwar

Sadat and Israeli Prime Minister Menachem Begin experienced great pressure from President Carter in 1978–79 to make peace. It is also noteworthy that European publics and governments were generally favorable to American leadership—even hegemony—when its policies supported and advanced European security. But Europeans were less willing to accept Washington's views when U.S. forces were used in combat in Vietnam and Iraq. This reflected the fact that their national interests were more narrowly defined than was the case for the United States, which had global security interests after World War II and carried out global policies to defend them.

In sum, while the Cold War threatened the security of allies around the world, the governments of Europe, Japan, South Korea, and most Latin American countries accepted a high degree of American hegemonic behavior because their own security and economic well-being depended on strong and dependable U.S. security policies. When the Cold War ended, however, what had previously been considered acceptable U.S. behavior was increasingly viewed as undesirable, even coercive, by certain governments and by large segments of European public opinion. That new view of America crystalized when the George W. Bush administration invaded Iraq without UN approval, causing Europeans to view his policy as displaying the "arrogance of power."

Bill Clinton and Secretary of State Madeleine Albright had frequently spoken about the importance of a multilateral approach in U.S. foreign policy. Their dealings with crises in Haiti, Bosnia, and Timor, as well as their handling of North Korea's missile threat and international environmental issues, were applauded by Europeans and Japanese as appropriate ways for America to exercise its hegemonic influence. But Clinton acted unilaterally in 1998 in ordering missile strikes against targets in Afghanistan and Sudan following Al Qaeda bombings of two American embassies in East Africa. Clinton also launched three days of missile strikes against military targets in Iraq in 1998, supported only by Britain, in retaliation for Saddam Hussein's ouster of the UN arms inspectors. In those cases Clinton's use of U.S. airpower without consulting the United Nations or most allies caused an exasperated French foreign minister to label the United States a "hyperpower." Nevertheless, Clinton's conduct of foreign policy was more acceptable to Europeans than the early policies of the new Bush administration, which rejected a popular global-warming treaty endorsed by the Clinton administration but was unlikely to be ratified by the Senate. Bush also notified Russia of his abrogation of the 1972 Anti-Ballistic Missile Treaty, a move strongly opposed in Europe because it might antagonize Russia's government.

UN PEACEKEEPING AND AMERICAN POLICY

Americans have long been ambivalent about the ability of the United Nations to keep peace in the world after the Cold War began and the Soviet Union exercised its authority to veto Security Council resolutions. As a result, in 1948 a yearlong American-British airlift to supply West Berlin during the Soviet blockade was accomplished without UN authorization. The U.S.-led military operation in Korea in 1950 obtained UN approval only because the Soviet Union had absented itself from the deliberations. Americans have been reluctant to join in military peacekeeping missions under UN auspices unless the operation has a U.S. commander, as was the case in Somalia, Haiti, Bosnia, Afghanistan, and Kuwait. The reality of the post-1945 era was that peace enforcing, as contrasted with peace-keeping, was not effectively accomplished by the United Nations unless the United States took the leadership in organizing combat forces to carry out the missions. On the other hand, when the United Nations did not authorize the United States to use force to deal with dangerous security threats that it viewed as vital, presidents have acted without the UN's blessing—for example, in Vietnam in 1965, Grenada in 1983, and Kosovo in 1999. In the 1970s and 1980s Congress grew weary of numerous General Assembly resolutions that criticized U.S. policies on Israel, South Africa, and even Panama in connection with control of the Panama Canal. Congress voted in the 1990s to hold back part of the annual U.S. contribution to the UN budget until its secretary general made serious efforts to reform the Secretariat's inefficient administration and the General Assembly agreed to reduce the disproportionately high U.S. dues. As American political scientist Inis L. Claude, Jr. observed in his book *States and the Global System,* "Performance as a great power in international politics and in the United Nations has not proved an exhilarating experience for the American people." He saw sharp disagreement among Americans as to whether "they have abused the world or been abused by it." In Claude's view, an illusion has grown up among Americans that the United Nations is an organization that can be a substitute for armed action by the United States in dealing with international crises. He cited Vice President Hubert Humphrey's statement during his 1968 campaign for president that he would reduce America's role in the world and work to equip the United Nations for taking up the tasks to be relinquished by the United States. Claude worried that "the existence of the United Nations now provides a convenient rationalization for the diminution of American responsibilities in world affairs."[14]

The breach in transatlantic relations resulting from America's unilateral decision to invade Iraq caused Americans to reduce further their regard for the United Nations. Although the Security Council's decision in 2004 to take the lead in helping Iraq to hold elections in 2005 and write a new constitution mitigated this criticism, the reality was that most Americans did not see the United Nations as a substitute for American power in times of crisis, when the five permanent members of the Security Council do not agree. The problem is acerbated by the emerging European drive, led by France and Germany, to create a distinctly European foreign policy and to curb what is seen as the unilateral policies of the Bush administration.

In this strained atmosphere in transatlantic relations, it is noteworthy that a British historian, Niall Ferguson, brought out a book in 2004 asserting that the world *needs* an American empire, or hegemon, to maintain order in an increasingly chaotic world. In *Colossus: The Price of America's Empire,* Ferguson is less concerned about America becoming too powerful and more that it might lose its will to exercise a crucial hegemonic role in international politics. "The problem," he asserts, "is that despite occasional flashes of self-knowledge, they [Americans] have remained absentminded—or rather, in denial—about their imperial power all along. Consequently, and very regrettably, it is quite conceivable that their empire could unravel as swiftly as the equally 'anti-imperial' empire that was the Soviet Union." He believes that the real threat to America's role in international politics emerges not from imperial overreach but "from the vacuum of power—the absence of a will to power—within."[15]

Ferguson also observes that the terms "empire" and "hegemony" have been used interchangeably and incorrectly, suggesting that they add up to the same thing: "the exercise of dominant political power." He prefers "empire" because it is closer to what Britain, as a liberal power, achieved in the nineteenth and early twentieth centuries. For the United States, however, my preference is "hegemony" because it implies less direct control over the decisions of other states, even though the outcome in terms of their policies may be similar.

CHAPTER 2

THE IMPACT OF 9/11 ON U.S. FOREIGN POLICY

Americans who were old enough on September 11, 2001, to remember Pearl Harbor, a massive Japanese attack on Hawaii sixty years earlier, knew that American history would be changed profoundly by the bombings of the World Trade Center in New York and of the Pentagon outside Washington. As the attack on Pearl Harbor had sent shock waves across the United States, so the terrorist aerial bombings of 9/11 stirred the country to outrage. In 1941 the public had learned about the Pearl Harbor disaster on their radios, not television, and waited several days before photos of the massive damage to the U.S. Pacific Fleet appeared in newspapers and magazines. In contrast, images of the September 11 attacks were seen live on television as the Twin Towers in New York imploded and trapped people jumped to their deaths from burning rooms. As they realized the magnitude of the disaster, Americans looked to Washington for leadership and reassurance. President George W. Bush, who was in Florida that morning, returned to Washington and addressed an anxious nation that evening. He reassured the country that the government was functioning, that everything possible would be done to help the victims, and that he would find the terrorists who had planned the attacks.

The question for many Americans on September 11, and citizens of other countries, was whether this new president was up to the job of exerting national leadership in a time of crisis. In 1941 Franklin Roosevelt had done so admirably. But Roosevelt had been president for nearly nine years, and most Americans already trusted his judgment. George W. Bush had been in office less than eight months and had become president after a disputed election that had showed the deep divisions in the country. His father, George H. W. Bush, had served for eight years as Ronald Reagan's vice president and then four years as president; the younger Bush, in contrast, was a relatively unknown quantity in terms of leadership. However, unlike many presidents who enter the White House unfamiliar with the complexities of running the federal government—for example, Jimmy Carter, Ronald Reagan, and Bill Clinton—the new president had worked in his father's political campaigns in 1988 and 1992 and understood how political power is used in Washington. Nevertheless, many Americans wondered whether George W. Bush fully appreciated the enormity of the problems he faced as both federal and state governments grappled with the severity of the economic and psychological aftermath of the 9/11 attacks. Many also questioned whether the new president was a serious enough person to lead the country at a time of great danger to the homeland.

BUSH AS WARTIME LEADER

Presidential leadership in time of crisis distinguishes great presidents from ordinary ones. Abraham Lincoln, despite enormous obstacles, provided steadfast leadership to the Union during the Civil War. Woodrow Wilson persuaded a reluctant Congress to declare war on Germany in 1917 but failed to convince the country that the United States should become a guarantor of the postwar peace in Europe. Franklin Roosevelt not only rallied an unprepared nation for war and led it to victory in 1945 but won its support for the new United Nations Organization in 1945 to keep the peace. On the other side, Presidents Harry Truman and Lyndon Johnson failed to convince the country that fighting inconclusive wars in Korea and Vietnam, respectively, was in the country's vital national interest, and both of them retired without seeking reelection. How would George W. Bush be judged by historians for his leadership in dealing with both domestic and foreign policy following the 9/11 disaster?

His address to the nation on September 11 was reassuring. The media gave him high marks for showing steadiness and resolve in a time of crisis. Nine days later, on September 20, he addressed a joint session of Congress and outlined how he planned to deal with possible additional terrorist threats to the country. He recalled that only once before, in 1941, had the United States been attacked without warning: "Americans have known the casualties of war but not at the center of a great city on a peaceful morning. Americans have known surprise attacks, but never before on thousands of civilians." The formulation of a new U.S. foreign policy was contained in these statements:

> This war will not be like the war against Iraq a decade ago, with a decisive liberation of territory and a swift conclusion. It will not look like the air war above Kosovo two years ago, where no ground troops were used and not a single American was lost in combat. Our response involves far more than instant retaliation and isolated strikes. Americans should not expect one battle, but a lengthy campaign, unlike any other we have ever seen. It may include dramatic strikes, visible on TV, and covert operations, secret even in success. We will starve terrorists of funding, turn them one against another, drive them from place to place, until there is no refuge or no rest. And we will pursue nations that provide aid or safe haven to terrorism. Every nation, in every region, now has a decision to make. Either you are with us, or you are with the terrorists. From this day forward, any nation that continues to harbor or support terrorism will be regarded by the United States as a hostile regime.

This speech was a major departure from what the president had said on foreign policy during both the election campaign in 2000 and his first months in office. As a candidate for president, Mr. Bush had campaigned as one determined to restore integrity to the Oval Office, following Bill Clinton's scandalous behavior with a White House intern. He also wanted Congress to enact large tax cuts to stimulate the sluggish economy. He had proposed a smaller and less intrusive federal government but had little to say on foreign policy except that U.S. troops should not be part of UN peacekeeping operations or engage in "nation building." During his first seven and a half months in office the new president focused almost entirely on his domestic agenda in Congress, including massive tax cuts and a federally funded education reform program for the nation's public schools. On several foreign policy issues the Bush administration took a tough stance—for example, disavowal of the Kyoto Treaty on Global Warming, which President Clinton had supported; refusal of concessions to induce North Korea to halt its nuclear weapons program; and a decision not to become involved as mediator in stalled Israeli-Palestinian negotiations to end their conflict. By September 2001, few in Washington guessed that within a few weeks this president would completely reverse his foreign policy priorities by launching a worldwide war against terrorism and assuming the role of a world policeman. Implicitly, Bush had asserted a U.S. intention to be the world's hegemonic superpower.

The president's enunciation of new foreign policy objectives caused critics to question whether he was overreacting by calling for a "war on terrorism." Some viewed the task as primarily a police action to apprehend criminals, not a military operation against states that harbored terrorists, specifically the Taliban government of Afghanistan. It had harbored the Al Qaeda terrorists, headed by Osama bin Laden, for six years. Mr. Bush now instructed the State Department and the Pentagon to prepare for an invasion of Afghanistan if its government refused to turn over bin Laden and other Al Qaeda leaders and close down their training camps. When Afghanistan refused, the United States launched a preemptive war that began with air strikes, followed by the insertion of special operations forces into both the southern and northern parts of the country. The attack in the north was facilitated by opposition Afghan tribal forces under the control of local warlords who formed a grouping known as the Northern Alliance. These hardened fighters, aided by CIA operatives and U.S. air strikes, moved southward at the end of November and within two weeks captured the capital, Kabul. British special forces and Australian commando units joined American troops in southern Afghanistan; these forces soon seized control of the provincial capital at Kandahar and pursued retreating Al Qaeda forces into the mountains on the Pakistani border. Osama bin Laden escaped, but many of his lieutenants were captured or killed. At the end of December, President Bush could claim a major military success in the war on terrorism, even though the task of organizing a new government in Kabul and pacifying the country had just begun.

BUILDING A COALITION FOR WAR

In order to launch a successful invasion of Afghanistan and overthrow its radical Islamic regime, the Bush administration needed the cooperation of the countries in Southwest Asia as well as its NATO allies. European governments, especially Germany, where the 9/11 terrorists had planned their attacks, urgently needed to crack down on Al Qaeda terrorist cells in their countries. But the Europeans' help was also needed to provide security for Kabul and other northern towns in Afghanistan once they were liberated. Britain provided the largest continent of allied forces, but France, Germany, Spain, Canada, Italy, and Australia, among others, participated. The State Department's task was to obtain the cooperation of neighboring Pakistan, which previously had given political and some material support to the Taliban government because of strong ethnic ties between Pushtun tribes living on both sides of the border between Pakistan and Afghanistan. Two years earlier Pakistan's army had seized control of its government and installed Gen. Pervez Musharraf as president. Musharraf was disposed to cooperate with the United States in 2001 against the Taliban government and Al Qaeda terrorists in return for large U.S. economic aid, to which the Bush administration agreed. Musharraf assumed a pivotal role in helping the United States launch its war in Afghanistan, an action that was highly unpopular in Pakistan. In addition, Secretary of State Powell and President Bush obtained Russian president Vladimir Putin's agreement for U.S. planes to use Russian airspace to transport special forces and supplies to Uzbekistan and Tajikistan, both of which had formerly been part of the Soviet Union. Without Russia's cooperation, Washington could not have supported the Northern Alliance with arms or inserted U.S. and British special forces into northern Afghanistan to prepare for the assault on Kabul. In return for Putin's cooperation, the U.S. government muted criticism of Russia's military crackdown in the rebellious province of Chechnya, even though both the Bush and Clinton administrations had previously condemned the operation because of human rights violations. China's government was persuaded not to hinder U.S. plans to attack Afghanistan.

In mid-September the president had ordered Secretary of Defense Donald Rumsfeld and the Joint Chiefs of Staff to devise quickly a plan to invade Afghanistan, oust its government, capture the Al Qaeda leadership—especially Osama bin Laden—and eliminate its base of operations. From a domestic political standpoint, the president needed to show Americans, once he announced his intention to use force in Afghanistan, that he would move quickly to crush the Al Qaeda base of operations. In a series of interviews with *Washington Post* writer Bob Woodward, the president later provided insights into his thinking. In a carefully researched and widely read book, *Bush at War,* Woodward wrote that the president pressed hard on the Pentagon to start the bombing and get ground forces into Afghanistan. He told his national security adviser, Condoleezza Rice, "I have to have a good sense of this time, of when we really are going to be ready to go." The American people had been through a terrible shock, he said, and "I have to know when something's going to get started." Bush told Woodward that Americans needed to know "where we're headed. There was a certain rhythm and flow on this, and I was beginning to get a little frustrated."[1]

European public support for the United States in the aftermath of the 9/11 attacks was overwhelming. Critics in Britain, France, and Germany who had denounced the president for abandoning the Kyoto Treaty now supported his call for an international coalition to crush the Al Qaeda terrorist network, which had been active in major European cities. Many of the Arab hijackers who carried out the attacks in the United States had made their plans in Hamburg, Germany. Other cells were discovered in Paris, Madrid, Milan, and London. When the president declared that he might use force in Afghanistan, European governments pledged their support and offered military forces. There was some criticism that Gen. Tommy Franks, head of the U.S. Central Command, chose not to integrate these forces into the initial invasion force, choosing instead to rely on U.S. and British special forces. Russia provided valuable intelligence support to the Central Intelligence Agency (CIA) and the Pentagon, based on its experience in Afghanistan in the 1980s.

By the end of 2001, just three months after the war in Afghanistan started, U.S. military forces had succeeded impressively in crushing the Al Qaeda base of operations and the Taliban regime. President Bush's prestige at home and abroad soared. Most other governments applauded the way he had built a coalition to win the war. Only in Arab countries and several others with large Muslim populations was public opinion critical of the United States. In several Arab capitals demonstrators even applauded the attacks on the United States as retaliation for its support of Israel's actions against the Palestinians. Nevertheless, Bush was now in a position to exert strong influence on the world to support America's continuing war on terrorism, including, he hoped, his emerging plan to oust Saddam Hussein's regime in Iraq.

CONFRONTING THE "AXIS OF EVIL"

A new chapter in the evolution of the Bush foreign policy unfolded in his first State of the Union address to Congress, on January 29, 2002. In it he sounded an optimistic, bordering on triumphal, tone, in sharp contrast to his somber mood in September. His opening statement was reassuring: "We last met in an hour of shock and suffering," he said. "In four short months, our nation has comforted the victims, begun to rebuild New York and the Pentagon, rallied a great coalition, captured, arrested, and rid the world of thousands of terrorists, destroyed Afghanistan's terrorist training camps, saved a people from starvation, and freed a country from brutal oppression. The American flag flies again over our embassy in Kabul." He also told the assembled legislators and dignitaries that he hoped all nations would "heed our call and eliminate the terrorist parasites who threaten other countries and our own." But he also declared that if some governments remained "timid" in the face of terror, he wanted there to be no mistaking U.S. intentions: "If they fail to act, America will." The assembled leaders of Congress burst into sustained applause when the president thus announced a new policy of unilateral military action against the sources of terrorism.

The most remarkable statement in this January 20 address was Mr. Bush's singling out of three countries—North Korea, Iraq, and Iran—as special threats to international security. He branded them an "axis of evil." The context of this statement was his description of the dangers that confronted the world after the defeat of Taliban and Al Qaeda forces in Afghanistan:

Our second goal is to prevent regimes that sponsor terror from threatening America or our friends and allies with weapons of mass destruction. Some of these regimes have been pretty quiet since September the 11th. But we know their true nature.

North Korea is a regime arming with missiles and weapons of mass destruction, while starving its citizens. Iran aggressively pursues these weapons and exports terror, while an unelected few repress the Iranian people's hope for freedom. Iraq continues to flaunt its hostility toward America and to support terror. The Iraqi regime has plotted to develop anthrax, and nerve gas, and nuclear weapons for over a decade. This is a regime that has already used poison gas to murder thousands of its own citizens—leaving the bodies of mothers huddled over their dead children. This is a regime that agreed to international inspections—then kicked out the inspectors. This is a regime that has something to hide from the civilized world.

States like these, and their terrorist allies, constitute an axis of evil, arming to threaten the peace of the world. By seeking weapons of mass destruction, these regimes pose a grave and growing danger. They could provide these arms to terrorists, giving them the means to match their hatred. They could attack our allies or attempt to blackmail the United States. In any of these cases, the price of indifference would be catastrophic.

The president identified Iraq as the next target of American attention in the war on terrorism, but he included Iran and North Korea in the "axis" because they too had been enemies of the United States in the past and continued to threaten its interests. All three countries were what previous administrations had branded "rogue states." The United States had fought Iraq in Kuwait in 1991; it had been in a quasi-war with Iran since 1979–80, when its revolutionary Islamic regime imprisoned fifty-two American diplomats; and it had fought a costly war with North Korea from 1950 to 1953. All three countries supported terrorism, but there was no clear evidence that any of them had close links to Al Qaeda.

One other statement in the State of the Union address that caused much concern abroad, especially in Europe, was Mr. Bush's announcement that he would take preemptive action against states that seriously threatened U.S. interests abroad: "America will do what is necessary to ensure our nation's security. We'll be deliberate, yet time is not on our side. I will not wait on events, while dangers gather. I will not stand by, as peril draws closer and closer. The United States of America will not permit the world's most dangerous regimes to threaten us with the world's most destructive weapons." Europeans were stunned by the president's declaration of America's intention to exercise unilateral hegemonic power in its war on terrorism.

In his 2004 book *Plan of Attack,* Bob Woodward described the deliberations that went into writing the president's 2002 State of the Union address and Mr. Bush's personal involvement. White House speechwriter Michael Gerson knew that the president wanted an ambitious speech, one that would set out the new rules of the game and the direction he was heading in foreign policy. The term "axis of evil" had evolved from an earlier "axis of hatred" comprising the three countries that the president had mentioned as promoting terrorism and seeking to acquire weapons of mass destruction. The president's deputy national security adviser, Stephen Hadley, questioned whether Iran should be included; it had a democratically elected government, even if real power was in the hands of religious extremists. When he and his national security adviser, Condoleezza Rice, suggested that Iran be dropped, the president said, "No, I want it in." In an interview with Woodward, Bush explained why: "It is very important for the American president at this point in history to speak very clearly about the evils the world faces. . . . No question about it, North Korea, Iraq and Iran are the biggest threats to peace at this time."[2]

The new aggressive U.S. policy caused serious political problems in NATO capitals. The president's enunciation of what some dubbed the "Bush Doctrine" startled European governments and contributed to growing public apprehension regarding an enlargement of the Afghanistan intervention to include other countries, specifically in the Middle East. January 2002 thus marked the beginning of a serious divergence of national interests and policies among the NATO allies. This split reached a crucial stage in early 2003, when Germany and France openly rejected U.S. plans to invade Iraq in order to bring about a regime change.

What lay behind the president's decision to enlarge the war on terrorism and confront Iraq and perhaps even Iran, so-called rogue states that Washington had tolerated during the 1990s? Why was North Korea's reclusive regime made a part of the axis of evil, even though former President Clinton had successfully negotiated in 1994 an arrangement that seemed to curtail Pyongyang's drive to build nuclear weapons? Three factors explain the president's decision. First, he had received alarming intelligence reports that each of them was working secretly to acquire nuclear weapons and become nuclear powers, as India and Pakistan had done in 1999 despite strong pressure by Washington to abandon their programs. Second, the president considered Iraq to be "unfinished business" dating from his father's presidency, when Washington expected Saddam Hussein to be overthrown by his military, following the disastrous war. Also, Saddam posed a continuing danger to his neighbors and to Israel. Third, the administration's success in Afghanistan and the president's high approval ratings emboldened him to believe that he had an opportunity to remove Saddam Hussein, install a democratic regime, and then force Iran's hardline revolutionary ayatollahs to halt their efforts to build nuclear weapons. Iran also supported terrorists against Israel and threatened U.S. economic interests in the Persian Gulf region. North Korea was included because of its nuclear program and the danger it posed to South Korea and Japan.

Conservatives in the Bush administration, led by Vice President Cheney and Defense Secretary Rumsfeld, were determined to reverse what they saw as President Clinton's weakness in dealing with North Korea's nuclear "blackmail" and with Saddam Hussein's manipulation of a divided UN Security Council in order to oust the arms inspectors and have its economic sanctions lifted. His suspected acquisition of weapons of mass destruction (WMD) led George W. Bush to conclude that his father had erred in 1991 by permitting Saddam to remain in power and continue to threaten U.S. interests in the broader Middle East. The UN had sanctioned no-fly zones over northern and southern Iraq, patrolled by U.S. and British warplanes, but this did not hinder Saddam's ability to build or acquire WMD. A personal factor could also have played a part—President Bush may have desired to avenge an assassination attempt on his father's life by Iraqi agents during the former president's official visit to Kuwait in 1993.

PUTTING OFF THE ISSUE OF PALESTINE

A new and dangerous crisis erupted in the Middle East on March 27, 2002, when a Palestinian female blew herself up at a hotel celebration in

Natanya, killing 29 Israelis and wounding 140. Israelis were outraged by a suicide bombing in their own country, not the occupied territories, and demanded retaliation. A conservative government headed by Prime Minister Ariel Sharon was not likely to be intimidated by this escalation of violence, which Sharon asserted had been sanctioned by Palestinian leader Yasser Arafat. He ordered Israeli troops to occupy West Bank cities, which Palestinians had administered for six years, and confine Arafat permanently to his headquarters at Ramallah. Europeans and Americans were alarmed at the escalation of violence and called on President Bush to exert U.S. leadership to stop the killing on both sides. During his first year in office he had taken a hands-off posture toward the conflict in Palestine, focusing instead on domestic priorities and, after September 11, on the war on terrorism. From the White House's point of view, there was little the president could accomplish by trying to resolve this conflict until the two sides agreed upon what could be negotiated. Earlier, in September 2000, Arafat had rejected a generous peace offer by then Israeli Prime Minister Ehud Barak, which had been strongly endorsed by President Clinton. Clinton was aware that President Jimmy Carter had facilitated the 1979 peace accords between Israel and Egypt, and he hoped that his personal involvement in negotiations might do the same. But these efforts failed.

If George Bush had expected to avoid becoming involved in the intractable and frustrating struggle, the March 27 suicide bombing in Israel shattered his hope. Additional suicide bombings in subsequent weeks and Sharon's forceful response raised the Middle East violence to a new level of public awareness in the United States. Dramatic television footage of the carnage caused American and world opinion to demand action, and congressional leaders called on Bush to show leadership. However, dealing with Ariel Sharon was bound to be a challenge. As a former army general, he had long been an advocate of expanding Jewish settlements in the West Bank and Gaza, and of using force against the Palestine Liberation Organization (PLO) in order to force it to accept Israel's demands. As defense minister in 1982, Sharon had ordered an ill-fated Israeli invasion of Lebanon in pursuit of PLO fighters who were harassing Jewish settlements in northern Israel. He strongly opposed the 1993 Oslo Peace Plan, which Prime Minister Yitzak Rabin had negotiated with Yasser Arafat. Now, in 2002, Sharon was Israel's prime minister and controlled its foreign policy and armed forces. He had announced some months earlier that his government would not deal with Arafat, whom he accused of supporting terrorists, and he called on Palestinians to elect a new leader who would clean up the corruption in Palestinian Authority (PA) and negotiate a real peace. By April 2002 contacts between Israel and the PA were at an end.

President Bush took the initiative in a Rose Garden address on April 4, 2002. He adopted a tough line against terrorism, deplored the suicide bombing of March 27, and announced that Secretary of State Colin Powell would go to the region and consult with the various leaders and try to arrange a cease-fire. The president's intent was to persuade Sharon to withdraw Israeli troops from Palestinian cities and start negotiations with the PA under U.S. mediation. Powell saw little chance that U.S. diplomacy could succeed in the existing environment, but he was persuaded by the president that the journey was necessary in order to assuage growing criticism of the administration's inaction. When Powell asked what he should say to the Israelis, Bush replied, according to Woodward's account: "You're going to have to look Sharon in the eye and say get out." The president may have been reflecting on criticism that Sharon had leveled at his administration the previous October—that Bush was repeating the mistakes made by Britain and France at Munich in 1938 by pressuring Israel to make concessions to the Palestinians in order to win Arab support for the war on terrorism. "Do not try to appease the Arabs at our expense," Sharon had declared. "Israel will not be Czechoslovakia."[3]

In his April 4 address the president accepted the reality that he could no longer follow a hands-off policy on Palestine. He called for a regional approach that envisioned a broad peace that provided Israel a security treaty with its Arab neighbors and the creation of an independent Palestinian state that would live at peace with Israel. He also called on Middle East countries to combat terrorism: "Since September the 11th I've delivered this message: everyone must choose; you're either with the civilized world, or you're with the terrorists. All in the Middle East also must choose and must move decisively in word and deed against terrorist acts." For Palestinian leader Yasser Arafat, Bush had this admonition: "The Chairman of the Palestinian Authority has not consistently opposed or confronted terrorists. At Oslo and elsewhere, Chairman Arafat renounced terror as an instrument of his cause, and he agreed to control it. He's not done so." The most newsworthy portion of the president's remarks, however, was addressed to Israel's leadership. As reported by the White House on April 4, 2002, Mr. Bush said:

> Israel faces hard choices of its own. Its government has supported the creation of a Palestinian state that is not a haven for terrorism. Yet, Israel also must recognize that such a state needs to be politically and economically viable.

> Consistent with the Mitchell plan, Israeli settlement activity in occupied territories must stop. And the occupation must end through withdrawal to secure and recognized boundaries consistent with United Nations Resolutions 242 and 338. Ultimately, this approach should be the basis of agreements between Israel and Syria and Israel and Lebanon.

The president coupled these tough words with others that conveyed understanding for the plight of the Israeli people. "I speak as a committed friend of Israel," he said. "I speak out of a concern for its long-term security, a security that will come with a genuine peace. As Israel steps back, responsible Palestinian leaders and Israel's Arab neighbors must step forward and show the world that they are truly on the side of peace." He also voiced his expectations for Arab leaders: "The world expects an immediate cease-fire, immediate resumption of security cooperation with Israel against terrorism, an immediate order to crack down on terrorist networks. I expect better leadership, and I expect results."

In making these pronouncements, the U.S. president sounded the tone of a world hegemonic superpower, one that expected that his words would produce results. Yet, Prime Minister Sharon chose to ignore Bush's demand that he withdraw Israeli forces from Palestinian cities; in fact, Israeli incursions into the occupied territories intensified over the ensuing weeks. Colin Powell's mission to the Middle East was to arrange a cease-fire and persuade the two sides to renew peace talks. But his diplomatic efforts were undercut by hard-liners in Washington who opposed pressuring Sharon. Powell's two-week diplomacy ended in failure because Sharon refused to halt Israeli attacks on Palestinian lands without a complete halt to Palestinian violence. Rumors circulated in Washington that

Powell would soon be forced to resign. According to Bob Woodward's account, Powell told his deputy, Richard Armitage, that officials in the Pentagon and the vice president's office thought he was not tough enough on Arafat and expected too much from Sharon. Powell believed that "no one wanted to step up, face reality. They wanted to be pro-Israel and leave him holding the Palestinian bag by himself."[4] President Bush quickly expressed satisfaction that Powell had done what was asked of him, and the rumors of resignation ended. For his part, Sharon was convinced that if he held firm against negotiations, the Palestinians would eventually realize that violence would not produce results and would oust Arafat. In May Sharon visited Washington and made a strong case to the president and his national security team that Israel should not withdraw from Palestinian cities until there was new PA leadership with which he could negotiate. Sharon wanted to deport Arafat, but Bush opposed this because, he said, Arafat had been freely elected as president by the Palestinians and his fate should be decided by them. Sharon had stood his ground successfully against any negotiations with Arafat.

On June 24, again in the White House Rose Garden, President Bush made public a major shift in U.S. foreign policy in the Middle East. To emphasize its importance, he brought Secretary of State Powell, Secretary of Defense Rumsfeld, and National Security Adviser Rice to the occasion. His remarks focused on the Israeli-Palestinian crisis and were designed to answer criticism in the United States and Europe that his administration was not exercising leadership in stopping the escalating violence. Although his speech was framed in broad terms, the heart of the statement was that no progress would be made on achieving Palestinian statehood until there was a complete halt to terrorism. He agreed with Sharon that negotiations to end the Israeli occupation could not take place until there was new Palestinian leadership that was fully committed to ending terrorism. The essence of the president's policy was contained in a White House news release June 24:

> It is untenable for Israeli citizens to live in terror. It is untenable for Palestinians to live in squalor and occupation. And the current situation offers no prospect that life will improve. Israeli citizens will continue to be victimized by terrorists, and so Israel will continue to defend herself.

In this situation the Palestinian people will grow more and more miserable. My vision is two states, living side by side in peace and security. There is simply no way to achieve that peace until all parties fight terror. Yet, at this critical moment, if all parties will break with the past and set out on a new path, we can overcome the darkness with the light of hope. Peace requires a new and different Palestinian leadership, so that a Palestinian state can be born.

I call on the Palestinian people to elect new leaders, leaders not compromised by terror. I call upon them to build a practicing democracy, based on tolerance and liberty. If the Palestinian people actively pursue these goals, America and the world will actively support their efforts. If the Palestinian people meet these goals, they will be able to reach agreement with Israel and Egypt and Jordan on security and other arrangements for independence.

And when the Palestinian people have new leaders, new institutions and new security arrangements with their neighbors, the United States of America will support the creation of a Palestinian state whose borders and certain aspects of its sovereignty will be provisional until resolved as part of a final settlement in the Middle East.

The president also said that if the Palestinians "embrace the effort to confront corruption and firmly reject terror, they can count on American support for the creation of a provisional state of Palestine."

To the dismay of many in Washington and Europe, Bush had publicly backed away from his tough talk of April 4 and given full support to Ariel Sharon's method of dealing with Palestinian terrorism. He apparently had concluded that it was not politically prudent to pressure Israel for negotiations until the terrorist attacks on Israelis stopped and Palestinians chose new leaders. In effect, the president hoped that moderate Palestinians would find a way to remove Arafat from power.

PLANNING FOR WAR

A major reason that George Bush decided to step back from the conflict in Palestine was that his administration was secretly preparing to use military force to oust Saddam Hussein from power in Iraq. He had instructed Secretary Rumsfeld eight months earlier to work quietly with the commander of the U.S. Central Command, General Franks, to prepare a war plan that could be used when the president decided that force should be employed in Iraq.[5] During the spring of 2002 the Pentagon, with cooperation from the British, quietly built up forces in the Persian Gulf, even as the president told the press and foreign visitors that he had not seen any war plans. Some thought the buildup was a large show of force to persuade Saddam Hussein to accept the return of UN arms inspectors, whom he had ousted in 1998. But the president seemed intent on forcing a confrontation with Saddam that would persuade him to leave the country rather than face an American invasion. Unlike his earlier effort to line up international support for the invasion of Afghanistan, the president now proceeded on the assumption that the United States and Great Britain, under Prime Minister Tony Blair's leadership, would eventually be obliged to act forcefully in Iraq, with possible support from Australia and Spain. Speculation about the U.S. arms buildup in the Gulf alarmed European leaders and public opinion, which opposed using force against Iraq. Most Europeans thought the Bush administration should instead make greater efforts to pressure Israel and the Palestinians to end their conflict before precipitating an armed confrontation with an Arab country. For Bush, however, the conflict in Palestine would remain on the back burner of his priorities until he had forced Saddam Hussein's regime from power.

By July 2002, ten months after the attacks of 9/11 and seven months after the overthrow of the Taliban government in Afghanistan, the United States was in the process of expanding the war on terrorism to include one of the "axis of evil" states, on the assumption that Saddam Hussein had weapons of mass destruction and was seeking to acquire a nuclear arms capability. It became clear later that some officials in the administration entered office in 2001 with the intention of settling scores from 1991 with Saddam Hussein's regime but at the time lacked the pretext for doing so. The 9/11 attacks and the subsequent war on terrorism gave these "hawks" an opportunity to plan a confrontation with Saddam's regime, one they hoped would result in his ouster by his own military.

Whether the international coalition that had supported the U.S. war in Afghanistan would join in another war to topple Saddam was problematical. America's aspiration to be the world's hegemonic superpower would be at stake in the outcome of the looming confrontation with the Iraqi dictatorship.

CHAPTER 3

PREPARING FOR REGIME
CHANGE IN IRAQ

Planning for the ouster of Saddam Hussein's regime began soon after the 9/11 attacks in New York and Washington. Richard Clarke, the former White House official in charge of counterterrorism in 2001, recounts in his book *Against All Enemies* a brief conversation he had with President Bush on September 12 outside the White House Situation Room: "He grabbed a few of us and closed the door to the conference room. 'Look,' he told us, 'I know you have a lot to do and all . . . but I want you, as soon as you can, to go back over everything, everything. See if Saddam did this. See if he's linked in any way.'" Clarke said he was taken aback by the president's words and replied: "But, Mr. President, al Qaeda did this." The president persisted: "'I know, I know, but . . . see if Saddam was involved. Just look. I want to know any shred.'"[1] Clarke was convinced that key members of the new administration were determined to oust Saddam Hussein even before they took office in 2001. He thought that Vice President Cheney, who had been secretary of defense in 1991 during the Gulf War, and Paul Wolfowitz, the current deputy secretary, who had been undersecretary for policy at the Pentagon in 1991, were the principal advocates of war with Iraq and had pressed their views in the National Security Council (NSC) soon after the administration took office in January.[2] The events of 9/11 brought the question of Iraq to a head on November 21, 2001. That is when the president instructed Secretary of Defense Donald Rumsfeld to begin secret planning for an invasion of Iraq. Two months later, in his January State of the Union address, Mr. Bush cited Iraq as part of the "axis of evil."

Iraq had long sought to acquire nuclear weapons, and Saddam Hussein had viewed himself before the 1991 Gulf War as a modern-day Saladin who would lead the Arab nations in a holy war against new Western crusaders, led by the United States. In 1981 Israel had decided that Iraq's nuclear program was so dangerous to its security that it launched a risky preemptive bombing attack on Baghdad and destroyed a nuclear plant that Israeli intelligence had determined was near to producing nuclear weapons. Similarly, in 1991 President George H. W. Bush had launched a war against Iraq to force it to withdraw from Kuwait and to ensure that Saddam did not invade Saudi Arabia and control of the flow of Persian Gulf oil to world markets. Washington hoped in 1991 that Iraq's military would overthrow Saddam's regime, but the Iraqi dictator prevailed and continued his repressive policies against domestic enemies. In 1998 President Clinton signed legislation expanding economic and military sanctions against Iraq, a measure that also called for "regime change." George W. Bush laid the groundwork for another military confrontation with Saddam after concluding, based on CIA estimates, that covert action alone was not likely to result in regime change. The president may also have calculated that removing Saddam would strengthen his hand in dealing with the Israelis and Palestinians in resolving their conflict in Palestine, because Israel considered Iraq to be its most dangerous enemy.

LAYING THE GROUNDWORK FOR WAR

A significant turning point in the evolution of Bush's policy in the Middle East was a major address he delivered to the graduating class at the U.S. Military Academy in West Point on June 1, 2002. He talked expansively about America's mission to uphold freedom and promote democracy in the world: "Our nation's cause has always been larger than our nation's defense. We fight, as we always fight, for a just peace, a peace that favors human liberty. We will defend the peace against threats from terrorists and tyrants. We will preserve the peace by building good relations among the great powers. And we will extend the peace by encouraging free and open societies on every continent." The words were reminiscent of President John Kennedy's ringing pledge in his January 1961 Inaugural Address that "we shall pay any price, bear any burden, meet any hardship, support any friend, oppose any foe to assure the survival and the success of liberty." President Bush now asserted: "Building this just peace is America's responsibility, and America's duty." He added: "America has no empire to extend or establish. We wish for others only what we wish for ourselves—safety from violence, the rewards of liberty, and the hope for a better life."

A major aspect of the West Point address was the sharpening of Bush's determination to confront other states that he believed were threats to vital U.S. interests. This was the first official statement of the administration's intention to employ preemptive military action when necessary to prevent further attacks on the United States or its installations abroad. An excerpt from the important speech, released by the White House on June 1, underlines the president's intent to go beyond his war on terrorism and prepare the country for war with Iraq:

> We cannot defend America and our friends by hoping for the best. We cannot put our faith in the word of tyrants, who solemnly sign non-proliferation treaties, and then systematically break them. If we wait for threats to fully materialize, we will have waited too long. Homeland defense and missile defense are part of stronger security, and they're essential priorities for America. Yet the war on terror will not be won on the defensive. We must take the battle to the enemy, disrupt his plans, and confront the worst threats before they emerge. In the world we have entered, the only path to safety is the path of action. And this nation will act.
>
> Our security will require the best intelligence, to reveal threats hidden in caves and growing in laboratories. Our security will require modernizing domestic agencies such as the FBI, so they're prepared to act, and act quickly, against danger. Our security will require transforming the military you will lead—a military that must be ready to strike at a moment's notice in any dark corner of the world. *And our security will require all Americans to be forward-looking and resolute, to be ready for preemptive action when necessary to defend our liberty and to defend our lives* [emphasis added].[3]

Most Europeans and Americans realized after reading this speech that the U.S. president was not content to defeat the Taliban regime in Afghanistan and oust the Al Qaeda organization but that, in addition, he was intent on using success in that war to confront Iraq militarily as one of the axis of evil states he had identified five months earlier. In July his administration launched a media campaign, including leaks to the press, to alert the country to the danger posed by Saddam Hussein and the need for strong action, including the possibility of military force. There were several reasons why he waited six months after highlighting the "axis of evil" theme to start the public information campaign. First, he wanted to announce his support for a Palestinian state, as a way to persuade the leaders of Saudi Arabia, Egypt, and Jordan to cooperate with his plan to use force against Saddam if he did not leave Iraq voluntarily; although Bush did not achieve a cease-fire between Israelis and Palestinians, he hoped to mollify Arab leaders by pledging to recognize a new Palestinian state in 2005. Second, he needed time to persuade the European allies and Congress that launching a new Persian Gulf war was a necessary course in view of Saddam's continued defiance of numerous UN resolutions to disarm. Third, the president needed time to resolve a serious disagreement within his administration on how to accomplish regime change in Iraq, with the State Department pressing for negotiations and the secretary of defense's powerful staff advocating military confrontation. Vice President Cheney's office often sided with the Defense Department's "hawks," while the National Security Council's staff tried, mostly unsuccessfully, to resolve the conflicting advice to the president.

The Joint Chiefs of Staff and the U.S. Central Command under General Franks had by July developed a detailed plan to invade Iraq and oust its government. The top-secret plan envisioned an invasion by a force numbering more than 100,000 troops during the early months of 2003, when weather conditions in the Persian Gulf would be favorable. General Franks had already expanded U.S. military facilities in Kuwait, Qatar, and Bahrain, with full support from the host governments. However, Saudi Arabia, a participant in the first Gulf War, opposed an invasion of Iraq even though it considered Saddam Hussein a menace in the region. Its government denied U.S. forces use of its bases for combat operations but acquiesced in overflight rights for U.S. aircraft. It also agreed to give noncombat support to U.S. forces if the invasion occurred. Egypt and Syria, two other Arab states that supported the 1991 Gulf War, also opposed an invasion of a fellow Arab state, even though they too had no respect for the Iraqi dictator. Jordan's King Abdullah was equivocal but indicated he might permit his territory to be used. As for Turkey, a crucial country if a northern front was to be opened against Iraq, the Pentagon seemed optimistic that it would be persuaded to join the U.S.-British coalition and permit U.S. ground forces to use its territory for an invasion. Middle East experts were skeptical, however, that Turkey would permit its land to be used by foreign troops. In the end, these experts were proved correct.

Many officials in Washington and in Europe, but not at the Pentagon, believed that if the United States demonstrated a determination to use its military power against him, Saddam would change his policy and allow UN arms inspectors to return. Some thought that a large buildup of U.S. forces in the Gulf would stimulate Iraq's military to oust Saddam, establish a friendly government, and thereby avoid the need for invasion. Neoconservative policy makers at the Pentagon, including Donald Rumsfeld and Paul Wolfowitz, were convinced that nothing short of an invasion would bring a real change in policy in Baghdad, that it was a waste of time to negotiate with Saddam or with the United Nations on this issue.

The campaign to build public support for war began in July with leaks from the Pentagon about the buildup of U.S. and British forces in the Persian Gulf. Prime Minister Tony Blair and President Bush were in agreement, after watching Saddam Hussein flout UN sanctions and after years of patrolling no-fly zones over northern and southern Iraq, that military force would probably have to be used to oust him. The debate within the administration was intense, but, according to Woodward's inside account, the president encouraged debate because it clarified the differing viewpoints he needed before deciding how to proceed. "I'm the kind of person that wants to make sure that all risk is assessed," Bush told Woodward in a private interview later. "A president is constantly analyzing, making decisions based upon risk, particularly in a war—risk taken relative to what can be achieved."[4] Although the president had been telling reporters and foreign visitors that no decisions had been made, Secretary Rumsfeld and his staff were now advising the media that the time had come for the United States to face the reality that Saddam was acquiring

WMD and therefore posed a dangerous threat to the security of the Middle East and the United States.

The internal debate came down to a disagreement on the tactics for removing Saddam Hussein, not the importance of doing so. Hard-liners in the administration had long argued that Saddam was a dangerous threat and that he had thwarted UN arms inspections and the economic sanctions imposed after the 1991 Gulf War. Reports from arms inspectors before their ouster in 1998 showed that Saddam had built a chemical and biological warfare capability, which had by 1998 been mostly destroyed. If he could now acquire nuclear weapons, civilian and military leaders at the Pentagon argued, Saddam would use them to intimidate his Arab neighbors and try to force the evacuation of U.S. forces from the entire Middle East. The State Department argued against precipitous action, and it had some support from members of the NSC staff. This cautious view, enunciated in a measured manner by Secretary Powell, focused on the important need to have allies in Europe and the Arab countries join a coalition to confront Iraq, as they had done twelve years earlier after Iraq's invasion of Kuwait. Powell and others argued that the United States should not operate unilaterally but should instead take its case to the UN Security Council, as it had in 1990, and persuade others to join. Advocates of the go-slow approach had support from key members of Congress who insisted that the president also needed to make his case to Congress and obtain approval before launching a war in the Persian Gulf. Some hard-liners did not think this was necessary.

The media debate reached a crescendo at the end of August with op-ed articles contributed by two former secretaries of state, Henry Kissinger and James Baker, and a third by Brent Scowcroft, the president's national security adviser at the time of the Gulf War. Their cautionary views were aired in three of the country's most influential newspapers and received wide attention. Kissinger argued in a *Washington Post* commentary, "Our Intervention in Iraq" (August 12): "America's special responsibility, as the most powerful nation in the world, is to work toward an international system that rests on more than military power—indeed, that strives to translate power into cooperation. Any other attitude gradually will isolate and exhaust us." Scowcroft wrote in the *Wall Street Journal*, "Don't Attack Saddam" (August 15), that "an attack on Iraq now would seriously jeopardize our counter-terror campaign." He cited the "obsession" among Arabs with the Israeli-Palestinian conflict and observed: "If we were seen to be turning our backs on that bitter conflict—which the region, rightly or wrongly, perceives to be clearly within our power to resolve—in order to go after Iraq, there would be an explosion of outrage against us." James Baker, secretary of state during the first Gulf War, wrote in the *New York Times*, "The Right Way to Change a Regime" (August 25), that although regime change in Baghdad was desirable, the real issue for policy makers "is not whether to use military force to achieve this, but how to go about it." He advocated taking the issue to the UN Security Council and obtaining a resolution that required Iraq to submit to "intrusive inspections anytime, anywhere . . . and authorizing all necessary means to enforce it." Baker acknowledged those who were opposed to involving the United Nations: "Some will argue, as was done in 1990, that going for United Nations authority and not getting it will weaken our case. I disagree. By proposing to proceed in such a way, we will be doing the right thing, both politically and substantively."

CONSULTING THE UN SECURITY COUNCIL

While the public debate raged over how to confront Iraq, President Bush held private talks with Colin Powell and Condoleezza Rice on the desirability of asking the United Nations for a strong resolution regarding Iraq's noncompliance with previous UN demands that it disarm. The president was scheduled to address the General Assembly in New York on September 12, a day after the first anniversary of the 9/11 attacks. Powell had persuaded him that launching a unilateral war on Iraq without asking for UN authority would be ill advised if he hoped to have a coalition of countries to support the war. Powell, a decorated Vietnam War veteran and former chairman of the Joint Chiefs of Staff, cautioned the president about taking responsibility for administering Iraq without the help of allies after Saddam's regime was ousted. "You are going to be the proud owner of 25 million people," he said. "You will own all their hopes, aspirations and problems. You'll own it all." Powell reminded the president that Iraq had never been a democracy, "so you need to understand that this is not going to be a walk in the woods." He urged him to make his case before the General Assembly and thought that most countries would support his efforts.[5] On this Powell was mistaken.

At an NSC meeting on August 16, the question of taking the Iraq issue to the United Nations was discussed. The president decided to go ahead with the plan to do so and instructed his staff to prepare a speech for his presentation to the General Assembly on September 12 laying out the case against Iraq. However, Vice President Cheney was not reconciled to taking the UN route, and he decided, apparently with the president's general approval, to state his concerns publicly. His strong dissent regarding the UN option was highlighted in a speech to the Veterans of Foreign Wars in Nashville, Tennessee, on August 26. Cheney asserted that the risks of inaction on Iraq were far greater than those of action, arguing that "it would be useless, if not a dangerous delay, to seek a United Nations resolution requiring that Iraq submit to weapons inspectors." He said that Iraq had refused to cooperate with earlier UN weapons inspectors who sought to certify that it did not possess WMD and he saw no point in sending them back: "A return of inspectors would provide no assurance whatsoever of his [Saddam's] compliance with U.N. resolutions. On the contrary, there is a great danger that it would provide false comfort that Saddam was somehow back in his box." Cheney warned that Saddam Hussein already had WMD: "There is no doubt that Saddam Hussein now has weapons of mass destruction and that he is assembling them to use against our friends, our allies, and ourselves." Cheney was convinced that "preemptive action" against Iraq was imperative.[6] His hard-line address was designed to reassure the administration's conservative supporters that the president was not backing off his plan to force a confrontation with Saddam Hussein on the WMD issue.

When he read the press accounts, Colin Powell was "astonished" by Cheney's speech; the vice president was now contradicting what the president had approved at an NSC meeting just ten days earlier. The press spent several days speculating about who was speaking for Bush on Iraq policy, and neoconservatives charged that Powell was not following administration policy. In sum, this was a case where President Bush seemed to be pursuing a two-track policy and hoping to keep both hawks and doves in his administration on edge.

A day after Cheney's speech, Secretary of Defense Rumsfeld roiled the waters further by telling three thousand Marines at Camp Pendleton, California, "I don't know how many countries will participate in the event the president does decide that the risks of our not acting are greater than the risks of acting." But, he said, "I've found over the years that when our country does make the right judgments, the right decisions, that other countries do cooperate and they do participate." The defense secretary observed, "It's less important to have unanimity than it is to be making the right decisions and doing the right thing, even though at the outset it may seem lonesome."[7] Rumsfeld's speech added to the confusion in Washington about who spoke for the president.

Another issue that received media attention in August was the administration's tentative claim that it was not necessary to obtain a new authorization from Congress for the use of force in Iraq. White House lawyers concluded that Congress's authorization in 1991 for the use of force to disarm Iraq remained in effect and would cover a new presidential order. The claim got a swift reaction from Capitol Hill, where both Republican and Democratic leaders counseled the White House to seek congressional approval for any military action in Iraq. The White House soon passed the word to reporters that the president was prepared to ask Congress for a resolution of support, even though it might not be legally required. As the first anniversary of September 11, 2001, approached, the president decided not only to seek a strong UN resolution to resume arms inspections in Iraq but also to challenge the United Nations. Meanwhile, he continued to assert that no final decision about the use of force had been made, even though military plans for doing so were far advanced. For the moment, Bush was willing to try returning the UN inspectors to Iraq even though press reports showed that the military buildup in the Persian Gulf was progressing at a rapid rate. This led skeptics to wonder whether Bush actually believed that war with Iraq could be avoided. Divisions within the administration did not dissipate as Bush's speechwriters worked on details of his address before the General Assembly.

The confusion in Washington over the president's intentions toward Iraq, the United Nations, and the European allies caused a political firestorm in Europe. This was especially so in Germany, where Chancellor Gerhard Schroeder faced a close election within a few weeks. A day after Cheney's tough Nashville speech, Schroeder declared publicly that Germany would not support a war in Iraq, even if the United Nations approved. Schroeder thought he had been assured by Washington that U.S. policy at the United Nations would not go beyond demanding the return of arms inspectors. Cheney's blunt dismissal of inspections and his call for action alarmed the Germans, and it also startled the British and French governments. They called on the Bush administration to work through the United Nations and not to pursue a unilateral policy on Iraq. On September 5 the *New York Times* carried a front-page story and an extensive interview with Schroeder entitled "German Leader's Warning: War Plan Is a Huge Mistake." It quoted him as predicting, "No one has a clear idea about what the effect would be." He felt that a new war in the Middle East would put at risk all that had been gained so far in the unfinished battle against Al Qaeda and would be a "terrible mistake." Critics in Washington charged that Schroeder was jeopardizing Germany's close relationship with its American ally in order to gain a few votes in the upcoming elections. However, the reality was that German public opinion was strongly opposed to Bush's war plans, and Schroeder's stand turned enough antiwar votes to the governing coalition's parties to give them a very close victory in the election. Schroeder remained as Germany's chancellor, to the disappointment of the Bush White House.

BUSH CHALLENGES THE UNITED NATIONS AND CONGRESS

George Bush's speech before the General Assembly on September 12 was viewed by most media pundits as a masterful attempt to make the case that Saddam Hussein had repeatedly violated previous UN resolutions and that unless the international body acted promptly to enforce its instructions it would, like the League of Nations, become "irrelevant." Speaking of Saddam's duplicity in dealing with arms inspectors, the president asserted: "He has proven . . . his contempt for the United Nations, and for all his pledges. By breaking every pledge—by his deceptions, and by his cruelties—Saddam Hussein has made the case against himself."

Mr. Bush also assured assembled members that "America stands committed to an independent and democratic Palestine, living side by side with Israel in peace and security." The key part of his address called for UN action on Iraq:

> My nation will work with the U.N. Security Council to meet our common challenge. If Iraq's regime defies us again, the world must move deliberately, decisively to hold Iraq to account. We will work with the U.N. Security Council for the necessary resolutions. But the purposes of the United States should not be doubted. The Security Council resolutions will be enforced—the just demands of peace and security will be met—or action will be unavoidable. And a regime that has lost its legitimacy will also lose its power. Events can turn in one of two ways: If we fail to act in the face of danger, the people of Iraq will continue to live in brutal submission. The regime will have new power to bully and dominate and conquer its neighbors, condemning the Middle East to more years of bloodshed and fear. The regime will remain unstable—the region will remain unstable, with little hope of freedom, and isolated from the progress of our times. With every step the Iraqi regime takes toward gaining and deploying the most terrible weapons, our own options to confront that regime will narrow. And if an emboldened regime were to supply these weapons to terrorist allies, then the attacks of September the 11th would be a prelude to far greater horrors.
>
> If we meet our responsibilities, if we overcome this danger, we can arrive at a very different future. The people of Iraq can shake off their captivity. They can one day join a democratic Afghanistan and a democratic Palestine, inspiring reforms throughout the Muslim world. These nations can show by their example that honest government, and respect for women, and the great Islamic tradition of learning can triumph in the Middle East and beyond. And we will show that the promise of the United Nations can be fulfilled in our time.[8]

The president's remarks were well received by many in Europe and other regions, but Muslim countries, especially the Arab states, were skeptical if not scornful. Still, the president accomplished what Secretary Powell, many influential Republicans, and the British and French governments had urged him to do. Even though he remained unconvinced that the UN Security Council would heed his call for tough action on inspections, the president had given the world body and the arms inspectors time to demonstrate what they could accomplish without the use of force on Iraq. Meanwhile, American and British troops assembled in growing numbers at bases in the Persian Gulf.

Soon after Bush's September 12 appeal to the United Nations, the administration launched a concerted campaign to obtain congressional authority for military action if new UN efforts to disarm Iraq failed. The White House calculated that if Congress provided the president with a strong vote of support for a war measure, this would help Secretary Powell's efforts to convince other members of the Security Council to support a tough resolution warning Saddam of strong action if he did not submit to UN demands. The White House believed it would be easier to get approval from the House of Representatives, where Republicans held a slim majority, than in the Senate, where Democrats had a bare majority. Although most House Democrats strongly opposed a war resolution, the party's unity on this issue was broken when Representative Richard Gephardt of Missouri, the party's House leader, announced his support for the resolution. In 1991 Gephardt had voted against a similar measure that authorized President George H. W. Bush to use force in the Gulf War, but he now declared, "September 11 had made all the difference." Saddam Hussein had to be prevented, he said, from developing WMD and that "events of that tragic day jolted us to the enduring reality that terrorists not only seek to attack our interests abroad, but to strike us here at home."[9]

The final vote in the House of Representatives was 296 in favor and 133 opposed. A majority of Democrats, 126 to 81, voted against the resolution, most of them from districts in the Northeast, the West Coast, and large urban centers. Richard Gephardt came under strong criticism from his party for joining the Republicans and appearing later with President Bush in the Rose Garden. He subsequently stepped down as House minority leader and was replaced by a vocal opponent of the war measure, Nancy Pelosi of California. A few weeks later Gephardt announced that he would run for president in 2004.

The Senate's debate lasted a week; a filibuster was averted only when cloture was eventually voted. The final outcome was not in doubt, however—seventy-seven in favor and twenty-three opposed. That represented more than a three-fourths majority of the Senate, a resounding victory for the president. One of the most vocal opponents was Robert Byrd of West Virginia, who warned Congress against turning over its authority on matters of war and peace to the president. Other senior senators who joined him in opposition were Carl Levin of Michigan, chairman of the Armed Service Committee; Edward Kennedy of Massachusetts; and Bob Graham of Florida. Among Democrats voting for the war measure were several who had presidential aspirations, including John Kerry of Massachusetts, Joseph Lieberman of Connecticut, Joseph Biden of Delaware, and John Edwards of North Carolina. Hillary Clinton of New York, a possible candidate for the White House, also voted for the resolution. Democratic Majority Leader Tom Daschle of South Dakota reluctantly said yes after expressing serious misgivings about granting the president sweeping authority to take the nation to war. Some senators recalled regretfully the 1964 Tonkin Gulf Resolution, which had given President Lyndon Johnson authority to wage war in Southeast Asia.

The war resolution on Iraq, approved by the House on October 10 and the Senate on October 11, contained this key language: "The president is authorized to use the armed forces of the United States as he determines to be necessary and appropriate in order to: (1) defend the national security of the United States against the continuing threat posed by Iraq; and (2) enforce all relevant United Nations Security Council resolutions regarding Iraq." A section of the resolution titled "War Powers Resolution Requirements" stated: "Consistent with section 8(a)(1) of the War Powers Resolution, the Congress declares that this section is intended to constitute specific statutory authorization within the meaning of section 5(b)."[10] It was clear from this language that the president was granted firm legal authority to act unilaterally against Iraq if, in his judgment, it failed to comply with all UN resolutions regarding disarmament.[11] President Bush greeted the votes with great pleasure: "With tonight's vote in the United States Senate, America speaks with one voice."

Armed with firm congressional support for war, the president was in a strong position to press his case, that the Security Council should vote on a new tough resolution on Iraq threatening force if Saddam Hussein failed to comply fully with arms inspections. The *New York Times* quoted an unnamed "senior administration official" as saying of the Senate vote: "Right now we have accomplished what we had to do to take action we need to take, and we don't need the Security Council. So, if the Security Council wants to stay relevant, then it has to give us similar authority."[12] The paper also reported that some Security Council members acknowledged privately that the vote on Capitol Hill put obvious pressure on them "to bend to the will of the Bush administration" and support a single resolution. But France was insisting that there should be two separate resolutions, one to send the arms inspectors back to Iraq and a second to decide what to do if Saddam interfered with their mission. With the strong congressional resolution in his hand, however, President Bush had the legal authority to ignore a second Security Council deliberation if he chose to attack Iraq. In reality, Mr. Bush could legally launch an invasion of Iraq without the UN's blessing; the political question for him was whether it would be wise to do so. On that point, the deep divisions in the administration that had been aired publicly in August continued into the autumn.

On November 8, following seven weeks of painstaking negotiations in New York, Secretary Powell got a unanimous vote in the Security Council for a resolution to send the weapons inspectors back to Iraq, with full authority to search for prohibited weapons and carrying a warning to Saddam that he would face "strong consequences" if he did not comply. As American and British troops massed in the Persian Gulf for an invasion, George Bush had much reason to feel satisfaction that his decision to go to the United Nations had produced a consensus there for serious measures to force Iraq to comply with its resolutions. The White House believed it now had the momentum for a showdown with Saddam Hussein that would result in either his overthrow or an invasion by American and British troops to oust him.

Political observers raised two important questions about President Bush's tactics in this process. The first involved his motivation in supporting Colin Powell's recommendation that he seek the UN's blessing before going to war; the second was whether the president would agree with key allies on the Security Council, specifically France and Russia, that weapons inspectors should be given all the time they needed in order to verify whether Saddam had destroyed his WMD. Skeptics wondered whether the president had already decided to use force and was simply waiting for the military buildup in Kuwait, Qatar, and elsewhere in the Gulf to be completed and then launch an attack in early 2003 when the weather in Iraq was most favorable. Before the U.S.-led invasion was launched in March 2003, it can reasonably be argued, the president had already concluded that he was unlikely to receive French and German support for war no matter what the inspectors found, and that he would in the end have to invade Iraq without the UN's support but with a coalition consisting of Britain, Spain, Australia, and a few others. It is also reasonable to conclude that if Bush had not accepted Powell's advice to take his case to the United Nations, he would have had serious difficulty persuading Congress to pass its war resolution and obtaining British support. The president appreciated that Prime Minister Blair was under intense pressure in his Labour Party to reject war and that this was why he had urged the president to seek United Nations approval.

My conclusion is that George Bush was reasonably certain already in June 2002 that an invasion of Iraq was his only means to achieve Saddam Hussein's ouster. But in order to build American and international support for that eventuality, it was necessary to go through the process of consulting with the United Nations, even though he was aware that France and Germany would use their influence to block a resolution to use force. The preparations for war showed that the administration had skillfully laid the political groundwork, first persuading Congress to grant it authority to act unilaterally if necessary, then, through Colin Powell's diplomacy, inducing the skeptical Security Council to vote unanimously to threaten Saddam Hussein with serious action if he did not comply with arms inspections. However, Powell had failed to convince France, Germany, or Russia, key members of the council, to authorize the use of force if Saddam Hussein did not comply. There existed a critical gap between the view of major European governments, led by France, that no time limit should be imposed on the inspectors to complete their work, and the American-British position that unless Saddam complied promptly with the weapons inspectors' demands, the international community could use force without a second UN vote. In this crucial situation, America's assertion of hegemonic influence on its allies in Europe and friendly governments in the Middle East was rejected. The seeds of a split in the Atlantic Alliance were planted.

CHAPTER 4

REDEFINING U.S. GLOBAL INTERESTS: THE CASE OF IRAQ

One year after the 9/11 attacks and just ten days after President Bush delivered his address at the United Nations, the White House published a remarkable presidential document entitled "The National Security Strategy of the United States of America." This thirty-one-page blueprint of the president's vision of America's role in the world startled many in Washington, in the capitals of Europe and elsewhere. The boldly crafted redefinition of U.S. national interests put America's adversaries on notice that the United States intended to take whatever measures the president found necessary to deal with international terrorists and the governments that harbored them. It gave warning to states that aspired to obtain WMD, in order to intimidate their neighbors and the United States, that they would be confronted with the full range of U.S. policy options, including military force. To impress leaders of rival powers who might be tempted to contest America's hegemonic aspirations, the president reiterated his plan to increase U.S. military superiority over any potential enemy or group of adversaries. In effect, he was asserting the responsibility of the United States to exercise global hegemonic influence in the twenty-first century, even though he had denied in earlier statements that this was his intent. Some called the new national strategy the "Bush Doctrine."[1]

The president's covering letter cited the importance of American values, liberty, and freedom in the shaping of his strategy. "The great struggles of the twentieth century between liberty and totalitarianism ended with a decisive victory for the forces of freedom—and a single sustainable model for national success: freedom, democracy, and free enterprise." He asserted that "only nations that share a commitment to protecting basic human rights and guaranteeing political and economic freedom" would be able to assure their people's future prosperity. His covering letter to the policy paper continued:

> These values of freedom are right and true for every person, in every society—and the people across the globe and across the ages. Today the United States enjoys a position of unparalled military strength and great economic and political influence. In keeping with our heritage and principles, we do not use our strength to press for unilateral advantage. We seek instead to create a balance of power that favors human freedom: conditions in which all nations and all societies can choose for themselves the rewards and challenges of political and economic liberty. . . . We will extend the peace by encouraging free and open societies on every continent.

The president cited the new situation in national defense created by the events of 9/11 and argued that defending the country against its enemies was the government's "fundamental commitment." He envisioned an enemy with networks that "can bring great chaos and suffering to our shores for less than it costs to produce a single tank." Asserting that such groups had declared their intention to acquire WMD, the president said he would not allow them to succeed. He then outlined his new policy: "We will cooperate with other nations to deny, contain, and curtail our enemies' efforts to acquire dangerous technologies. And as a matter of common sense and self-defense, America will act against such emerging threats before they are fully formed. We cannot defend America and our friends by hoping for the best. . . . History will judge harshly those who saw this coming danger but failed to act. *In the new world we have entered, the only path to peace and security is the path of action*" (emphasis added).[2]

Mr. Bush thus placed other governments on notice that he would use preemptive military action against any country he decided was a serious threat to the United States and its allies. He also said he would act unilaterally if his administration was unable to persuade others to follow its lead in confronting dangerous adversaries. He seemed to have France and Germany in mind.

Critics had earlier raised the question of how the United States could build a stable world order when its overwhelming military power might tempt some policy makers to think they could act unilaterally to achieve America's objectives, with or without major allies or the United Nations. They also questioned how the United States would accomplish its international security goals, promote freedom abroad, and enjoy flourishing trade and commerce without the cooperation of other states. This case was argued by Joseph S. Nye, Jr., in *The Paradox of American Power: The World's Only Superpower Can't Go It Alone.*[3]

The introduction to Bush's National Security Strategy did not argue against the desirability of a multilateral approach to policy:

> We are also guided by the conviction that no nation can build a safer, better world alone. Alliances and multilateral institutions can multiply the strength of freedom-loving nations. The United States is committed to lasting institutions like the United Nations, the World Trade Organization, the Organization of American States, and NATO as well as other long-standing alliances. Coalitions of the willing can augment these permanent institutions. In all cases, international obligations are to be taken seriously. They are not to be undertaken symbolically to rally support for an ideal without furthering its attainment.

But skeptics wondered if these were just words designed to placate domestic and foreign critics of the president's new strategy. The words would be put to a test when the president launched the war against Iraq six months later, without the support of the United Nations or of a group of major allies, among them France, Germany, Canada, Mexico, and Turkey. The administration's desire to gain wide allied support conflicted with the president's decision to act unilaterally when the UN Security Council declined to endorse his plan to invade Iraq (see below).

A CONCEPTUAL FRAMEWORK FOR DEFINING
U.S. NATIONAL INTERESTS

Before analyzing the president's national security strategy, we will consider a conceptual framework for defining national interests that will assist in that discussion. This framework is based on the premise that the United States, like all great powers, has four basic, long-term national interests that guide its policy makers in deciding foreign and national security policies. They are providing for defense of the homeland, supporting the economic well-being of the nation, building a favorable world order, and promoting the nation's value system abroad. These basic interests interact and compete in the United States for the attention of the president and Congress and for the large financial resources needed to enhance them. These basic interests rise and decline in importance over decades, not months, in response to changing international challenges and changing domestic priorities.[4]

Defense of homeland is the first priority for most countries, especially great powers, and requires a substantial outlay of national resources. This is true for China, Great Britain, France, Russia, and the United States, all nuclear powers and permanent members of the UN Security Council. Other powers—like Germany, Japan, Italy, Iran, India, and Pakistan—also fit into this category, because all of them allocate substantial resources to national defense. The United States, because of its global interests, has military expenditures larger than those of all other great powers combined. America maintains a worldwide network of military bases and facilities, as well as aid missions in more than one hundred countries. A significant part of the U.S. defense budget, which in fiscal year (FY) 2005 was expected to reach $500 billion, also supports the country's third basic interest, the building of a favorable world order (see below). Since the attacks of 9/11, the federal government has allocated a large budget for the new Department of Homeland Security, which is responsible solely for defense of the United States. In FY 2004 its budget was $30 billion. Additional sums for domestic intelligence activities were allocated to the FBI and the CIA (see chapter 5).

The *economic well-being* interest guided U.S. presidents during the early part of the twentieth century, but World War II and the subsequent

Cold War caused succeeding presidents to subordinate this interest to building an international security system that promoted America's third basic interest, building a favorable world order. In the 1990s, however, with the Cold War over, Washington shifted its priorities and gave greater attention to the nation's economic needs. This was because of an increased awareness that the United States had fallen behind Japan and other industrialized countries during the Cold War in productivity growth and expansion of its manufacturing sector. The administration of George H. W. Bush decided, with strong support from the business community, to focus government attention on strengthening the nation's economy and promoting free trade in North America and Asia. Bill Clinton continued to give economic policy a high priority and promoted balanced budgets and lower interest rates to stimulate private investment. He also expanded U.S. trade agreements under the General Agreement on Tariffs and Trade (GATT) and its successor, the World Trade Organization (WTO). This led to a major expansion in U.S. exports and imports and increased foreign investments in the United States. By the end of the twentieth century the United States had once again become the undisputed economic superpower, surpassing Japan and the countries of the European Union. The American people enjoyed a major increase in their standard of living, and the country's unemployment rate in 2000 dropped to a record low of 3.9 percent (see chapter 6).

Building a *favorable world order* was a top priority of every president after 1945 because of the Cold War's confrontations with the Soviet Union and China. The U.S. government took on major responsibility for building international security through the establishment of the United Nations and, by an elaborate alliance system with countries in Europe, East Asia, the Middle East, and Latin America. These were designed to protect the United States and other noncommunist countries against the political and military pressure exerted on them by the Soviet Union and China. In the process the United States assumed the trappings of a hegemonic power, working collaboratively with allies in most cases but occasionally exercising unilateral power during crises—for example, the Suez Crisis in 1956 and the Cuban Missile Crisis in 1962. When the Cold War ended in 1990, the president and Congress substantially reduced troop deployments abroad and financial assistance to many countries. Yet, both the earlier Bush and Clinton administrations built up an American military presence in the Persian Gulf region designed to protect vital oil reserves in Saudi Arabia and deter the nuclear ambitions of Iraq and Iran. Although budget outlays to support the country's world-order interests declined during this period, those supporting strictly defense of homeland operations did not. Large amounts were allocated for new sophisticated weapons systems that greatly increased the effectiveness of U.S. arms and lessened the need for large military forces, especially ground troops. In response to the terrorist attacks on U.S. embassies in East Africa and military installations in Saudi Arabia and Yemen in the late 1990s, additional funds were allocated for covert activities under the Central Intelligence Agency. After 9/11, the resources allocated to world-order interests increased dramatically as the United States took on new security responsibilities in Central Asia and the Middle East (see chapter 7).

Promotion of values received increased attention from the U.S. government in the late 1970s when Jimmy Carter made this a top priority of his foreign policy. Succeeding presidents have given it public expression, although Republicans Ronald Reagan and George H. W. Bush were less vocal in their public criticism of other countries' human rights shortcomings than were Democrats Carter and Clinton. This basic national interest might be called the "ideological component" of American foreign policy, with an emphasis on liberty, human rights, and the advantages of democracy. The focus on human rights occasionally is in conflict with U.S. world-order interests, in which case the president and Congress wrestle with its policy implications. For example, when the Chinese government used brutal force to suppress a massive protest demonstration in Beijing in 1989 (Tiananmen Square), Congress voted overwhelmingly for tough economic sanctions that became a source of major foreign policy difficulties for George H. W. Bush and Bill Clinton in their efforts to avoid confrontations with China, a nuclear power that held a permanent seat in the UN Security Council. Similarly, the White House was restrained in its criticism of Russia for human rights abuses in Chechnya because of its desire to build good relations with the governments of Boris Yeltsin and, more recently, Vladimir Putin. In general, however, promotion of human rights and American values abroad is an important national interest that most Americans support (see chapter 8).

NATIONAL INTERESTS AND BUSH'S
NATIONAL SECURITY STRATEGY

In analyzing President Bush's national security strategy, it is useful to compare specific sections of the White House document with the four basic national interests described above. Figure 2 provides a matrix showing how these basic interests relate to four *intensities,* or degrees, of danger that international events and crises pose for policy makers. An event that falls into the category "vital interest," a dangerous threat to the country's interests, may well result in a presidential decision to use force.

A reading of President Bush's speeches after the 9/11 attacks shows that he began immediately to reorder priorities among the basic national interests. *Defense of the homeland* and *favorable world order* became the basis of his war on terrorism. He focused on invading the remote country of Afghanistan, a whole new region for the American military, and he confronted other governments that were suspected of aiding Al Qaeda terrorists by providing financial support. The White House argued that the best way of defending the homeland against Al Qaeda terrorists was to crush their sanctuaries before they could mount additional attacks on the United States. It would be done through intelligence operations abroad, financial pressure on friendly governments, and the use of military force against governments that were suspected of acquiring WMD or providing these weapons to Al Qaeda. This forward strategy had undergirded U.S. defense policy since the Second World War and promoted the expanded

FIGURE 2
ASSESSING THE INTENSITY OF BASIC NATIONAL INTERESTS

	Intensity of Interest			
Basic Interest	*Survival*	*Vital*	*Major*	*Peripheral*
Defense of Homeland				
Economic Well-Being				
Favorable World Order				
Promotion of Values				

world-order interests of the country. In sum, George Bush's reassessment of U.S. national interests shifted attention and resources away from the previous emphasis on economic priorities and focused them on his new national security strategy, which included an ideological agenda as well as the imperative to crush Al Qaeda.

An examination of the president's strategy document shows a correlation between its section headings and the basic national interests described above. For example, one section titled "Prevent Our Enemies from Threatening Us, Our Allies, and Our Friends with Weapons of Mass Destruction" fits the *defense of the homeland* interest, namely, a military threat to the United States or its allies. Another section headed "Ignite a New Era of Global Economic Growth through Free Markets and Free Trade" correlates with *economic well-being.* A third, "Champion Aspirations for Human Dignity," falls into the *promotion-of-values* category. Still another one bridges economic well-being and promotion of values: "Expand the Circle of Development by Opening Societies and Building the Infrastructure of Democracy."

The strategy's major emphasis, however, is on building a more *favorable international environment, or world order,* in which the United States and its allies would be more secure. Three sections addressed this national interest: "Strengthen Alliances to Defeat Global Terrorism," and "Work to Prevent Attacks against Us and Our Friends"; "Work with Others to Defuse Regional Conflicts"; and "Develop Agendas for Cooperative Action with the Other Main Centers of Global Power." An examination of these sections illustrates how the president intended to enhance U.S. world-order interests during his tenure in the White House.

On strengthening alliances to defeat terrorism, the strategy paper asserted, "The United States will continue to work with our allies to disrupt the financing of terrorism." It pledged to "identify and block the sources of funding for terrorism, freeze the assets of terrorists and those who support them, deny terrorists access to the international financial system, protect legitimate charities from being abused by terrorists, and prevent the movement of terrorists' assets through alternative financial networks." The strategy also took account of the reality that preventive action cannot be successful without the cooperation of many other countries: "While our focus is protecting America, we know that to deter terrorism in today's globalized world we need support from our allies and friends." Where possible, Bush said he would rely on regional organizations and other countries to fight terrorism; in cases where the task was beyond their capacities, the United States would be willing to assist "with whatever help we and our allies can provide."

In the section entitled "Work with Others to Defuse Regional Conflicts," the strategy discussed regional problems that required U.S. attention. These included the Israeli-Palestinian conflict, border tensions between India and Pakistan, an insurgency in Colombia, and civil wars in parts of Africa. Strangely, North Korea's threat to the security of Northeast Asia was not among the issues cited. While pledging that "the United States would work with friends and partners to alleviate suffering and restore stability" in troubled areas, the strategy paper cautioned, "We have finite political, economic and military resources to meet our global priorities" and that the United States should "be realistic about its ability to help those who are unwilling or unready to help themselves."

Another section, "Develop Agendas for Cooperative Action," raised an intriguing question about Bush's strategy on U.S. policy on Iraq. In a statement about future relations with America's friends and allies, the paper declared, "America will implement its strategies by organizing coalitions—as broad as practicable—of states able and willing to promote a balance of power that favors freedom. Effective coalition leadership requires clear priorities, *an appreciation of others' interests, and consultations among partners with a spirit of humility*" (emphasis added). Five months later, four NATO allies, France, Germany, Canada, and Turkey, which had supported the president when he asked for help in Afghanistan, refused to support his decision to invade Iraq. One reason alleged by observers was that Washington had failed to consult with the allies about its military plans; instead, it had simply informed them of its decisions and expected at least political support, if not military and economic assistance, from them.

The document had anticipated this difficulty: "There is little of lasting consequence that the United States can accomplish in the world without the sustained cooperation of its allies and friends in Canada and Europe. Europe is also the seat of two of the strongest and most able international institutions in the world: the North Atlantic Treaty Organization

(NATO), which has, since its inception, been the fulcrum of transatlantic and inter-European security, and the European Union (EU), our partner in opening world trade." This wording suggested that the State Department's priority was on using diplomacy to build a broad coalition of nations and was thus at odds with the Pentagon's view, stated elsewhere, that favored unilateral action if allies failed to support the United States.

This raised the crucial issue of whether Iraq was a truly vital national interest—so important to the United States that the president would be justified in acting unilaterally if allies refused to join. The major policy dispute, clearly visible in July and August before the president took the Iraq issue to the United Nations, was not reconciled in the national security strategy paper. The internal debate would continue on the key question of whether the United States was so powerful and so mobilized by the 9/11 disaster that it should be willing to "go it alone" if necessary. The issue reached a climax in January and February 2003, when UN weapons inspectors failed to find a "smoking gun" in Iraq and the Security Council declined to authorize the United States to use force. President Bush would eventually have to decide whether cooperation with major European allies was essential to protecting U.S. interests in 2003, or whether France and Germany should be downgraded as allies and replaced by a "coalition of the willing."[5]

A final section of the strategy paper was entitled "Transform America's National Security Institutions to Meet the Challenges and Opportunities of the Twenty-First Century." After stating, "It is time to reaffirm the essential role of American military strength," the president pledged to "build and maintain our defenses beyond challenge." Anticipating a debate on whether America was taking on a role similar to that of Imperial Rome, the presidential document declared:

The presence of American forces overseas is one of the most profound symbols of the U.S. commitments to allies and friends. Through our willingness to use forces in our own defense and in the defense of others, the United States demonstrates its resolve to maintain a balance of power that favors freedom. To contend with uncertainty and to meet the many security challenges we face, the United States will require bases and stations within and beyond Western Europe and Northeast Asia, as well as temporary access arrangements for the long-distance deployment of U.S. forces. . . . We must prepare for more such deployments by developing assets such as advanced remote sensing, long-range precision strike capabilities, and transformed maneuver and expeditionary forces. This broad portfolio of military capabilities must also include the ability to defend the homeland, conduct information operations, ensure U.S. access to distant theaters, and protect critical U.S. infrastructure and assets in outer space.

One could reasonably conclude that the president intended to expand America's military reach to all parts of the world, wherever he determined that there were security threats to the United States and its allies. It was a breathtaking claim of a new American hegemony.

WHAT ISSUES CONSTITUTE "VITAL" INTERESTS?

The strategy document laid out in clear prose the president's goals and objectives. What the new strategy did not do was define which international issues are so crucial—vital—to the interests of the United States that a president would be justified in taking military action if all nonmilitary actions failed. A fundamental question for policy makers, congressional leaders, and experts on international relations is: what criteria should be used in deciding whether a specific security threat is so dangerous that a president should act militarily, without allies if necessary? At what point should he conclude that a potential enemy's policies have reached the threshold of vital interest and may require military measures to counter them? International terrorism is such a danger, and the attack on Afghanistan's Taliban government had logically followed. A second threat is a rogue state's intention to build or acquire WMD, especially nuclear weapons. The strategy document implied this in regard to Iraq, Iran, North Korea, and potentially Libya, when it cited an "axis of evil." An additional issue is whether a president should approve the intervention of American forces in civil wars where no strategic and economic interests are at stake but where the killing of civilians is widespread, as in Bosnia in 1995 and Kosovo in 1999, or mass starvation is rampant, as in Somalia in 1991.

Both George W. Bush in 2003 and his father in 1991 had decided that

Saddam Hussein was so dangerous to U.S. world-order and economic interests in the Middle East that he had to be stopped with force. Whereas former president Bush sought to build a broad coalition of European and Arab states to assist in the war to oust Saddam's troops from Kuwait, George W. Bush decided to crush Saddam's regime even without the approval of the UN Security Council and major allies because he considered him such a dangerous threat. Bush was influenced in this view by Prime Minister Tony Blair of Britain, who was one of the few major allies that supplied troops for the 2003 invasion. An important question that historians will address is whether George Bush would have launched the Iraq war unilaterally if Tony Blair had not persuaded the House of Commons to approve his plan to join the United States.

The strategy document did not address another key question: Is the president justified in acting preemptively to deal with *potentially* dangerous threats to U.S. vital interests, whether or not major allies approve the use of military force? Is the United States, because of its overwhelming military and economic power, justified in ignoring allies and the United Nations when Washington is convinced that the danger of waiting is greater than the risks of a preemptive attack against an enemy? Few Americans question the proposition that a president must be able to act unilaterally whenever a threat borders on the "survival" level—that is, an imminent attack on the homeland, as was seen in the Cuban Missile Crisis. Similarly, a possible Soviet-instigated communist takeover in Grenada in 1983 prompted President Reagan to invade that island because of its potential threat to the U.S. homeland.

THE DECISION TO REMOVE SADDAM HUSSEIN

By February 2003 the United States had nearly 200,000 military personnel, and the British another 40,000, positioned in the Persian Gulf for an invasion of Iraq if Saddam Hussein failed to cooperate fully with UN weapons inspectors who had returned to Iraq three months earlier. Bob Woodward writes in *Plan of Attack* that President Bush told Condoleezza Rice in January that he probably would have to go to war, because Saddam Hussein was "playing for time" to avoid revealing the location of his WMD. "He's getting more confident, not less," the president said. "He can manipulate the international system again. We're not winning. . . . Time is not on our side here, we're going to have to go to war."[6]

In his State of the Union address on January 28 the president devoted the last portion of his remarks to Iraq. Recalling twelve years of failed UN efforts to force the Iraqi dictator to disarm, Bush declared, "Nothing to date has restrained him from his pursuit of these weapons, not economic sanctions, not isolation from the civilized world, not even cruise missile strikes on his military facilities." He said that although Saddam Hussein had had almost three months to comply with the latest UN resolution, he showed "his utter contempt for the United Nations and for the opinion of the world." The president issued this warning: "The world has waited 12 years for Iraq to disarm. America will not accept a serious and mounting threat to our country, our friends, and our allies. The United States will ask the U.N. Security Council to convene on February 5th to consider the fact of Iraq's ongoing defiance of the world. . . . If Saddam Hussein does not fully disarm, for the safety of our people, and for the peace of the world, we will lead a coalition to disarm him."[7]

Secretary of State Powell delivered a long address to the Security Council on February 5 laying out the Bush administration's case for why it was necessary that the world body deal urgently with the threat to peace posed by Saddam Hussein. He divided his arguments into three categories, matching three of the four basic national interests described above: Saddam's determination to acquire and use WMD to threaten the United States and its allies (defense of homeland), Saddam's alleged links to the Al Qaeda terrorist network and his plans to destabilize the entire Persian Gulf area (favorable world order), and Saddam's abhorrent human rights record in dealing with his own people and those of Kuwait (promotion of values). Powell did not address Saddam's threat to Persian Gulf oil reserves, but many observers believed that America's economic well-being was also a prime reason for the administration's decision to oust him. On Iraq's weapons acquisition efforts, Powell stated that, on the basis of his careful examination of all the intelligence available to the United States and other governments, "there's no doubt in my mind that these illicit procurement efforts show that Saddam Hussein is very much focused on putting in place the key missing piece from his nuclear weapons program, the ability to produce fissile material." He noted that "over the last 18 months, Saddam Hussein has paid increasing personal attention to Iraq's top nuclear scientists, a group that the government press calls openly his 'nuclear mujahedeen.'" Powell also cited the Iraqi dictator's program to develop missiles to carry these weapons: "Saddam Hussein's intentions have never changed. He is not developing the missiles for self-defense. These are missiles that Iraq wants in order to project power to threaten, and to deliver chemical, biological and, if we let him, nuclear warheads."[8] Regarding Saddam's plans to dominate the Persian Gulf region and his ties to international terrorists, Powell cited intelligence indicating links between Iraqi intelligence services and a top operative of the Al Qaeda network: "Iraq today harbors a deadly terrorist network headed by Abu Mussab al-Zarqawi, an associate and collaborator of Osama bin Laden and his Al Qaeda lieutenants." Powell said that after the Taliban government was ousted in Afghanistan, "the Zarqawi network helped establish another poison and explosives training camp in northeast Iraq" and that it had become a safe haven for Al Qaeda members who were ousted from Afghanistan. "They remain there today," Powell asserted. Regarding the matter of Saddam's human rights record, he observed: "Nothing points more clearly to Saddam's dangerous intentions and the threat he poses to all of us than his calculated cruelty to his own citizens and to his neighbors. Clearly, Saddam Hussein and his regime will stop at nothing until something stops him." Powell's address went far to persuade many skeptical Americans who had questioned the Bush administration's preparations for war that the threat posed by Saddam was real and that it needed to be confronted, sooner rather than later.[9]

President Bush addressed the nation from the White House on March 17 and issued an ultimatum to Saddam Hussein and his sons to leave Iraq within forty-eight hours. "Their refusal to do so," he said, "will result in military conflict to commence at a time of our choosing." Two days later, American, British, and Australian forces based in Kuwait launched an invasion. The expected opening of a northern front did not materialize, however, because Turkey's parliament failed to allow large numbers of U.S. troops to use its territory for an invasion.

Figure 3 shows my assessment of the national interests of the principal countries that had an important stake in the 2003 decision to invade Iraq to force the ouster of Saddam Hussein. This breakout of the major countries' conflicting interests in the Iraq war illustrates why six of them decided *not* to join the United States in the invasion, while five others did. It also indicates that the United States and Britain, under the leadership of George Bush and Tony Blair, shared a vital national interest in three of the four basic interests: economic well-being, favorable world order, and promotion of values. This intensity of interest was what drove their policies in the period leading up to war, and why they were prepared to defy the opposition of five NATO partners and Russia. Iraq was the only country with a survival interest at stake—defense of homeland—because a successful invasion meant the end of its government. Neighboring Arab countries and Iran had either a vital or major defense interest because of the effects that regime change and a continuing U.S. presence in Iraq would have on their own security.

FIGURE 3

NATIONAL INTERESTS OF KEY NATIONS ON WAR IN IRAQ

	Intensity of Interest			
Basic Interest	*Survival*	*Vital*	*Major*	*Peripheral*
Defense of Homeland	**Iraq**	**Iran** **Syria**	**S. Arabia** **Jordan** **Kuwait**	
Economic Well-Being		**U.S.** **Britain** **Turkey**	**Russia** **France** **Germany**	
Favorable World Order		**U.S.** **Britain** **Spain** **Italy** **Poland** **Australia**	**Russia** **France** **Germany** **Turkey** **Canada** **Belgium**	
Promotion of Values		**U.S.** **Britain**		

Those who argue that the United States should always act multilaterally when it uses military force abroad deny the reality that, as the paramount power in world politics, America has a responsibility to deal effectively with dangerous threats to world order, even if some key allies object. The crucial question is this: Should the fact that France, Germany, Belgium, Turkey, and Canada, five important NATO allies, refused in 2003 to accept the U.S. assessment that Saddam Hussein was a dangerous threat in the Middle East and must be removed from power *automatically* have required President Bush to abandon, or modify, his plan to invade Iraq, even after he had received the backing of Congress for this course? I think not. Although one may rightly criticize the Bush administration's diplomacy when trying to persuade allies, notably Turkey, to join the coalition, France's blatant threat to veto any UN resolution authorizing the use of force constituted a frontal challenge from an ally that no responsible U.S. president should have been obliged to accept. That was especially so in view of Saddam's previous intimidation of neighboring countries and his open support of terrorism against Israel. The president's decision to invade Iraq despite France's veto threat put the allies and the world on notice that America would act unilaterally whenever it concluded that a dangerous threat—a vital national interest—was at stake. And in making this point clear, George W. Bush underlined the reality that the United States considered itself the world's hegemonic superpower.

REACTION TO BUSH'S NATIONAL SECURITY STRATEGY

Many columnists and editorial writers commented on President Bush's National Security Strategy of the United States, published in September 2002. Conservatives supported its main thrust, including the option of preemptive war, while moderates and liberals deplored its unilateralist approach to foreign policy. One of the latter was former national security adviser to President George H. W. Bush, Gen. Brent Scowcroft. In August 2002 he had counseled the administration against invading Iraq, arguing that it would unleash forces in the Middle East that would be difficult to contain (see chapter 3). Two years later, in an interview with the London *Financial Times,* Scowcroft called the U.S. intervention in Iraq a "failing venture" and claimed that relations with Europe were "in general bad." Like many experts, he believed that the United States needed Europe to help deal with the world's major security problems.[10]

In their book *America Unbound: The Bush Revolution in Foreign Policy*, Ivo Daalder and James Lindsay analyzed Bush's grand strategy and concluded: "Although Bush's imperious style entailed great costs for American foreign policy, that was not the only shortcoming in this revolution. . . . The deeper problem was that the fundamental premise of the Bush revolution—that America's security rested on an America unbound—was mistaken." The authors wrote that the "premise would have been right if the unilateral exercise of American power could have achieved America's major foreign policy goals." But they argued that the most important challenges facing the country "could not be solved by Washington alone. They required the active cooperation of others." These writers recalled that when George Bush returned home from a successful trip to Europe in June 2003, his arrival resembled "a victory lap to celebrate America's win in the Iraq War—a war that many of the leaders Bush met on his trip had opposed."[11]

By the summer of 2004 an increasingly serious security situation emerged in Iraq requiring the deployment of additional U.S. troops. No additional help was forthcoming from the NATO allies. President Bush's national security strategy of unilateral action, including preemptive warfare when necessary to protect U.S. national interests, was being criticized by many foreign policy experts during the presidential election campaign. John Kerry, the Democratic Party nominee, launched a vigorous attack on the administration for ignoring the allies and bungling the occupation of Iraq after winning an impressive military victory. Bush strongly defended his decision to oust Saddam Hussein, even though no WMD were found. The November 2004 presidential election would provide American voters an opportunity to decide whether the president was justified in this decision and should be given another four years in office (see Epilogue).

CHAPTER 5

DEFENDING THE HOMELAND AFTER 9/11

The primary national interest of every sovereign state is the protection of its territory, its citizens, and its political system. This "Defense of Homeland Interest" is more pressing for the United States now than at any other time since 1941. Americans have lived for most of their lives with the notion that their homeland was protected against foreign attack by two oceans to the east and west, by a friendly country—Canada—to the north, and by a U.S.-dominated Caribbean Basin area and Mexico to the south. The Japanese attack on Pearl Harbor in 1941 did not damage the continental United States, and as a result, in the early post–World War II period Americans resumed their complacency. This was in contrast to the way World War II impacted all the other major powers—Britain, France, Germany, Italy, the Soviet Union, China, and Japan. America's sole possession of the atomic bomb (until 1949) persuaded most Americans that it was safe to cut drastically the budgets of the Army and Navy and withdraw most U.S. forces from Europe and the Far East.

The Soviet Union's development of nuclear weapons in the 1950s and its successful testing of long-range missiles in the 1960s profoundly changed the public's attitude on homeland defense. Consequently, Congress voted large increases in the Defense Department budget. In the summer of 1961, after a stormy meeting with Soviet President Nikita Khrushchev in Vienna, President Kennedy warned the nation of the threat of attack on the United States and the need for civil defense. People built bomb shelters, and their children were drilled at school on how to protect themselves in case of a nuclear attack. Public apprehension was heightened in October 1962 when it was discovered that Moscow had secretly installed medium-range nuclear missiles in Cuba, thereby placing all of the United States east of the Mississippi River within range. President Kennedy then put the military on the highest state of readiness. War seemed imminent but was averted when Khrushchev agreed to remove the missiles in return for a U.S. pledge not to invade Cuba. Subsequent presidents—Johnson, Nixon, Ford, Carter, and Reagan—negotiated nuclear arms control agreements with the Soviet Union. In 1985 a new Soviet leader, Mikhail Gorbachev, came to power and worked with Reagan to end the Cold War. When the Soviet Union disintegrated in 1991 and was replaced by a smaller Russian Federation, most Americans were convinced that the nuclear danger to their homeland had passed and that the defense budget as well as U.S. troops stationed abroad could be substantially reduced.

A New Priority for Homeland Defense

For fifty-five years after World War II the United States based its national defense strategy on a "forward defense." Washington acquired allies and established military bases in many countries far from U.S. territory and in proximity to its enemies, the Soviet Union and the People's Republic of China. This strategy was successful in containing the military power of these competitors for world hegemony and it eventually resulted in the Soviet Union's demise in 1991 and China's transformation into a market economy. The ten-year period of calm came to a sudden end on September 11, 2001. Now the danger to the country came not from missiles fired from the oceans or another continent but from sophisticated international terrorists who could operate inside the United States and be armed potentially with WMD.

Fighting international terrorism, a struggle that President Bush called "a war on terrorism," required a far different concept of national defense.

The president's first priority was to destroy the Al Qaeda terrorist bases in Afghanistan, which U.S. forces accomplished in November and December 2001, but it also included confronting countries with governments that had not previously taken action against terrorists. Washington now took strong steps, including tough financial measures, to close off funding channels through which the Al Qaeda network operated. The new concept of national defense caused Washington, for the first time in half a century, to reorganize the numerous national security agencies of the executive branch and assemble them in the new Department of Homeland Security. Some twenty-two government agencies were affected, including the Coast Guard, Immigration Service, Customs Service, Border Patrol, and the Transportation Security Administration, which provided security screening at the nation's airports. This new department, authorized by Congress in 2002, had as its major responsibility making the United States more secure internally. Another significant change was the Patriot Act, passed by Congress in late 2001, which greatly increased the powers of the Justice Department to monitor, apprehend, and prosecute persons within the United States, especially aliens, suspected of terrorist activities. With growing pressure from Congress for changes in the nation's intelligence agencies, the president ordered closer cooperation between the FBI and the CIA to provide timely warning of terrorist threats to the United States. During the congressional debate on the Patriot Act and after its enactment, critics charged that Congress had granted too much authority to the Justice Department to interfere with the civil liberties of both American citizens and legal residents of the country, including thousands of foreign students. Some complained that the Homeland Security Act gave too much power to that department to decide when to raise the level of national emergency in response to intelligence alerts. Other critics claimed that the Bush administration had not provided sufficient funding to the fifty states to carry out their increased responsibilities for homeland security, including those of local police, medical staffs, and firefighters. Nevertheless, the federal government was willing to spend billions of dollars for homeland defense to fight terrorists at home, strengthen the country's internal security, and provide additional funding for the Defense Department and the CIA.

MILITARY THREATS TO THE HOMELAND

The Department of Homeland Security had the mandate to provide security to Americans within the fifty states, and that work began even before Congress approved the organization of the new department. But responsibility for defending the homeland against enemies outside the country, including the Al Qaeda terrorist network, fell to the Department of Defense and the CIA. To defend the homeland against external attack, America's strategic plans have always included the adjacent areas in North America and the Caribbean as part of its defense perimeter. This includes Canada, Mexico, the countries of Central America, the island states in the Caribbean, as well as Venezuela and Colombia. A threat to these countries by a hostile foreign power would normally be considered a threat to the homeland, as was demonstrated during the Cuban Missile Crisis (1962), by the Soviet-supported communist coup in Grenada (1983), and by Soviet military support for the Sandinista government in Nicaragua (1984–86). The strategic location of Iceland and Greenland in the North Atlantic has long made them a part of U.S. North American defense.

By far the most important country in North America in terms of homeland defense is Canada. That is because of its size, strategic location, four-thousand-mile border with the United States (including Alaska), and its huge two-way trade relationship with the United States. During the Cold War, Canada was an integral part of the North American Air Defense system, which provided early warning of bombers and missiles that could be launched from the Soviet Union and sent across the Arctic. The relatively open U.S. borders between the two countries continued during the Cold War years, because Canadian and American officials controlled the flow of travelers and trade and ensured that security was maintained. Many Americans took Canada for granted and assumed that its government agreed with Washington on defense issues and on most foreign policy ones. Events after the 9/11 attacks challenged that assumption.

The principal external military threats to the United States at the beginning of the twenty-first century fall into three categories: (1) nuclear-armed states with the capability and the intention to launch WMD on the United States, (2) countries that do not produce these weapons but seek to acquire them in order to threaten the U.S. homeland, and (3) revolutionary forces that seize control of a country within the U.S. defense of homeland perimeter or one that provides support to parties that threaten to harm the homeland. Examples of each category are (1) North Korea, potentially Iran, possibly China; (2) countries where officials are susceptible to bribes in exchange for providing terrorists with WMD—for example, Russia and Pakistan; and (3) Fidel Castro's regime in Cuba, a classic case of a North American state providing military bases to a U.S. enemy (Soviet Union) and supporting communist forces in Nicaragua and El Salvador. President Reagan was convinced in the 1980s that Nicaragua under its Marxist government was providing a base of operations for Soviet and Cuban military operatives who fostered revolutions in nearby countries, including Mexico. In 1999 the Clinton administration became deeply concerned about a growing danger in Colombia that it feared would lead to the establishment of an anti-American regime that threatened the Panama Canal. Venezuela is another potential defense of homeland problem because its leftist government headed by Hugo Chavez has close ties to Cuba's Fidel Castro and calls for social revolutions in Latin America (see chapter 7).

In 2004 the world's acknowledged nuclear powers were the United States, Russia, Britain, France, China, India, and Pakistan. Israel does not admit that it has nuclear weapons, although its arsenal of them is an accepted reality. President Bush identified Iraq, Iran, and North Korea as countries that were developing nuclear weapons, and in 2003 North Korea admitted that it had them and would produce more. Iraq had constructed facilities to produce nuclear weapons, but these were dismantled after the Gulf War. In 2002 the U.S. intelligence community debated whether the Iraqi government had resumed its quest for nuclear weapons after UN inspectors were forced out of the country in 1998. Following extensive searches after the invasion of Iraq in March 2003, no nuclear weapons or facilities were discovered. In 2004 two independent inspection teams, one headed by David Kay and another by Charles Duelfer, reported that they had found no evidence of WMD in Iraq, concluding that they probably had been destroyed in the 1990s and that Saddam Hussein had not rebuilt his arsenal. As for Iran, UN inspectors found evidence in 2003 that it was secretly building a nuclear weapons facility. At first the Tehran government denied it, saying its nuclear reactors were producing energy only for civilian use. But in October, under prodding from Britain, France, and Germany, Iran's highest authority admitted the existence of a nuclear weapons program. Iran was reprimanded by the UN's International Atomic Energy Agency (IAEA), and it pledged to stop the program. However, in 2004 Iran's government resisted intrusive inspections by the IAEA.

In 2004 the likelihood that any of the world's nuclear powers would use WMD against the United States was small, even though that could change within a few years. Only China and Russia had a capability to launch intercontinental ballistic missiles, but neither showed any sign of an intention to do so. My assessment of the threat of nuclear attack on the U.S. homeland is shown on the national matrix in figure 4. An assessment of economic well-being, favorable world order, and promotion-of-values interests is contained in the following chapters.

The fundamental issue for U.S. defense of homeland policy is whether the United States should risk permitting additional countries to become nuclear powers. After the Clinton administration failed to persuade India and Pakistan to stop their quests for nuclear weapons, the Bush administration concluded that the United States should use its power to prevent additional countries from acquiring them and potentially destabilizing

FIGURE 4
THREATS TO THE U.S. HOMELAND FROM NUCLEAR STATES

Basic Interest	Intensity of Interest			
	Survival	Vital	Major	Peripheral
DEFENSE OF HOMELAND			China Russia N. Korea Iran	Britain France India Pakistan Israel
Economic Well-Being				
Favorable World Order				
Promotion of Values				

whole regions. This policy was reflected in President Bush's 2002 State of the Union Address and in his National Security Strategy document published later in the year. Iraq, Iran, and North Korea were singled out as countries that were seeking nuclear weapons in order to challenge U.S. hegemony in the Middle East and East Asia. Regarding Iraq, the threat was diminished when U.S. and British troops invaded in 2003. On North Korea, Bush chose to use diplomacy instead of military confrontation, enlisting China, Japan, Russia, and South Korea in a joint effort to defuse a dangerous situation in their region. As for Iran, the administration believed that after U.S. forces had established a firm presence in neighboring Iraq, Tehran's Islamic regime would bow to international pressure and allow UN inspectors to monitor its nuclear program, to ensure that it was not for military purposes. In 2004 that assumption was questionable.

Of the seven acknowledged nuclear powers, only China had the capability and potential willingness to threaten the United States with nuclear weapons. North Korea reportedly had a few such weapons but not a delivery capability. However, if diplomacy failed to resolve the dangerous issue of Taiwan's pressure for independence, or if the United States threatened to attack North Korea, a war with China might result and reopen the nuclear question. In 2002 President Bush canceled the 1972 Anti-Ballistic Missile (ABM) treaty with the Soviet Union, with the consent of Russia's government, and began to implement a long-range plan to build a continental missile defense system designed to protect the United States and its Asian allies against attack from North Korea or China. To reduce criticism of this change in U.S. strategic policy, Washington offered to share the new system with allies, among them Britain, Canada, and Japan. Beijing voiced strong opposition to the system, charging that it was directed against China. The Pentagon argued that the main threat was from North Korea and that U.S. forces were prepared to counter its missile threats to Japan and South Korea. Regarding Russia, some defense experts worried that it had retained a large, if aging, nuclear missile capability and might in the future become a threat. Presidents Clinton and Bush worked with Russia's new leaders to reassure them about U.S. intentions, and the two governments also negotiated significant reductions in their nuclear stockpiles.

NONMILITARY THREATS TO HOMELAND DEFENSE

Terrorism directed by organizations located in other countries was the most immediate and dangerous threat to the U.S. homeland at the beginning of the new century. That fact was underlined by Congress's creation of the Department of Homeland Security and by the frequent national terrorist alerts that were called by its head, Secretary Thomas Ridge. The danger was underlined by a congressional investigation undertaken after the 9/11 terrorist attacks to determine why U.S. intelligence agencies had not anticipated them and what needed to be done to improve the agencies' performance in homeland security. A joint panel of House and Senate intelligence committees issued its report on July 24, 2003. According to the *New York Times,* it "found that the F.B.I. and C.I.A. had failed to heed repeated warnings that al Qaeda intended to strike in the United States." The *Times* reported that the document "referred to one newly disclosed intelligence document from December 1998 that said: 'Plans to attack U.S. aircraft proceeding well.' Two individuals had successfully invaded checkpoints 'in a dry run at New York's airport.'"[1] The congressional report also cited evidence that Al Qaeda had carried out an earlier (1993) attack on the World Trade Center and that lack of coordination among the intelligence agencies and the U.S. Immigration Service had raised the threat of a major attack on the U.S. homeland to the dangerous—vital—level. Two conclusions to be drawn from the congressional report were that Al Qaeda terrorists had been operating in the United States for at least six or seven years and that the 9/11 highjackers had proceeded with their plans undetected. The report made clear, however, that it had uncovered no information "that would have provided specific, advance warning of the details of the [9/11] attacks." Because of the public's demand for a fuller investigation into the reasons for the attacks, the president and Congress established a bipartisan independent commission in 2003 to investigate thoroughly the government's role and report its finding in the summer of 2004.[2]

Congressional criticism of intelligence failures resembled in some ways an earlier investigation into the intelligence failure prior to the attack on Pearl Harbor on December 7, 1941. In that case the commanders of Navy and Army forces in Hawaii were charged with negligence in not having taken appropriate security precautions. Now, in 2003, some members of Congress called for the resignation of CIA Director George Tenet, who had headed the agency for four years. Some called for detaching the FBI from the Justice Department in order to refocus its attention on domestic intelligence instead of its traditional function of law enforcement. However, the president expressed confidence in both Tenet and FBI Director Robert Mueller for their work after 9/11. Bush decided against detaching the FBI from the Justice Department, and both agencies were given larger resources to focus on domestic intelligence and antiterrorism. He also directed them to provide intelligence to Secretary Ridge, who had been appointed a full member of the president's NSC.

Although the administration supported creation of the Department of Homeland Security and enactment of the Patriot Act to strengthen the Justice Department's ability to apprehend individuals suspected of terrorist activities, the president did not approve creation of a new department of national intelligence to bring under one jurisdiction all the intelligence agencies, now spread among half a dozen separate departments. Among these were the Defense Intelligence Agency (DIA), National Security Agency (NSA), National Geospatial Intelligence Agency, and CIA. Some members of Congress had urged him to consolidate under one agency all the intelligence functions, including those of the FBI. But the Defense Department strongly resisted giving the director of CIA or any other agency funding authority over DIA and NSA, which controlled a far higher proportion of the total intelligence budget than did CIA. Secretary Donald Rumsfeld not only opposed any new agency headed by a "czar" but had already created a small intelligence evaluation group within the Office of Secretary of Defense to challenge, critics claimed, the findings of CIA national intelligence estimates (NIEs) that did not support his department's view of the existence of WMD in Iraq prior to the war.[3]

The intelligence failure before September 2001 made it obvious that the federal government would not only need to spend far more money on intelligence work, both at home and abroad, but it would have to strengthen greatly the capability of state and local governments to provide the security and health resources needed to prevent future terrorist attacks. This was a job for the Department of Homeland Security, and it required far greater intelligence about domestic security and better coordination among intelligence agencies than had been in place before September 2001. Both President Bush and Secretary Ridge told the nation that there was no way to make the country completely safe from terrorist attacks, given the size of the country and the magnitude of the challenge. But they made progress in bringing state and local officials into planning how best to cope with another national disaster. Still, there was criticism in Congress that the administration had not requested sufficient funding in FY 2004 for state and local officials to organize effectively to cope with the many tasks levied on them by Washington. The outbreak of anthrax in 2002 in Florida and the Washington, D.C., area, including at one of the Senate office buildings, put a severe scare into residents of the nation's capital and showed how massive the problem could become if the country were faced with a widespread attack of biological and chemical weapons. Another 9/11-type terrorist attack would surely propel Congress to spend far greater amounts on homeland security and strengthen the Patriot Act further to meet the public's demands for action.

In July 2003 *The Economist* published an article written by several former experts from U.S. agencies that dealt with intelligence. They called for far greater emphasis on "human intelligence," spies, to penetrate terrorist groups within the United States. The report stated: "Despite the best efforts of our law enforcement and intelligence agencies, the fact remains that secret members of a conspiratorial foreign organization operated clandestinely abroad and in the country for almost a decade before September 11th to plan, lay the groundwork for and successfully carry out a surprise attack on the United States." These experts recommended, among other things: "Our collective experience makes it absolutely clear that the only way to uncover and destroy terrorist activity is to penetrate the organizations engaged in it. And the best way to do this is to place spies in their innermost councils." They observed that "Americans do not like spies, especially within the United States; but we have used them successfully in the past and, if we are to succeed in the war against terrorism, we need to again."[4]

LOWER-LEVEL THREATS TO HOMELAND SECURITY

Americans have long considered threats to the homeland primarily in terms of military attack. Since mid-1993, when the first terrorist bombing of the Twin Towers in New York occurred, the public has been aware of the danger of international terrorism. But another serious threat from outside the country was the massive flow of illegal drugs into the United States. These were channeled by powerful drug lords operating primarily from Latin American countries. In some cases, as in Colombia and Mexico, the drug lords were so wealthy and powerful that they were able to buy off corrupt government officials and persuade them to condone, even facilitate, the flow of cocaine and other drugs to American cities. Another potential threat to the country's internal security is posed by illegal aliens who are involved in drug trafficking. Creation of the Department of Homeland Security was intended to help the government cope with this problem; for that reason it included the transfer of the Immigration and Naturalization Service from the Justice Department. Similarly, the U.S. Secret Service and Customs Service were moved from the Treasury Department, and the Coast Guard and Transportation Security Administration were transferred from the Department of Transportation. These moves were expected to improve the campaign to control the flow of illegal drugs into the United States. Congress and the American public needed to be persuaded that these were not short-term measures to deal with a short-term threat; sustained public awareness and willingness to support these new efforts were needed over many years in order to reduce the drug trade.

Federal authorities admit that the government has all but lost the war on illegal drugs, despite the large sums of money and personnel provided to drug enforcement agencies during the 1990s. The reality was that, because of the country's long coastlines and porous southern border, apprehending illegal traffickers was a nearly impossible task. The Coast Guard and Drug Enforcement Agency substantially increased their activities in 2002 and 2003, but officials acknowledged that they could not seriously curtail the flow of illegal substances so long as a huge demand for them persist in U.S. cities, and because the profits are so huge. The drug trade causes harm to the public health, financial stability, and law enforcement resources of many states and local communities as they attempt to cope with drug addicts who often engage in serious crime.

Another threat to internal security, particularly after the 9/11 attacks, is the presence in the United States of millions of illegal aliens whose activities and whereabouts are unknown to U.S. authorities. Monitoring these residents to determine whether they are security risks is the province of the U.S. Immigration Service and the Justice Department. The large numbers of foreign students overstaying their visa limits became a source of concern to U.S. authorities after 9/11, because some of them could be in terrorist "sleeper cells" waiting to be activated. The threat to internal security posed by lack of efficient enforcement of immigration laws lies in the huge number of persons who are in the United States on temporary visas and remain in the country illegally when their visas expire. These persons are almost beyond the ability of the Immigration Service to monitor. For example, millions of visas are issued each year for foreign students to attend U.S. colleges and universities, but in the past little was known about them after they entered the country, or even whether they were actually enrolled in school and whether they left when their visas expired. The vast majority of foreign students are not a threat to the country's security, but lack of monitoring by state and federal agencies has opened the likelihood that some may be potential terrorists who slipped through the screening process before their visas were issued. It is noteworthy that nearly all of the nineteen hijackers who attacked the World Trade Center and the Pentagon were in the country *legally* on student visas.

CHOOSING NEW PRIORITIES AMONG NATIONAL INTERESTS

For most of forty-five years after World War II, eight American presidents and successive congresses gave top priority, among the four basic U.S. national interests, to building a favorable world order to make America's external environment more secure. Although the hundreds of billions of dollars appropriated by Congress for the Department of Defense during the Cold War years were justified in terms of defending North America, a large proportion of the military budget was used to build and support alliances with over forty countries and to obtain military bases abroad from which U.S. power could be projected to contain the expansionist policies of the Soviet Union and China. Huge amounts of foreign aid, financial and military, were expended in an effort to bolster the economies and upgrade the military capabilities of countries willing to join the

United States in "fighting communism." The "promotion-of-values" interest was given a low priority during the 1950s and 1960s as the government gave most attention to building defense relationships with Asian countries. Many of these were governed by military governments, as in Thailand and South Vietnam, or authoritarian regimes run by undemocratic oligarchies, as in many Latin American countries. In the late 1970s and 1980s, however, the promotion-of-values interest, especially emphasis on human rights, was accorded a higher priority by policy makers. President Carter made human rights an important part of his foreign policy and created a new post in the State Department to emphasize it. The government's promotion of freedom and democracy in Soviet-dominated Eastern Europe contributed to the breakdown of Soviet control there in the 1980s, beginning with Poland and Hungary and spreading across the area. In his book *From the Shadows,* Robert Gates, director of the CIA near the end of the Cold War, highlighted this effort.[5]

With the Cold War over and America emerging in the 1990s as the world's only superpower, presidents George H. W. Bush and Bill Clinton adjusted the priorities among the four basic U.S. interests. The number of American forces in Europe and East Asia was substantially reduced, and many bases were closed. Both presidents gave a high priority to promoting free trade and rebuilding America's economic strength, which had fallen behind that of Japan and Germany with respect to capital investment and productivity. By 2000 the restructuring of the U.S. economy had succeeded remarkably. An astonishing number of new jobs was created, and the gains in productivity became the envy of the world. A feeling of hubris set in among American business and financial leaders. Many economists and politicians concluded that America could continue to expand the economy indefinitely and pay for both new social programs and a sizeable defense establishment and thereby support its world-order obligations. As a result, the 1990s became a period of optimism bordering on euphoria about the future, resembling the first years following World War II. A great surge in consumer spending and a booming stock market led Federal Reserve Chairman Alan Greenspan to remark about the dangers of "irrational exuberance." The optimism ended in 2000 with a sharp decline in the stock market; it was dealt a stunning blow a year later by the economic effects of the 9/11 attacks. President Bush and Congress then shifted national priorities away from a focus on the economy and promotion of values and toward a far greater emphasis on defense of the homeland and establishment of a safer world order. Renewed attention was given to expanding the military's worldwide network of bases and to providing financial aid to countries and groups that joined the U.S. war on terrorism. Pakistan, for example, though a military-run regime, received more than $1 billion in aid, and in return cooperated with the U.S.-led war in Afghanistan. Russia, which provided overflight rights and intelligence support for the war, received indirect financial aid from Washington and a reduction in the Bush administration's criticism of Russia's military operation in Chechnya.

In sum, a fundamental shift in America's national priorities occurred in 2001–2002, away from emphasis on balanced budgets and domestic social programs and toward major support for homeland defense and fighting international terrorism. A commitment to expand U.S. military power and the financial outlays required to launch the war and occupation of Iraq raised this fundamental political question: Would Congress and the public support the president's shift in priorities required by his war on terrorism if the price turned out to be ballooning federal deficits, a reduction in social programs at home, and a prolonged insurgency in Iraq that would require a long-term commitment of American forces?

CHAPTER 6

ENSURING THE COUNTRY'S ECONOMIC WELL-BEING

The second important national interest pursued by most major powers is securing the economic well-being of the country. The United States had this as its primary national interest for more than a century after George Washington became its first president. During most of the nineteenth and early twentieth centuries, promoting trade and commerce dominated the foreign policies of both Republican and Democratic administrations. Early in the twentieth century, however, presidents Theodore Roosevelt and Woodrow Wilson vastly enlarged America's role in international politics by, respectively, precipitating war with Spain in 1898 and joining France and Britain in 1917 to defeat Germany in World War I. But the American public was not persuaded that the country should play a great power role, and following the European war it elected an isolationist Congress that promoted protectionism in trade policy and isolationism in defense policy, with emphasis on "no entangling alliances." A nationalist version of economic well-being became the primary focus of U.S. foreign policy, with "dollar diplomacy" and protective tariffs forming the basis of America's relationships with the world during the 1920s and 1930s. The outbreak of war in Europe, however, and Germany's defeat of France in 1940 stunned the country and resulted in a fundamental change in national priorities. Beginning in 1941, defeating Germany and Japan and thereafter establishing a lasting peace became

America's overriding national interest. Economic well-being took a secondary role behind defense of homeland and world order as the basis of President Franklin Roosevelt's wartime foreign policy. Promotion of values also was subordinated to winning a war in which allies—for example, the Soviet Union and Nationalist China—had not the kind of governments that epitomized American values. By 1945 a "sleeping giant" had been awakened, and the result was a fundamental turn in U.S. foreign policy.

ECONOMIC INTERESTS DURING THE COLD WAR

The economic well-being interest had a prominent role in foreign policy immediately after the war because the country needed to return the economy to peacetime production and reestablish trade and commerce with the world. World-order interests were also important in the postwar period; the United States took the lead in creating the United Nations to help keep the peace. It also supported other international institutions, such as the World Bank and the International Monetary Fund, as means by which to assist countries with their postwar reconstruction. However, the economies of European countries had been heavily damaged by war, and they faced serious political threats from local communist parties, which capitalized on public disillusionment. Rebuilding Europe's productive capacity became a high priority of the Truman administration, for both economic and world-order reasons. The Marshall Plan, approved by Congress in 1948, was President Truman's response to Europe's need to rebuild economically and to prevent communist groups under Moscow's direction from gaining control of key countries, specifically France and Italy. When the huge four-year Marshall aid program was launched in 1948, however, a serious security threat emerged in Eastern Europe. The Soviet Union imposed the Berlin Blockade in an effort to force the Western Allies to abandon their plan to integrate West Germany into the Marshall Plan and force them to withdraw their occupation forces from Berlin. For the next two years economic interests—rebuilding Western Europe and stimulating international trade and commerce—shared top priority with international security interests (world order) in Truman's response to the postwar crisis that gripped Western Europe. In 1949 he proposed the Point-4 Program of Technical Assistance to Developing Countries in order to promote trade and investment in the so-called Third World. He also responded to mounting Soviet pressures in Europe by agreeing to join the North Atlantic Alliance to guarantee the security of ten Western European countries. The huge Soviet armies that occupied all of Eastern Europe did not demobilize, as the United States had done in the postwar years, and by 1949 Europe was divided into two hostile political and economic systems. The Cold War had started.

North Korea's invasion of South Korea in June 1950 stunned Washington and caused President Truman to give U.S. defense-of-homeland and world-order interests far higher priorities than economic interests. He reacted swiftly to North Korea's attack, assuming correctly (as shown later) that the Soviet Union had encouraged that nation's communist leaders to test America's willingness to act militarily in Asia, where its armed forces were weak. This was a dangerous threat to U.S. interests in Japan, and the president, with UN support, immediately sent troops to repel the North Korean aggression. He asked Congress for a substantial increase in the defense budget to rebuild the armed forces, and both he and his successor, Dwight Eisenhower, continued on that course during the 1950s. Large amounts of economic and military assistance were offered to many countries to enlist their support in the Cold War struggle with the Soviet Union and, after 1949, with Communist China. The Eisenhower administration concluded large aid programs with many nations in East Asia and the Middle East, and it formed defense pacts with some of them to help contain Soviet and Chinese influence.

The subordination of economic interests to world-order and defense-of-homeland priorities continued throughout the 1950s and 1960s, with growing strains on the economy. The Vietnam War had a major negative impact on the U.S. economy because of the Johnson administration's unwillingness either to raise taxes or to cut nondefense spending. The result was an international financial crisis in 1971, forcing the Nixon administration to abandon the gold standard and adopt flexible exchange rates as the basis for conducting international trade. The United States also had to persuade its trading partners to accept a devaluation of the dollar, which resulted in inflation at home, a rise in interest rates, and growing unemployment. These factors were exacerbated by an Arab oil embargo in 1973–74, the result of President Nixon's strong support of Israel during its 1973 "October War" with Egypt. Although Nixon sought to strengthen the U.S. economy, his efforts failed, and the economic problems persisted. They worsened during the Carter administration because of soaring inflation, high interest rates, and a slowing economy. Carter's defeat in the election of 1980 brought to the White House a conservative Republican, Ronald Reagan, who was determined to turn the economy around, restore America's military power, and force an end to the Cold War. He cut taxes and spent heavily on the military. However, because Reagan could not persuade Congress to reduce domestic spending to offset tax cuts and expanded defense budgets, his administration ran up large federal deficits, and the Treasury Department was forced to borrow heavily. Reagan was convinced that the Soviet Union's economy could not match America's military buildup and that its leaders would eventually have to negotiate an end to the Cold War. His and the Federal Reserve Board's tough economic policies led to a serious recession in 1982–83 and large unemployment, but the president's attitude was that economic considerations were far less important to U.S. national interests than was ending the Cold War on America's terms. In the election of 1984 he was able to convince the public that his policies were working, and he won reelection with an increased majority.

By the time Reagan left office in 1989, the Cold War was near an end and the Soviet Union was withdrawing forces from Afghanistan and parts of Eastern Europe. Still, the economic price of winning the Cold War was a U.S. economy in serious need of repair. Reagan's successor, George H. W. Bush, began reducing the defense budget and American armed forces stationed in Europe and East Asia. This was intended to permit American firms to compete more effectively with rising industrial powers, notably Japan, Germany, and South Korea, which had greatly expanded their economies and exports during the Cold War. In automobiles, for example, Japanese and German cars not only competed successfully abroad with U.S.-made products but steadily increased their market shares in the United States.

In 1992 Bill Clinton campaigned for the presidency on the theme that Reagan and Bush had seriously neglected the country's domestic needs and that it was time to shift national priorities away from heavy U.S. involvement abroad and concentrate instead on providing jobs and expanding the economy. Clinton's message resonated with the electorate because it concluded that the successful Gulf War in 1991 and the demise of the Soviet Union a few months later had made it safe for the country to reduce further defense and foreign aid budgets and to spend far more on domestic social programs. Clinton succeeded impressively in stimulating the economy during his eight years in office and in reducing the unsustainable costs of a ballooning welfare system. However, the price Clinton paid for his early concentration on domestic issues was tardiness in coming to grips with a major foreign policy crisis in the Balkans, specifically in Bosnia, which vitally affected America's NATO allies. He was also late in recognizing the growing menace posed by international terrorism. The Al Qaeda network had set up training camps in Afghanistan in the mid-1990s, and it carried out deadly attacks on U.S. embassies in East Africa and U.S. military facilities in Saudi Arabia. On the other hand, Clinton established good working relations with the new leaders of Russia and China, Boris Yeltsin and Jiang Zemin, respectively, and persuaded the leaders of Israel and the PLO to begin the Oslo peace process. Despite his personal involvement in final negotiations between Israel and the PA in 2000, however, Clinton was unable to persuade their leaders to reach a final settlement, and hostilities then resumed.

When Clinton left office in 2001, the United States had achieved the status of economic superpower with no serious rivals; during his tenure more new jobs had been created than in any other period in U.S. history. The unemployment rate of 3.9 percent in 1999 was the lowest on record. Except for a few experts, such as Federal Reserve Chairman Alan Greenspan, who had warned earlier about "irrational exuberance" in the stock market, many Americans had come to believe that the unbounded prosperity generated by the economy in the 1990s would continue indefinitely. However, when the stock markets began a steady fall in 2000 and 2001, many companies were forced into bankruptcy and a mild recession followed.

The term "globalization" entered the public's vocabulary during the 1990s and remained a preoccupation of policy makers, economists, and pundits during that decade. The goal was free trade worldwide, based on the assumption that expanding trade would benefit all nations, including the United States, by encouraging them to produce those goods in which they had comparative advantages. The movement toward a global application of free trade was enhanced by conclusion of the North American Free Trade Agreement (NAFTA) in 1993 by Canada, Mexico, and the United States. NAFTA produced a rapid increase in trade and jobs in all three countries, even though some high-cost U.S. industries moved their production to lower-cost Mexico. Some policy makers talked optimistically about extending the NAFTA arrangement to other Latin American countries, but the loss of many manufacturing jobs in the United States that resulted from NAFTA caused American labor organizations to oppose its expansion to other countries. The European Common Market's evolution into the EU during the late 1990s contributed to America's support for globalization. The Senate's ratification of a new WTO, replacing the GATT, also facilitated the trend. Nevertheless, Congress had serious reservations about the desirability of additional free trade agreements, because some aspects were proving detrimental to many American industries—for example, steel. Critics cited alleged unfair foreign competition, both overseas and in the U.S. market. By the end of the decade additional U.S. corporations were moving production to lower-cost countries, one of them China, which had adopted a market economy despite the tight political controls exercised by its communist regime.

A widely known proponent of globalization was *New York Times* columnist Thomas Friedman. His best-selling book *The Lexus and the Olive Tree* described the wide differences that exist in the way people live in the developed world and in most countries of the Middle East, Africa, and parts of Asia. His thesis was that free trade and the free flow of capital around the world are virtually uncontrollable, because banks and global traders, the "electronic herd," can transfer hundreds of millions of dollars instantaneously as the result of the revolution in telecommunications. Friedman argued that governments could not stop the "herd"; he concluded that international free markets are inevitable. "There is just one global market today," he wrote, "and the only way you can grow at the speed your people want to grow is by tapping into the global stock and bond markets, by seeking out multinationals to invest in your country and by selling into the global trading system goods which your factories produce."[1]

THE IMPACT OF 9/11 ON U.S. ECONOMIC WELL-BEING

The Al Qaeda terrorist attacks of September 11, 2001, occurred at a time when the U.S. economy was headed into recession. The seriousness of the downturn was not apparent until after George W. Bush entered the White House in January 2001, however. In order to provide stimulus to the economy, he pressed Congress to pass a huge cut in individual income taxes; after bitter debate, Congress enacted a ten-year $1.3 trillion reduction in income taxes and also agreed to a refund on excess taxes paid from the beginning of that year. As a result, what had previously been projected by the Congressional Budget Office as large annual fiscal surpluses for the foreseeable future now became huge budget deficits. For the administration's policy makers, cutting the growth of the federal government was an essential means of strengthening the U.S. economy in the face of increasing foreign competition while allowing for an increase in defense spending. These budget projections were upset by the 9/11 attacks and the president's decision to go to war with Afghanistan. Congress quickly provided $20 billion to help New York cope with the economic damage caused by the 9/11 attacks, and it provided additional billions to aid U.S. airlines, which were economically devastated by the closing of U.S. airports for nearly a week and a sharp drop in passenger traffic. What had appeared in early 2001 to be a mild recession now turned into a more serious threat of economic dislocation due to increased defense and homeland security spending and a sharp drop in travel.

The huge tax cuts enacted in June 2001 now appeared to be premature to many in Congress, in light of the new realities in national security. Unemployment began to rise as many companies played it safe and cut their workforces in anticipation of a deeper recession. What had been the lowest unemployment level on record in 1999 now climbed steadily until June 2003, when it stood at 6.4 percent. Inflation remained low, however,

near 1 percent, and this stimulated the home-building industry by producing the lowest mortgage rates in memory. The economy grew slowly
in 2002 and 2003, but not at a fast enough pace to stem a rise in unemployment or provide additional revenues for the U.S. Treasury. As a result, President Bush's budget office projected a deficit for FY 2004 of $450
billion, the highest in history and an astonishing turnaround from the
surpluses that had been predicted by the Clinton administration. (The
final 2004 figure stood at $413 billion.)

By July 31, 2003, the country had lost 2.7 million manufacturing jobs
(from the beginning of the economic downturn in 2000). Many of them
had moved overseas as U.S. industries sought to reduce costs. A drop of
seventy-one thousand occurred at a time when the economy was expanding at 2.4 percent, producing a situation that some analysts called the
"jobless recovery." Democrats pointed out that 2.5 million of the industrial jobs had been lost since George Bush became president in 2001. One
of them, Senator Joseph Lieberman, the Democrats' vice-presidential
nominee in 2000, warned: "We are hemorrhaging manufacturing jobs,
which is a great threat to our future economic security and, more personally, to the reality of America as an opportunity country in which the
American dream, the promise of America, is still alive."[2] Even when
third-quarter statistics for 2003 indicated that the economy had expanded
by 8.2 percent, unemployment dropped only marginally, to 5.9 percent.
Economists suggested that a 9.4 percent growth in productivity accounted
for a large part of the modest increase in jobs. By 2004 the unemployment
had dropped somewhat, but the slowness in creation of new jobs, particularly in manufacturing, became a presidential election issue.

What was more troubling about the health of the U.S. economy, however, was the country's massive current-account deficit, which in 2003
and 2004 showed no signs of abating. The country was consuming foreign-
made products, including oil, at a rate that was far beyond the value of
goods and services exported to pay for them. This meant that the United
States was living considerably beyond its means, and there was no serious
effort by the government or the media to dampen Americans' desire for
imported goods. Globalization seemed to be working too well. Americans
appreciated the lower prices they paid for foreign products; however, U.S.
workers were losing well-paying jobs because they could not compete

with low-paid foreign workers. The trade deficit for just one month, May 2003, hit $41.34 billion, and analysts predicted it would go higher, as imports of cars, televisions, business equipment, and crude oil were running ahead of the previous year. In December 2003 the trade deficit in goods and services stood at $489.4 billion for the year, a substantial increase over the 2002 total of $419 billion. The trend in 2004 continued upward, as the monthly figure for April reached $48.3 billion, an increase from $46.6 billion the month before. The April 2004 deficit was $5.8 billion larger than a year earlier, in April 2003. By December 2004 the annual trade deficit had soared 24 percent, to $617 billion. Clearly, the vaunted American economy could not sustain for long such massive imbalances without risking a major devaluation of the dollar, a large increase in the cost of living, and the loss of U.S. economic influence abroad. Some experts worried that the euro, which passed the dollar in value in 2003 and reached $1.30 in 2004, would one day replace the dollar as the world's major reserve currency. This was not likely to happen in the near term, they believed.

Six trading partners accounted for most of the U.S. deficit for May 2003. They were China, with a $9.86 billion surplus; Japan, $4.48 billion; Canada, $4.08 billion; Mexico, $3.42 billion; Germany, $3.25 billion; and Venezuela, whose trade surplus was $1.36 billion. These six accounted for two-thirds of the total U.S. trade deficit; China alone comprised 20 percent of the total. Despite a gradual devaluation of the dollar in 2003 and 2004, these percentages changed little in 2004.

Figure 5 places these six countries on a national-interest matrix, in terms of their economic importance to America's economic well-being.

Canada, Japan, China, and Mexico are, respectively, the largest and most important trading partners of the United States, and they are also vital to U.S. world-order interests. Moreover, Canada and Mexico, which share long borders with the United States, are vital to the defense of its homeland as well. Canada, Mexico, and Venezuela are major suppliers of crude oil to the United States, making it less dependent than Europe and Japan on Persian Gulf oil. Although China is neither a U.S. ally nor a producer of oil, it is highly important to U.S. interests in Asia and has cooperated with the Bush administration in five-power negotiations with North Korea to stop its production of nuclear weapons. Each American

FIGURE 5
U.S. TRADE DEFICIT BY MAJOR TRADING PARTNER

Basic Interest	*Intensity of Interest*			
	Survival	*Vital*	*Major*	*Peripheral*
Defense of Homeland				
ECONOMIC WELL-BEING		Canada	Germany	
		Japan	Venezuela	
		China		
		Mexico		
Favorable World Order				
Promotion of Values				

president starting with Richard Nixon has determined that China is a major, perhaps vital, world-order interest and that great efforts should be made with it to reach an accommodation of policies in Asia. This was particularly important when major security issues of concern to Washington were before the UN Security Council, where China has a permanent seat and veto power. Germany, the fifth of the trade-surplus countries, remains a major U.S. ally in Europe despite its refusal to support the U.S. invasion of Iraq in 2003.

Crude oil imports are a major factor in the continuing U.S. trade imbalances, a problem that becomes acute whenever international prices rise in response to foreign crises, especially in the Persian Gulf. The latest occurred in the spring of 2004, when the price went to forty dollars a barrel and gasoline prices in the United States topped two dollars a gallon. The huge import of oil into the United States was spurred by the driving habits of American motorists, who in the late 1990s purchased larger and less fuel-efficient cars and trucks. The insatiable demand for oil resulted in an increase of 20 percent in imports during the 1990s. By 2003 oil imports accounted for more than 50 percent of U.S. oil consumption. However, when the U.S. Senate debated a proposal to increase the fuel efficiency of automobiles by 2010, including on gas-consuming sport utility vehicles, the measure was rejected because it was considered too sensitive politically. Six countries that accounted for most U.S. oil imports, in millions of barrels per day, were Canada (1.9), Saudi Arabia (1.5), Mexico (1.5), Venezuela (1.4), Nigeria (0.6), and Iraq (0.5).

TRADE POLICY AND WORLD-ORDER INTERESTS

A case can reasonably be made that since the 1970s, in terms of U.S. trade policy toward major trading partners, the United States has subordinated its interest in economic well-being to an emphasis on defense of homeland and world-order interests. A discussion of the six trade deficit countries listed above elaborates this reality.

CANADA

Canada offers a particularly interesting case of a major trading partner that benefited significantly from free trade with the United States. It is also America's largest trading partner and dwarfs that with Japan and with Mexico. Total U.S.-Canada trade in 2003 amounted to $441 billion. Approximately 80 percent of Canada's exports are to the United States, an astonishing figure. But the U.S. trade deficit with Canada in 2003 and 2004 was also remarkable. In 2003 the trade deficit was $54 billion, and in 2004 it ballooned to $65 billion, a 27% increase. Statistics for 2003 and 2004 show there was no improvement in the figures, despite a devaluation of the U.S. dollar against the Canadian currency. Oil imports accounted for a part of the increase, but imports of autos and auto parts, mainly from Ontario, were a large factor.

The steep rise in Canadian exports to the United States began in the mid-1990s as a result of NAFTA. A contributing factor was the Canadian dollar's weakness, which created a favorable exchange rate during the late 1990s. From a high of about eighty cents for the U.S. dollar in 1994, the Canadian "loonie," as it is called, depreciated by 25 percent over a decade, trading at less than sixty cents in 2002. Obviously, with a 25 percent price advantage, Canadian products competed successfully against American-made goods, causing U.S. auto manufacturers to increase production in Canada instead of the United States as consumer demand for cars increased. However, when the U.S. dollar fell sharply in 2003, producers in Canada complained that they could not compete with American products.

NAFTA caused a political backlash among protectionist segments in the United States, particularly labor organizations, which protested manufacturing jobs moving to Mexico. The issue became a major theme in the 1992 presidential election, when Independence Party candidate Ross Perot warned of a "huge sucking sound" of U.S. jobs going to Mexico if NAFTA was approved by Congress. Since 1940 Canadian and American governments have agreed that their vast continental territories should be treated as a single defense zone. During the 1950s the United States built an early warning defense system in the Canadian Arctic to protect the continent against incoming Soviet bombers. Later these bases became capable of tracking incoming Soviet missiles if nuclear war broke out. The North American Aerospace Defense Command, located at Colorado Springs, Colorado, is the symbol of joint U.S.-Canadian operations in defense of both homelands. Canadian territory is also used by the United States for testing missiles and training troops. Canada and America share a deep interest in promoting free and democratic governments abroad and in providing humanitarian assistance to less developed countries. However, Ottawa often does not share the American view of creating a favorable world order. For example, it did not break diplomatic relations with Fidel Castro's communist regime in Cuba, even though it was a ruthless dictatorship and had concluded a defense alliance with Moscow. Also, Canada did not support the U.S. war in Vietnam and it was among the first countries to recognize the new communist regime in China when it took control in 1949. Although it joined the UN coalition, led by the United States, during the Korean War, it did not break relations when China entered that war on the side of North Korea against UN forces.

During the Cold War, Washington's policy makers considered Canadian cooperation so important to the defense of North America that they were reluctant on some issues to risk alienating the Canadian public and bringing to power a government that actively opposed U.S. foreign policy. During the 1970s, for example, there were hints of this possibility during the long tenure of Pierre Trudeau, the Liberal Party's leader and a prime minister who sought to forge an independent Canadian foreign policy and diminish its growing economic dependence on the U.S. market and on American investments. An additional factor was the growth in Quebec of an independence movement that brought to power in 1976 the Parti Quebecois on an avowedly secessionist platform. The damage that could be caused by an independent, French-speaking, sovereign country on America's northern border, one that held neutralist sentiments in foreign policy, was a prospect that Washington's policy makers were not willing to confront as the Cold War neared its climax in the early 1980s.

When Conservative Party leader Brian Mulroney became prime minister in 1985, relations with the United States improved markedly. He proposed to President Reagan a free trade pact between their countries that would greatly increase mutual trade and force Canadian industries that were protected by high tariffs to modernize or fail. The Free Trade Agreement (FTA) was signed just before Reagan left office, and it quickly enhanced the trade relationship as well as political ties. Mulroney, a native of Quebec, helped to dampen the sentiment for independence in that province, a major objective of U.S. policy. However, as the Canadian dollar declined against the U.S. currency in the 1990s, tensions rose around claims by U.S. producers, particularly in lumber, that Canada provided illegal subsidies to its producers. American labor groups complained that U.S. auto companies were transferring production to Canada because of the cheaper wage rates; Canadians countered that their workforce was better trained and more reliable than in many American industries.

In sum, Canada benefited hugely from free trade with the United States, while Washington gained by continuing to have a peaceful, cooperative defense partner on its northern border. As the European Union gained members and political cohesiveness at the turn of the century, it was clearly in the U.S. political as well as economic interest to move toward a closer relationship not only with Canada and Mexico in NAFTA but also with Central and South American countries. For this, Canada was a crucial ally whose political cooperation was more important to Washington than a large trade deficit. For the Bush administration a hopeful sign occurred in December 2003 when Finance Minister Paul Martin replaced Jean Chretien as Canada's prime minister. Chretien had openly disagreed with Bush's policy on Iraq and on some aspects of his homeland security policies. He was not among Bush's favorite foreign leaders. Martin indicated that he hoped to improve relations.

MEXICO

Like Canada, Mexico is crucial to the security of the United States, even though its territory was less exposed in military terms than was Canada's during the Cold War. Nevertheless, as noted in chapter 5, Mexico presents a serious security problem for the United States because of illegal drugs that originate in or pass through it on their way to U.S. cities. For example, in July 2003 U.S. and Mexican drug enforcement agents seized thirteen tons of cocaine and 240 traffickers, most of them in the United States, in a joint effort to break up Mexico's largest drug-smuggling network. Unlike Canada, Mexico has had a long history of fierce opposition to U.S. foreign policies stemming from the war in 1848, in which Mexico lost two-thirds of its territory, and from an American invasion in 1913. Until Mexico joined NAFTA in 1993, it was a poor Third World country with huge unemployment and high protective tariffs. Its government had been dominated since 1929 by the increasingly corrupt Institutional Revolutionary Party (PRI). The country has a strong anti-American Marxist minority that had a heavy influence on Mexico's foreign policy. During the 1950s, the Cuban revolutionary Fidel Castro was given sanctuary in Mexico, where he raised a small guerrilla force that eventually took over Cuba. Thereafter, Mexico provided support to the Castro government and refused to break relations despite great pressure from Washington. In the United Nations, Mexico usually voted with the nonaligned group of nations. This changed in the 1980s, when the country was on the verge of bankruptcy. The Reagan administration concluded that Mexico was too vital to U.S. interests to permit economic chaos to develop there, and the U.S. Treasury organized a large international loan to avoid that prospect.

As a result of American financial and political help in restoring the economy, Mexico's foreign policy became more accommodating. In 1989, when President Carlos Salinas proposed to President George H. W. Bush that Mexico should be accorded a free trade arrangement like the one with Canada, American labor organizations and farmers mounted strong opposition, arguing that because of its low wage rates, lack of labor organizations, and few environmental laws, free trade would result in American companies' transferring production south of the border. Independent Party candate Ross Perot campaigned on this issue and won 19 percent of the popular vote in the 1992 election. Political observers considered this outcome a serious challenge to the prevailing view of both Republican and Democratic leaders that, in the long run, free trade benefited the United States economically even though some industries and workers would be harmed in the short term. When Bill Clinton became president in 1993 he fully embraced the free trade policies of his Republican predecessors and pressed Congress to ratify the NAFTA arrangement. Clinton was convinced that Mexico was essential to U.S. economic and defense interests, but he made some concessions to U.S. labor by giving Mexican producers only gradual free access to the U.S. market. The expectation was that growing prosperity in Mexico would enhance both the economy and security of the United States. It was a courageous political judgment by a Democratic president against strong opposition from the U.S. labor movement. Defense and world-order interests trumped economic ones in Clinton's calculation.

VENEZUELA

Like Canada and Mexico, Venezuela is strategically located in the North American–Caribbean region and is a major oil supplier to the United States. It also accounts for a significant portion of the American trade deficit with the world. Since 1958, Venezuela has enjoyed a series of democratic governments following many years of military-dominated regimes. Like other countries in Latin America, it had opposed many U.S. policies that it believed were not in line with its national interests. Nevertheless, Venezuela is now heavily dependent on the American market, and from Washington's view, it constitutes a major factor in U.S. efforts to stabilize the political situation in neighboring Colombia, where drug traffickers and Marxist guerrillas are determined to bring down the democratic regime. Hugo Chavez, a former army officer, was elected Venezuela's president in 1999 by winning the support of the country's large poor population. He soon announced an agenda of social and economic revolution designed to break the grip of an entrenched oligarchy on the economy. Washington adopted a hands-off policy, believing that Chavez's policies would bankrupt the country and lead to his defeat in the next election. A more fundamental reason for Washington's caution was that, with the Cold War over, Venezuela did not constitute a security threat and that, as long as its oil exports were not interrupted, the country was also not an economic threat. Although Chavez's political and economic support to Cuba's Fidel Castro was irritating and his support of Colombia's rebels was troubling, both Bill Clinton and George W. Bush concluded they could live with a leftist government in Venezuela so long as it did not threaten its neighbors or U.S. interests in the Caribbean. Chavez apparently understands this and has been careful, as of 2004, not to cross a line that would trigger strong U.S. action.

CHINA

The People's Republic of China presents a far greater economic and political problem for the United States. Its trade surplus in 2004 was $162 billion, a 35 percent increase over 2003 and one-fourth of America's worldwide trade deficit. After Congress granted equal trade treatment to Chinese exports in the 1990s and Clinton supported Beijing's entry into the WTO, its exports to the United States exploded while its internal policies prevented a similar rapid importation of American products. By 2004, members of Congress, including Democratic presidential aspirants, were calling on the Bush administration to take action to stop the loss of U.S. jobs to low-wage factories in China. Part of the problem was the value of China's currency, the yuan, which was pegged to the U.S. dollar. It did not rise in strength as the U.S. currency declined in 2003 and 2004. As a result, not only was the total amount of Chinese goods entering the U.S. market not declining, but China continued to accumulate tens of billions of American dollars.

The mounting trade crisis with China was summed up in a *Wall Street Journal* news analysis: "With consumer confidence shaky and unemployment at a nine-year high, American anxiety about China's export prowess and the exodus of U.S. jobs overseas is emerging as a significant political issue."[3] *Washington Post* business columnist Steven Pearlstein commented on growing concerns in the U.S. business community: "We're talking here about China, now on the fast track to becoming a dominant player in the global economy and causing much disruption along the way." He asserted that entire U.S. industries were being wiped out as production was shifted across the Pacific by U.S.-based multinationals "that have concluded they have to abandon their U.S. workers and suppliers to squeeze out another penny to keep the order from Wal-Mart."[4]

Why did the U.S. government, beginning with the Reagan administration in the 1980s, give special consideration to China's drive to modernize its economy and enter the world of free trade? Unlike Canada, Mexico, or Venezuela, China is not a key oil exporter, and its trade with the United States is dwarfed by that of Canada, Mexico, or Japan. Two major political factors account for Washington's willingness to encourage China's rapid rise as an economic power. One is Taiwan; the other is North Korea. (These issues are discussed more fully in chapter 7.) In the case of Taiwan, the United States hoped to avoid war with China in the Taiwan Strait; on North Korea, it needed China's support in halting Pyongyang's drive to become a nuclear power. American policy makers calculated that if China prospered economically and its economy became heavily invested in the U.S. market, its leaders would be more willing than otherwise to accommodate Washington's political objectives in Asia. It was a calculated risk, and in 2003 it seemed to have paid dividends on both issues. In December, during a visit to Washington by Chinese Premier Wen Jia-bao, President Bush publicly warned the government of Taiwan not to proceed with a referendum that could lead to the island's declaring its independence. He asserted that neither China nor Taiwan should take unilateral actions that would upset the current balance in relations between them. In doing this, Bush was reiterating a U.S. policy that had been followed since 1971 of recognizing only one China and leaving it to Beijing and Taiwan to work out their future relations without either side threatening the other. As a result of Wen's visit, the expectation in Washington was that China would take the necessary steps to reduce the growing trade imbalance, which threatened to cause serious political problems in the United States and in U.S.-China relations. That situation did not improve in 2004.

JAPAN AND GERMANY

Japan and Germany are linked to the United States in similar ways. Both were totally defeated in 1945, but American policy made it possible for them to establish democratic systems and build thriving economies. In addition, both were indebted to the United States for protection during the Cold War, and each in a different way emerged as a responsible military power in its part of the world. Each became an economic powerhouse during the 1970s and 1980s, dominating trade and commerce with neighboring states. One large difference between Germany's and Japan's postwar experiences, however, was their political relations with neighbors. Germany made peace with France, with which it had fought three wars in seventy-five years, and with other European states through the European Common Market and later the EU, which took effect in the 1990s. Japan was not able to make a similar accommodation with its neighbors, China and Korea. It was also unable to settle a border dispute with the Soviet Union resulting from World War II. As a result, Japan depended on the United States for political and military help as it built itself into the world's second-largest economic power. After the Cold War, Germany turned to closer relations with France and its European neighbors while Japan continued close ties to Washington, in order to protect itself against North Korea's nuclear ambitions and China's determination to be the superpower in East Asia. This difference was highlighted in 2003 when Germany flatly refused to support either politically or financially the U.S. intervention in Iraq, whereas Japan agreed to send a contingent of troops and pledged $1.5 billion to help with reconstruction.

In sum, the reality of America's economic well-being interest in 2004 was that it was being subordinated to U.S. world-order interests abroad while the U.S. economy was going through severe strains at home. That raised a fundamental question about the hegemonic aspirations of the Clinton and Bush administrations: Could the United States continue to dominate the international system to the extent that it hoped if its economy did not return to the vibrancy that it had experienced in the 1990s? Put another way, was the United States prepared to endure a less than robust economy and a decline in its standard of living in order to pursue a coercive hegemonic foreign policy abroad? That question would be put to the test in 2004 when the economic and political costs of the Iraq war were debated in the 2004 presidential election campaign.[5]

Iraq in the Persian Gulf War and then watched the Soviet Union's dissolution. The United States no longer had a significant foreign enemy and the crucial Middle East oil supplies seemed secure. Optimism, even complacency, once again characterized the public's attitude on foreign policy and national security, and the nation's attention again turned to pressing domestic affairs. In the 1992 presidential election, voters chose Bill Clinton, a former governor of Arkansas who had pledged during the campaign to focus his attention on the country's domestic needs, especially its lagging economy. Even though Americans gave Ronald Reagan and George H. W. Bush much credit for bringing the Cold War to an end and for winning the Gulf War, they decided that it was time for change.

CLINTON'S VIEW OF U.S. WORLD-ORDER INTERESTS

During his eight years in the White House, Bill Clinton exhibited in his foreign policy both progress and drift. He succeeded in building good relations with the new leadership of Russia, the principal successor state of the defunct Soviet Union, and with the People's Republic of China, both of them nuclear powers. On Russia, Clinton supported the efforts of its president, Boris Yeltsin, to abandon a bankrupt state-run economy and institute free markets as well as to privatize major industries. He also encouraged Yeltsin to hold elections and permit political parties and a free press to operate without government interference. Clinton encouraged world lending agencies and private business to invest in Russia, in order to stimulate its economy and provide opportunities for a new class of private entrepreneurs. Regarding China, relations had been severely strained in 1989 by the communist regime's brutal suppression of massive student-led demonstrations in Beijing's Tiananmen Square, leaving hundreds dead. After Clinton came to office he persuaded a reluctant Congress not to impose economic sanctions and eventually to agree to a trade arrangement that produced large benefits to U.S. commercial interests. Although Clinton regularly criticized China for its poor human rights record, he did not permit the country's promotion-of-values interest to get in the way of efforts to build a favorable world-order relationship with Asia's preeminent power or hinder its efforts at economic reform. Clinton's multilateral approach to foreign policy during his first term was applauded by the NATO allies. His consultations even led them to acquiesce in Washington's plan to expand the alliance eastward to include Poland, the Czech Republic, and Hungary.

Nevertheless, the Clinton years were marked by uncertain leadership in other aspects of his drive to advance America's world-order and economic interests. The first was his 1993 withdrawal of American troops from Somalia under less than favorable circumstances. The second was his controversial military intervention in Haiti in 1994 to restore to power an elected leader, Bertrand Aristide, who indicated little inclination to run a democratic government. During the Bosnia crisis in 1994–95, Clinton showed ambivalence about intervening when European governments asked Washington to lead a coalition military force to stop the ethnic cleansing, which had caused massive killings of local Muslims by Serbs and Croats. Similarly, Clinton's response to terrorist attacks on U.S. embassies in Africa in 1998 and earlier ones on American installations in Saudi Arabia did not result in sustained action to deal with Al Qaeda terrorists.

Although it seemed unlikely that any president in 1995 could have persuaded a complacent public to support a large military action abroad, Bosnia turned out to be an exception. After weeks of daily television coverage of brutal ethnic killings occurring there, the public and Congress demanded action on humanitarian grounds. As a result, in December 1995 the United States and many European countries sent military forces to Bosnia to stop the civil war. The Pentagon sent twenty thousand troops and the Europeans contributed another forty thousand, a massive show of force that quickly forced a halt to the violence. The United States then brought the warring parties together in Dayton, Ohio, where they were persuaded to begin work on a constitutional arrangement for sharing power. Clinton was given much credit in Europe for his decision to intervene in Bosnia, but many members of Congress voiced concern that the United States had become "bogged down in the Balkans."

Neither American nor European governments were willing in the late 1990s to take strong action against a growing international terrorist threat after two U.S. embassies in Africa were attacked, with a large loss of life, or when France, Italy, and Spain experienced terrorist bombings associated with their large Muslim populations. In 1998, when Saddam Hussein's government in Iraq forced the withdrawal of UN arms inspectors who had been there since 1991 to monitor a UN agreement, only the United States and Britain responded by bombing Iraq military installations. Moreover, European governments, led by France, Germany, and Russia, which had large business dealings in Iraq, were anxious to lift sanctions rather than use force to achieve compliance with UN resolutions. Although Congress responded to the expulsion of the arms inspectors with legislation calling for "regime change" in Iraq, neither the American public nor America's allies seemed prepared to abandon the peaceful world order they thought had been ushered in when the Cold War ended.

By 1998, U.S. and British intelligence agencies understood the magnitude of the international terrorist threat posed by the Al Qaeda network, with its base in Afghanistan. But without sufficient public support for military action, Clinton was unwilling to undertake a major campaign to warn the country against the impending danger. In addition, Congressional impeachment proceedings against him at that time contributed to a period of drift in America's attention to a growing threat to its vital economic and world-order interests in the Persian Gulf.

BUSH'S VIEW OF WORLD-ORDER INTERESTS

George W. Bush came to the White House in 2001 primarily interested in reducing taxes and avoiding entanglements in "nation building" abroad. He tended to be unilateralist in his thinking on foreign policy and far less willing than Clinton to engage the NATO allies and others on major international issues, including a global-warming treaty, North Korea's nuclear weapons threat, relations with Russia and China, and numerous issues before the United Nations. On the threat posed by international terrorism, Bush's response was tentative at best. Two months before he took office, Al Qaeda sent a suicide bomber to attack the USS *Cole* while it was visiting Aden, Yemen, and nearly sank it, causing the loss of a score of American lives. Bill Clinton did not respond to this blatant attack, probably because of the impending transition to the new Bush administration and lack of clear evidence as to who had been responsible.

George Tenet, director of the CIA and the president's principal adviser on intelligence matters, warned the new president of the terrorist danger to the United States soon after he entered the White House in January 2001. But George Bush decided to avoid moving boldly against Al Qaeda until Congress enacted part of his domestic program, especially the huge tax cuts he had called for during the election campaign. Although by June that legislation and several others had been passed by Congress, the intelligence community and the president gave little attention to the possibility that a major terrorist attack on the United States itself was imminent. The nation later learned, during the April 2004 public hearings of the 9/11 Commission, that the intelligence community knew of Al Qaeda's heightened intention to attack U.S. targets. However, it believed the attacks would occur abroad, not in the United States—even though evidence showed that Al Qaeda had carried out the 1993 bombing of the Twin Towers in New York.[1]

Following the 9/11 attacks, President Bush abruptly changed course and enunciated a new, expansive definition of the country's world-order interests. In a series of speeches, notably his State of the Union address to Congress in January 2002, he called for regime change in Iraq, Iran, and North Korea, which, he charged, harbored terrorists and threatened neighbors with WMD. In September 2002 he outlined his vision of a new American strategy, *The National Security Strategy of the United States of America* (see chapter 4). It contained three major departures from previous presidential statements of strategy for defending U.S. world-order interests: the United States would act preemptively with military force against any country that it viewed as dangerous to its security; America would maintain a level of military power superior to that of any potential enemy; although the United States preferred to act in concert with allies and friends, it would decide unilaterally, if necessary, to defend its vital interests against any country that threatened them. This White House document was issued as the Pentagon prepared for an invasion of Iraq. The question was whether the president would act unilaterally in Iraq, without the UN's approval, and thereby sacrifice other world-order interests in his determination to eliminate the potential threat posed by Saddam Hussein's regime.

In March 2003 the rationale given by the White House for launching an attack on Iraq was that its defeat would remove a dangerous dictator who possessed WMD and threatened his neighbors as well as the United States. By the summer of 2003, with Saddam Hussein's government gone and no WMD found, a different rationale for the U.S. invasion was being enunciated by Condoleezza Rice, the president's national security adviser. In an op-ed column in August in the *Washington Post* entitled "Transforming the Middle East," she outlined the administration's grand strategy for expanding America's world-order interests in that region. Comparing the challenge facing the United States in the Middle East to the rebuilding of Europe after it defeated Nazi Germany in 1945, she observed:

> Today we and our friends and allies must commit ourselves to a long-term transformation in another part of the world: the Middle East. A region of 22 countries with a combined population of 300 million, the Middle East has a combined GDP less than that of Spain, population of 40 million. It is held back by what leading Arab intellectuals call a political and economic "freedom deficit." In many countries a sense of helplessness provides a fertile ground for ideologies of hatred. . . . These ingredients are a recipe for regional instability—and pose a continuing threat to America's security.

Rice cited the president's recent efforts to broker peace in meetings with Israeli Prime Minister Ariel Sharon and Palestinian Prime Minister Mahmoud Abbas to produce the basis of a two-state solution to the continuing conflict. She then outlined the administration's long-range plans: "The transformation of the Middle East will not be easy, and it will take time. It will require the broad engagement of America, Europe and all free nations working in full partnership with those in the region who share our belief in the power of human freedom. This is not primarily a military commitment but one that will require us to engage all aspects of our national power—diplomatic, economic and cultural." She concluded by citing an idealistic vision of the future, reminiscent of President Woodrow Wilson's vision expressed in 1918 after the end of World War I: "America is determined to help the people of the Middle East achieve their full potential. We will act because we want greater freedom and opportunity for the people of the region, as well as greater security for people in America and throughout the world."[2]

The notable aspect of Rice's commentary was the sweeping rhetoric regarding America's mission, even destiny, not just to crush tyranny in Iraq but to transform the entire Middle East to conform to America's version of a favorable world order. However, the comparison she drew between America's role in reconstructing Europe after World War II and the challenge of a post-Saddam Middle East was flawed. Defeated Germany, for example, was a culturally united society in 1945, even though Moscow soon sealed off its occupation zone in the east. Iraq was a country deeply divided by religious and ethnic tensions and in danger of civil war among Sunni, Shiite, and Kurdish populations. Also, in 1945 Germany was a totally defeated country. In linking the rebuilding of Europe after World War II with that of remaking the Middle East after the Iraq war, Rice seriously understated the task ahead.

President Bush reinforced the ideological thrust of his world-order strategy on Iraq in a major address to the National Endowment for Peace in Washington, D.C., on November 6, 2003. Echoing Ronald Reagan's call twenty-one years earlier for a "crusade for freedom" in the context of the Cold War struggle with the Soviet Union, Mr. Bush spoke of the spread of democracy in the world as a moral mission. America's war in Iraq, he declared, was an obligation to extend freedom, just as it had been in World War II and the Cold War: "Iraq democracy will succeed, and that success will send forth the news, from Damascus to Tehran, that freedom can be the future of every nation."[3]

WORLD-ORDER INTERESTS AFTER IRAQ

The "unfinished war" in Afghanistan, as critics called it, and the rapidly rising costs of the occupation and reconstruction of Iraq, raised major questions about the Bush administration's long-term foreign policy objectives. What had earlier been viewed as a short-term occupation and a rapid transition to a provisional Iraqi government had become by September 2003 a more uncertain matter because of mounting terrorist attacks in Baghdad and the Sunni Triangle and delays in getting the Governing Council to start the process of forming an interim government and writing a constitution. As a result, the Senate Foreign Relations Committee had searching questions for the Pentagon's leadership regarding the need to persuade America's allies to share the costs of reconstruction. A second question was how the Bush administration intended to pay for the new military commitments it had undertaken in Central Asia after the 9/11 attacks. Another was whether the president should request Congress to expand the size of the U.S. Army in order to accommodate its longer than anticipated tasks in Iraq. The president's 2002 national security strategy paper suggested a forward U.S. military presence that seemed beyond the ability of the armed forces to sustain. Senior army officers, strongly supported by Senator John McCain, argued that the Army was stretched too thin in Iraq and should be reinforced. Prewar Pentagon projections that many troops could be withdrawn by September 2003 had proven illusory, and the Army was having morale problems when soldiers' tours of duty in Iraq were extended to a full year in order to keep the force level at about 130,000 for another six months. In addition, the White House was facing a projected FY 2004 budget deficit of $450 billion, a stunning turnaround from the large surpluses that had been predicted just three years earlier.

While the United States dealt with the growing complexity of the occupation of Iraq, other countries—Indonesia, the Philippines, Russia, Jordan, Saudi Arabia—suffered the impact of Al Qaeda–linked terrorist attacks in their countries. Attorney General John Ashcroft and Homeland Security Secretary Tom Ridge warned Americans to be prepared for additional attacks on the homeland as well as U.S. embassies and bases abroad. Another task for the administration was how to persuade North Korea and Iran to stop their quests to produce nuclear weapons.

Figure 6, on the national-interest matrix, is my assessment of the threat level that a number of countries posed to U.S. world-order interests after the fall of Saddam Hussein's regime in 2003. The intensity of the danger from these countries is discussed below.

EAST ASIA

The principal threats to U.S. international security interests in this region are North Korea and China. Whereas North Korea is openly hostile to the United States, China is currently cooperative on most foreign policy

FIGURE 6
PRINCIPAL THREATS TO U.S. WORLD-ORDER INTERESTS

Basic Interest	Intensity of Interest			
	Survival	*Vital*	*Major*	*Peripheral*
Defense of Homeland				
Economic Well-Being				
FAVORABLE WORLD ORDER		China	Indonesia	
		N. Korea	Pakistan	
		Iraq	Afghanistan	
		Israel-PA	Iran	
			Turkey	
			Saudi Arabia	
			France	
			Russia	
			Colombia	
Promotion of Values				

matters, including North Korea's nuclear threat. Indonesia is a third country that potentially could reach the danger level with respect to world-order interests, but in 2003 and 2004 its government was generally cooperative with the United States in the war on terrorism.

North Korea is a dangerous (vital) threat to U.S. interests in East Asia because of its determination to build nuclear weapons and an intercontinental-missile capability. The Clinton administration wrestled with the threat during the 1990s but failed to dissuade Pyongyang from breaking a 1994 agreement with the United States under which it had suspended nuclear weapons production in return for large economic aid from the United States, Japan, and South Korea. President Bush refused to negotiate bilaterally with North Korea and stopped U.S. economic aid, arguing that its neighbors had equally important security interests at stake. In 2003, despite opposition from conservative groups, the president decided to pursue a diplomatic route with four Asian countries—Japan, South Korea, China, and Russia. This was an effort to convince the reclusive Pyongyang regime that it would find it a beneficial compromise to stop nuclear weapons production and submit to international inspections in return for a U.S. pledge not to attack North Korea and to resume economic assistance. China was the principal channel for communicating with North Korean leaders and arranging subsequent multinational meetings in Beijing, at which U.S. and North Korean representatives clarified their countries' positions. Japan and South Korea also made overtures to the North Korean government.

President Bush was at that time inclined toward negotiations instead of military confrontation because of heavy U.S. involvement in Iraq. If negotiations failed, however, and Pyongyang continued its nuclear weapons program, the United States reserved the option, under Bush's doctrine of preemptive war, to use force. As in the case of Iraq, a decision to do so would also aim at regime change in North Korea. A large question would then arise: would the other interested countries—China, Japan, Russia, and South Korea—oppose U.S. military action against North Korea? Washington would then have to decide whether its world-order interests were so threatened by North Korea's nuclear program that it should act unilaterally. An ominous view was introduced in 2003 by a Japanese political leader who suggested that Japan might one day find it necessary to become a nuclear power. This remark probably was designed to warn North Korea and China that Japan would not need to rely solely on the U.S. defense guarantee but would also have its own deterrent to Pyongyang's nuclear threat.

A new element was introduced into the Korean equation in May 2004 when Washington announced that it would withdraw about 12,000 troops from South Korea over the following year and that 3,600 would immediately be sent to Iraq to augment forces there. This followed an earlier decision reached by Washington and Seoul to move U.S. forces from their facilities in Seoul to new locations in the south of the country, thereby making them less conspicuous to the civilian population in South Korea's capital. The remaining U.S. force would then number about twenty-four thousand. These moves were intended in part to facilitate five-power discussions with North Korea about easing tensions as well as pressing Pyongyang to accept firm international guarantees regarding its nuclear program.

China is a potential challenge for the United States in Asia because of its size, military potential, and apparent determination to become the dominant power in East Asia. The near-term danger for U.S.-China relations is Taiwan, should its populace elect a government that pursues independence and asks for international recognition. China is adamant that such a move would mean war. The United States has a long-standing commitment to defend Taiwan if it is attacked, but since 1972 Washington has adhered to the view that Taiwan is a part of China. President Bush reiterated this policy when he became president. In December 2003 he reinforced this by warning Taiwan's leadership against a referendum that could open the way to declaring Taiwan's independence. He also stated that the United States opposed unilateral steps by either side to upset the current situation, in which Taiwan enjoyed autonomy and a democratic political system. Taiwan's national elections in March 2004 resulted in its government's decision not to press the issue of independence. Like Clinton's approach to China, the Bush administration sought to encourage China's economic and political development and to assure its leaders that it had no intention of seeking to contain China, as many Chinese suspected. The long-term reality is that China aspires to replace America eventually as the paramount power in East Asia. So long as the growth of Beijing's influence does not endanger the security of U.S. allies, such as Japan, South Korea, the Philippines, and Thailand, the gradual expansion of China's influence should not pose a dangerous threat to U.S. world-order interests.

Indonesia straddles the key waterways between the Indian Ocean, the South China Sea, and the Pacific Ocean—a vital strategic area for the United States and other maritime states. Founded in 1949, the country was ruled by a nationalist authoritarian government until 1965, when an attempted communist coup was crushed by the army led by General Suharto. He subsequently became president and his military-led government brought stability and extensive economic development but also rampant corruption. Suharto's regime was ousted in 1999 and replaced by a weak constitutional regime. The new elected government was slow to deal with an Indonesian terrorist organization linked to Al Qaeda that carried out devastating bombings in Bali and Jakarta in 2003. Unlike the neighboring Philippines, which sought security cooperation with Washington in order to crush its Muslim terrorist organization, Indonesia's government did not accept similar cooperation because of a reluctance to bolster the influence of its discredited military. In national elections held in October 2004, a new president, Susilo Bambang Yudhovono, was elected on a platform of cleaning up corruption. As a former military officer, he was also expected to be tougher than his predecessor in moving against Al Qaeda supporters in the country. Indonesia is currently a major world-order interest of the United States in the war on terrorism, but it could move to the *vital* interest level if Al Qaeda sinks deeper roots in the country and establishes a base of operations in its remote islands.

CENTRAL ASIA

Two countries, *Afghanistan* and *Pakistan,* represent major threats to U.S. world-order interests. Both are faced with serious security problems in dealing with the Al Qaeda terrorists who were ousted from their bases in Afghanistan by the U.S. invasion in 2001. In late 2003 and 2004, Pakistan's army moved against Al Qaeda fighters who had fled into the mountainous western border region, while U.S. and British forces pressed them from the Afghanistan side of the border. Despite these efforts, however, neither side was able to capture Osama bin Laden or his top lieutenants, a disappointment for the Bush administration, which needed to show progress in the war on terrorism. Afghanistan has long been dominated by local warlords. A central government was established in Kabul in 2002 under UN auspices but has not been strong enough to extend its rule into the southern and western areas of the country. NATO took over command of allied forces in Kabul in 2003 and provides security there and in a few other cities. But Afghanistan remains a poor unstable country in Central Asia and is a continuing problem for U.S. security interests there.

By contrast, Pakistan is a relatively stable country with a technically advanced economy. Its principal security problem is with neighboring India, with which it has fought several wars over the disputed northern area of Kashmir. In 1999 both India and Pakistan became nuclear powers, a stunning development that occurred in spite of strong efforts by the United States over fifteen years to dissaude them from building nuclear weapons. Since 2001 Pakistan's military-led government has cooperated with Washington in fighting terrorism in Afghanistan and, in return, Pakistan has received more than $1 billion in U.S. aid. Its government, headed by Gen. Pervez Musharraf, has pledged to hold free elections and permit political parties to operate freely again. Musharraf also took steps in 2003 to curb Muslim guerrilla attacks in Kashmir and thereby reduce tensions with India. He narrowly escaped assassination by Muslim extremists in December 2003, underlining the tenuous relationship Washington has with the leadership of this Central Asian nuclear power. Should a nuclear-armed Pakistan be taken over by extremists like those who in 1979 established the Islamic regime in Iran, Pakistan would quickly become a vital world-order interest for the United States. Afghanistan would also rise to the vital level.

MIDDLE EAST

The Middle East, running from Iran through Palestine to Egypt, constitutes one of the most dangerous areas for U.S. world-order interests, for three reasons: the huge oil reserves of the Persian Gulf, on which the United States, Japan, and Europe are heavily dependent; the security of Israel, which the United States is pledged to defend against hostile neighbors; and the radical form of Islam, known as Wahabism, which is promoted by radical clerics in Saudi Arabia and heavily influences Al Qaeda terrorists. For purposes of this discussion the area is divided into three parts: Iran, a non-Arab country; the Arab states of the Persian Gulf region; and the eastern Mediterranean area, where Israel, the PA, and Egypt are of principal concern to U.S. interests. A fourth country, Turkey, a non-Arab state, is included because of its importance to U.S. world-order interests in southeastern Europe and in the Middle East.

Iran

During Shah Reza Pahlavi's thirty-year reign, Iran was a U.S. ally in the struggle with the Soviet Union for influence in the Middle East. The loss of Iran as an ally occurred when a revolutionary Islamic regime headed by Ayatolla Khomeini seized power in 1979. This was a major strategic debacle for the United States. Relations sank to the danger point when the extremist regime sanctioned the imprisonment in 1979 of fifty-two

U.S. embassy employees by radicals, who held them under deplorable conditions for fourteen months. President Carter imposed economic sanctions and tried to isolate the country politically, to no avail. In the 1990s Tehran began building nuclear power plants with Russia's assistance and denied U.S. intelligence reports that it was surreptitiously acquiring a nuclear weapons capability. Iran's hostility toward the United States and its open support for terrorist groups in the Middle East made it one of President Bush's "axis of evil" countries. Its regime will remain a major threat to U.S. world-order interests and may quickly rise to the vital level if it continues its nuclear weapons program. Some observers in Washington suggested following Saddam Hussein's ouster in Iraq that the United States should use its military position there to help bring down Iran's regime. Others proposed that Washington support dissident Iranians, including students, to pressure Tehran's hard-line leaders to change their policies. In a 2003 modification of U.S. policy, President Bush decided to support a European initiative to persuade Iran's senior clerics that it was dangerous for them to pursue a nuclear weapons program and that cooperation with UN arms inspectors of the International Atomic Energy Agency would lead to better relations with Europe and the United States. This step, undertaken by the foreign ministers of Britain, France, and Germany, resulted in an agreement by Iran's top leadership to suspend efforts to build nuclear weapons and allow international weapons inspections. While many called it a diplomatic breakthrough, others doubted that Iran's drive to become a nuclear power would be shelved so long as Islamic hard-liners remained in power. Skeptics doubted it would follow Libya's example in 2003 and abandon its nuclear weapons program, a view that was confirmed in June 2004 when the IAEA issued a unanimous report rebuking Iran for failure to cooperate fully with its inspectors or to release important information. This issue could become a vital one for Europe and the United States in 2005.

Persian Gulf

The principal Arab states in the Persian Gulf region are Iraq, Saudi Arabia, and Kuwait, all major oil exporters. Smaller Gulf states—Oman, Qatar, the United Arab Emirates, and Bahrain—occupy collectively an important strategic position in the Persian Gulf but do not exercise a major influence on the regional balance of power. In 2003 all the smaller Gulf states helped the United States and Great Britain in the buildup for war in Iraq.

Saudi Arabia. In 2003 the Pentagon removed U.S. military personnel from the kingdom and transferred its Middle East headquarters to Qatar. This followed Saudi Arabia's decision not to support the U.S. attack on Iraq, unlike its positive stance in 1991 during the Gulf War. Saudi monarchs since World War II have made their country a strategic ally of Washington and provided stability in world oil markets through their ability to increase production when Iran and Iraq were at war and their oil production was cut. In return, Saudi leaders gained the tacit acquiescence from American presidents that the United States would not interfere with their traditional Islamic society, including a tightly controlled political system. The attacks of 9/11 diminished this amicable relationship because fifteen of the nineteen highjackers who carried out the attacks were Saudi nationals. After months of investigation it also became clear to U.S. leaders that elements of the Saudi royal family were financial backers of the Al Qaeda organization. Osama bin Laden, its leader, was a dissident Saudi millionaire who had been banned from the kingdom because of his radicalism and had then organized an international terrorist network in Sudan and later, in 1995, in Afghanistan. Bin Laden set up camps there, training thousands of Arabs and others to launch attacks on the United States and its allies, including Saudi Arabia. He planned to replace the Saudi monarchy with an Islamic regime.

U.S.-Saudi relations were further strained by the leadership's refusal to join the 2003 U.S. invasion of Iraq, even though it provided assistance in other ways. Some members of Congress and the American press criticized the relationship and questioned whether the Saudi government should be considered a friend and ally. When administration officials, including White House national security adviser Condoleezza Rice, spoke about transforming the Middle East into a collection of democratic societies, some believed that Saudi Arabia was a major target. If the country was a recruiting ground for Al Qaeda terrorists, the argument went, its political system needed overhauling so that its citizens could see the possibility of living in a free, modern society. The problem for U.S. policy was twofold: Should the kingdom continue to be treated like any other major oil producer needing to sell its oil? Would it be desirable for the United States to influence the transformation of Saudi society to resemble a modern nation? The answer to the first question was probably yes, but to the second, only slowly. Even though the Saudi leadership could not be relied on to give open support to U.S. strategic goals in the Middle East, it could nevertheless be viewed as a reliable supplier of oil to world markets. With Iraq under U.S. and British influence and the Gulf states supporting that policy, Saudi Arabia's strategic importance to the United States has diminished. By 2004 it was time for the United States to reevaluate the relationship and press the Saudi monarchy to institute reforms that would help it to avoid overthrow by an Al Qaeda–type Islamic revolution.

Iraq. In 2004 Iraq was the most important Middle East country for U.S. interests, and it will continue to be so as long as political instability persists in Baghdad. Rebuilding the country and assisting it to become a democratic political system will require years of effort and a long-term American presence. With Iraq no longer a threat to U.S. interests in the Middle East, it seemed that it should be easier for Washington to exert pressure on neighboring Syria and Iran to stop supporting terrorist organizations that threaten Israel, as well as U.S. interests in the region. A major problem, however, was the large financial burden that the United States was bearing for postwar Iraq without the help of other donor nations. Because the French, German, and Belgian governments had refused to support the invasion, they declined to provide reconstruction aid until a sovereign Iraqi government was formed and approved by the UN Security Council. The Pentagon was known to be opposed to sharing occupation authority with the United Nations because it would give other governments a major influence over the Iraqi economy, including its lucrative oil industry. However, in November 2003 President Bush decided, because of the serious security situation that had developed in major Iraqi cities, to speed the timetable for the transfer of sovereignty and establish an interim Iraqi government by June 2004. Critics suggested that the president was positioning himself for his 2004 reelection campaign and that the transfer of power might be premature. Administration supporters argued the reason was that Iraqis wanted their own government and an early end to the U.S. occupation.

In March 2004 the Bush administration won approval from the UN Security Council to play a major role in forming an interim Iraqi government, holding general elections early in 2005, and writing a new constitution that would permit a democratic government to emerge. The U.S. head of the Coalition Authority, Paul Bremer, who had exercised control in Iraq for over a year, was replaced on June 28, 2004, by a senior State Department ambassador, John Negroponte. He headed a large embassy staff that would supervise a massive U.S. aid program and be President Bush's representative to Iraq's new interim government headed by Prime Minister Ayad Allawi, formerly a prominent exile from Saddam Hussein's regime. Controversy arose at the United Nations over the future role of U.S. military forces, however, which in June numbered 138,000. Secretary of State Colin Powell expressed confidence that negotiations with Iraq's new government would clarify the conditions under which American forces would participate in dealing with the continuing insurgency and how they would relate to Iraq's newly trained army and police force.[4]

Israel and Palestine

The continuing violence between Israeli and Palestinian fighters, which claimed thousands of lives during three years of the *intifada*, was the second most serious foreign policy problem the United States faced in the Middle East. So long as the goal of Palestinians to achieve a viable and independent homeland was denied, continuing warfare between the two sides apparently would not decline. Late in 2003 Israeli Prime Minister Ariel Sharon announced, under increasing pressure from the Bush administration, that Israel would withdraw unilaterally from the Gaza Strip and evacuate the seventy-five hundred Jewish settlers who lived in enclaves protected by thousands of Israeli troops. Sharon also decided to build a wall between Israeli population centers and the West Bank territory in order to reduce terrorist attacks by Palestinian militants. Sharon's view was that since the Palestinians would not replace Yasser Arafat as leader of the PA, it was impossible to negotiate a peace settlement. Continuing violence in Gaza led to major Israeli military attacks in southern Gaza that resulted in hundreds of civilian casualties and brought international condemnation on the Sharon government, as well as growing protests within Israel over the government's policy.

The Bush administration continued to press for implementation of the "road map" that it had proposed in 2003 with the support of Russia, the EU, and the United Nations to arrange a just peace between Israel and the Palestinians. In March 2004 Bush suggested publicly that some Israeli settlements in the West Bank should be incorporated into Israel in a final peace settlement. This concession to Sharon was consistent with President Clinton's private suggestion in 2000 made during his negotiations with Israelis and Palestinians to find a breakthrough agreement before he left office. Some observers suggested that the only way to stop the continuing violence, which affected U.S. efforts to build support in the Middle East and Europe for its policies in Iraq, was for the United States to lead a peace-enforcing mission in Palestine, similar to President Clinton's action in Bosnia in 1995. This would in effect impose the "road map" on the warring parties. As in Bosnia, continuing warfare in Palestine and televised scenes of carnage could eventually persuade Americans that a U.S.-led intervention was desirable on humanitarian grounds. Arab states like Egypt, Saudi Arabia, and Jordan, and other Muslim countries, for example, Pakistan and Indonesia, would no doubt find it easier to cooperate with Mr. Bush's war on terrorism if Washington took a more forceful role in implementing the road map for peace. In reality, U.S. world-order interests in the entire Middle East and Asia suffered from lack of progress in the Arab-Israeli conflict. President Bush's reluctance to take a strong stance, critics argued, had much to do with his 2004 reelection campaign.

Turkey

During the entire Cold War, beginning with the Truman Doctrine in 1947, Turkey was one of America's staunchest allies. It hosted U.S. air bases for the containment of the Soviet Union and, after 1991, to enforce

UN sanctions against Saddam Hussein's regime in Iraq. Since then, because of its strategic location between Europe and the Middle East and the Ottoman Empire's four-hundred-year domination of Arab lands prior to 1918, this Western-oriented Muslim country has been an anchor of U.S. policy in the Persian Gulf and a counterweight to Iran's radical Islamic regime. In 2002 Washington's close relationship with Turkey was called into question after the election of a moderate leftist government. Ankara then decided not to authorize the introduction of U.S. troops into Turkey for the purpose of opening a northern front in the Iraq war. Despite a reported U.S. offer of $10 billion in aid, Turkey refused to permit the transit of U.S. troops through its territory or the bombing of Iraq from bases in Turkey. That was a significant blow to U.S. and British plans for the invasion, and it forced the Middle East commander, General Franks, to launch the attack on Iraq solely from Kuwait and Persian Gulf bases. Ankara's subsequent offer to contribute twenty thousand troops to assist in the occupation of Iraq was refused by Iraq's Governing Council, further complicating U.S. efforts to pacify the country. Turkey's refusal to sanction the U.S. invasion of Iraq underlined the reality that, on the decision to invade Iraq, Washington was isolated from allies and friends in the Middle East as well as Europe. In terms of U.S. world-order interests, Turkey's distancing of itself from this major U.S. policy was evidence of a serious erosion in American hegemonic influence. By 2004, relations between Washington and Ankara had improved somewhat.

EUROPE

After the collapse of the Soviet Union in 1991 and the pacification of the Balkans six years later, Europeans concluded that there were no serious external threats to their security. For the United States, the newly established Russian state was a potential competitor for influence in the Middle East and Eastern Europe, and as a result, President Clinton persuaded NATO to enlarge its membership into Eastern Europe to include Poland, the Czech Republic, Hungary, and the three Baltic states. France emerged as a major competitor for influence in Europe, seeking to be the political spokesman for the EU and a counterweight to growing American hegemonic influence. France and Russia, both permanent members of the UN

Security Council, and Germany, then a member, decided to oppose the U.S.-British plan to attack Iraq. This was a frontal challenge to vital U.S. world-order interests in both Europe and the Middle East, as well as a warning that continental Europe was openly displeased with the hegemonic exercise of U.S. power. The danger was that the new EU would follow France's leadership and gradually distance itself from the United States on political, economic, and military policy. Although Germany, Belgium, and Luxembourg joined France in opposition to U.S. policy in Iraq, other NATO countries—Poland, Spain, Italy, Denmark, and others—supported the U.S. and British invasion and sent troops to join the coalition in the occupation of Iraq.[5] This division within NATO led Secretary of Defense Donald Rumsfeld to make his controversial comment about an "Old Europe," out of touch with the views of a "New Europe," regarding NATO security policy. In 2004 Russia and France expressed willingness to consider assisting in the reconstruction of Iraq once sovereignty was turned over to an interim government. But neither of them, nor Germany, was ready to support America's wider vision of expanded hegemony in the Middle East.

Russia

Until the mid-1980s the Soviet Union was at the top of the list of countries threatening U.S. world-order and defense-of-homeland interests. In 2004 Russia was a severely weakened nuclear power that needed to rebuild its economy so that it might one day again play a major role in international affairs. Although it cooperated with President Bush on the war in Afghanistan, Vladimir Putin's government refused to go along with his decision to invade Iraq. Part of Moscow's opposition stemmed from its close relations with Saddam Hussein's regime during the Cold War and the accumulation of some $9 billion in Iraqi debt for arms sales. A previous president, Mikhail Gorbachev, had agreed reluctantly in 1991 to support Washington during the Gulf War, but Putin decided against the 2003 invasion. Instead, he joined the French and German effort to rein in U.S. hegemonic behavior in the Middle East and persuade the Bush administration to negotiate with other members of the UN Security Council to share responsibility for rebuilding Iraq. In other ways, however, Moscow cooperated with the United States, substantially reducing nuclear armed missiles and stabilizing the political situation in Eastern Europe. It even acquiesced in invitations to Poland and other former Warsaw Pact countries to join NATO. So long as Moscow presents no serious threat to U.S. interests in Europe and the Middle East and continues to cooperate in the war on terrorism, Russia will remain a major interest, but one that needs watching as it regains its economic and political strength.

France

For half a century France was a NATO member and partner of the United States in the effort to rebuild Europe and resist the Soviet threat to its security. Since the 1960s, however, France has refused to participate in the military planning of NATO or allow U.S. forces to be stationed there. President Charles de Gaulle's view of France's long-term interests envisioned a Europe that was free of American hegemony and could play an independent great-power role between the United States and the Soviet Union. For the plan to succeed, however, France needed the support of Germany and other continental states. Britain, which de Gaulle believed was part of an Anglo-American plot to dominate Europe, was not included in his vision. This French view of an independent Europe attracted the attention of Germany's government in August 2002 when Chancellor Gerhard Schroeder publicly opposed U.S. plans to invade Iraq and refused to pledge financial aid. France capitalized on Schroeder's opposition to Bush's policy and forged a working relationship with Germany to build the EU as a counterweight to the Americans and British. Earlier, French president Jacques Chirac had gotten agreement with other EU members, including Britain, to establish a joint rapid-reaction force that could operate separately from NATO when the United States chose not to participate—for example, in Africa. Some Bush administration officials saw this as a threat to the unity of NATO, a fear that was magnified in June 2004 when France publicly rejected a U.S. proposal that NATO take on responsibilities in Iraq when an interim Iraqi government assumed power. By mid-2004, France was viewed by a growing number of observers in Washington as an increasingly serious rival for international influence. If France, Germany, and the other countries in continental Europe continue their anti-American actions, they may eventually challenge U.S. interests not only in the Middle East but also in Europe.

LATIN AMERICA

Two countries in South America, *Colombia* and *Venezuela,* are major world-order interests for the United States, and both could quickly rise to vital interest if Venezuela should give material support to Marxist guerrillas operating against the government of Colombia. The latter country is currently a major, bordering on vital, interest for the United States because of the widespread violence precipitated by powerful drug lords and Marxist guerrillas, who formed an alliance to control the southern part of Colombia. The massive amounts of drugs that flow northward through Mexico to the United States have long been a serious problem for U.S. law enforcement. Wealthy drug barons until recently had virtual immunity from corrupt officials and the police, who were bought off by large bribes. President Clinton persuaded Congress to appropriate $1 billion to help Colombia's government cope with threats to its security, and in 2002 President Bush approved legislation that provided $2.5 billion in aid over three years. Venezuela became a problem for Washington in 2003 and 2004 because its leftist president, Hugo Chavez, indulged in anti-American rhetoric, was friendly with Cuba's Fidel Castro, and called for revolutionary reform elsewhere in Latin America. Still, Chavez was careful to avoid giving aid to Colombia's Marxist rebels because it would quickly force Washington to take counteractions. As long as Venezuela's oil exports to the United States are not endangered, Hugo Chavez will probably be tolerated by the United States.

CONCLUSION

The United States under presidents George H. W. Bush and Bill Clinton continued to enlarge America's world-order interests and influence following the end of the Cold War and the Soviet Union's collapse. But they conducted their policies in a manner that made American hegemony acceptable to most foreign leaders. The elder president Bush built a large coalition of European and Arab countries before he launched the Gulf War in 1991. Bill Clinton joined other NATO leaders in deploying troops to halt two ethnic wars in the Balkans and in welcoming several Eastern European countries into the alliance. Both presidents built good relations with Russia's and China's leaders even though major disagreements persisted over China's human rights problems. By 2000, however, France was complaining severely about American arrogance, and it began lobbying for an independent European foreign and defense policy. In the Middle East, two coalition partners in the Gulf War, Saudi Arabia and Egypt, complained about Washington's lack of an evenhanded policy in dealing with the Israeli-Palestinian conflict.

The evolution of American foreign policy from the exercise of cooperative hegemonic power to what many Europeans viewed as increasingly coercive superpower behavior was reinforced when George W. Bush came to the White House and asserted unilateral policies even before the events of 9/11. International disapproval of American hegemony finally came to a head at the United Nations in February and March 2003, when the Bush administration was unable to persuade the UN Security Council to approve its proposed armed intervention in Iraq. France even threatened to veto the resolution. In the end, only Britain, Spain, Italy, Poland, and Australia provided troops to support the invasion. The reality was hegemonic influence was waning as key European and Arab governments and Turkey failed to support the war. Washington's unsuccessful effort to exercise coercive diplomacy was probably the high-water mark in its effort to achieve the role of hegemonic superpower.

CHAPTER 8

PROMOTING FREEDOM AND AMERICAN VALUES ABROAD

Promoting liberty and justice abroad has long been a part of U.S. foreign policy, fostered by a strong sense of mission to promote freedom and democracy. Idealism and optimism about the future are additional attributes that foreign observers cite to distinguish American civilization from most others. In the nineteenth century America was a magnet for millions of immigrants from Europe who sought individual freedom and economic prosperity in this land of opportunity, and most succeeded beyond their expectations. By the century's end, the country had emerged from the Civil War period as a dynamic economic and political power that dominated the North American continent and the Caribbean Basin. It was perhaps predictable that many Americans came to think that their government should use its new power to promote freedom and markets outside North America. They found in President William McKinley a leader willing to annex the Philippines after a short war with Spain and give its people the opportunity to build a democracy and free market system. Later, on the eve of America's entry into World War I, President Woodrow Wilson declared that America intended to make the world "safe for democracy." When President Franklin Roosevelt took the nation to war in 1941, he proclaimed the "Four Freedoms" as America's objectives. During the Cold War all the presidents cited the worldwide struggle between freedom and communism as America's moral challenge. Jimmy Carter raised the promotion of human rights to a central objective of his foreign policy and appointed an assistant secretary in the State Department to press the program. Ronald Reagan repeatedly talked about America's special responsibility to defend freedom and defeat Moscow's "evil empire."

Critics of presidential calls for America to defend freedom abroad were vocal throughout the twentieth century. They claimed that rhetoric about America's moral responsibility to intervene in foreign conflicts was a tactic used to overcome public concerns about the potential costs of engaging in foreign wars. Some, like historian Charles A. Beard, charged that presidents McKinley, Wilson, and Franklin Roosevelt had engaged in wars as a means to enhance America's commercial and political interests abroad. Isolationist movements before both World War I and World War II resulted from the public's reaction against the expansionist policies of McKinley, Wilson's efforts to involve the United States in the League of Nations, and disillusionment over the costs of World War I. Americans, particularly in the Midwest, were simply opposed to getting involved in Europe's wars. So strong was isolationist sentiment before the disaster at Pearl Harbor that Franklin Roosevelt could not persuade the public and Congress that Nazi Germany posed a dangerous threat to U.S. interests. Beard, for example, charged that Roosevelt hid his true intentions when he declared during his reelection campaign in 1940 that he would not send U.S. troops to fight in Europe.[1] Still, during most of the twentieth century the public usually responded positively when the president made a strong case that force was needed to support noble purposes, such as to repel aggression in Korea, in Kuwait, and in Kosovo.

GEORGE BUSH AND PROMOTION OF VALUES

The president's National Security Strategy document in 2002 (see chapter 4) displayed this ambitious heading, "Champion Aspirations for Human Dignity," in the section on promotion of values:

> In pursuit of our goals, our first imperative is to clarify what we stand for: the United States must defend liberty and justice because these principles are right and true for all people everywhere. No nation owns these aspira-

tions, and no nation is exempt from them. Fathers and mothers in all societies want their children to be educated and to live free from poverty and violence. No people on earth yearn to be oppressed, aspire to servitude, or eagerly await the midnight knock of the secret police. America must stand firmly for the non-negotiable demands of human dignity: the rule of law; limits on the absolute power of the state; free speech; freedom of worship; equal justice; respect for women; religious and ethnic tolerance; and respect for private property.[2]

This sweeping commitment was a clear statement of President Bush's intent to promote U.S. values as part of his national strategy. But it was not unprecedented. For example, John Kennedy's eloquent promise at his January 1961 inauguration to "pay any price" to defend freedom in the world was even more sweeping in its commitment. What was striking about Bush's pronouncement was the prominence he gave it at the beginning of that 2002 document. It set the tone for the ensuing debate about the president's goal of ousting Saddam Hussein's regime in Iraq and liberating the Iraqi people from tyranny.

Condoleezza Rice, the president's national security adviser and principal author of the White House national security strategy paper, emerged in 2003 as one of the administration's staunchest promoters of American values in foreign policy. In a front-page story on August 8, "U.S. Promises Democracy to Middle East," the *Washington Post* quoted from a speech in which Rice had compared the struggle for freedom by people in the Middle East to the struggle of blacks in her home town of Birmingham, Alabama, who in the 1960s sought to throw off the yoke of white supremacists. Taking exception to experts who claimed that Arab cultures were not ready for freedom, Rice declared: "The view was wrong in 1963 in Birmingham and is wrong in 2003 in Baghdad and in the rest of the Middle East." In an op-ed commentary in the same newspaper, she wrote, "America is determined to help the people of the Middle East achieve their full potential. We will act because we want greater freedom and opportunity for the people of the region, as well as greater security for people in America and throughout the world."[3]

President Bush made a strong case for his promotion-of-values policies in a speech to the National Endowment for Democracy in Washington,

D.C., on November 6, 2003. He said that America had long promoted freedom as an important part of its foreign policy, and he claimed that many countries had adopted democratic systems over the past fifty years "at a time when the world's most influential nation was itself a democracy." He cited a speech by Ronald Reagan to the British parliament in 1982 in which he proclaimed a turning point in history, when "the day of Soviet tyranny was passing, that freedom had a momentum that would not be halted." Bush recalled American sacrifices in two world wars, in Korea, and in other countries to preserve freedom, and he cited Germany and Japan as examples where U.S. policy had brought democracy to replace dictatorships. However, his major message was about the need to promote freedom and democracy in the Middle East, where, he said, America had long accepted the idea that it could not flourish. That lengthy portion of his address is reproduced here:

> Securing democracy in Iraq is the work of many hands. . . . This is a massive and difficult undertaking—it is worth our effort, it is worth our sacrifice, because we know the stakes. The failure of Iraqi democracy would embolden terrorists around the world, increase dangers to the American people, and extinguish the hopes of millions in the region. Iraqi democracy will succeed—and that success will send forth the news, from Damascus to Teheran—that freedom can be the future of every nation. The establishment of a free Iraq at the heart of the Middle East will be a watershed event in the global democratic revolution.

> Sixty years of Western nations excusing and accommodating the lack of freedom in the Middle East did nothing to make us safe—because in the long run, stability cannot be purchased at the expense of liberty. As long as the Middle East remains a place where freedom does not flourish, it will remain a place of stagnation, resentment, and violence ready for export. And with the spread of weapons that can bring catastrophic harm to our country and to our friends, it would be reckless to accept the status quo.

> Therefore, the United States has adopted a new policy, a forward strategy of freedom in the Middle East. This strategy requires the same persistence and energy and idealism we have shown before. And it will yield the same results. As in Europe, as in Asia, as in every region of the world, the advance of freedom leads to peace.

The advance of freedom is the calling of our time; it is the calling of our country. From the Fourteen Points to the Four Freedoms, to the Speech at Westminster, America has put our power at the service of principle. We believe that liberty is the design of nature; we believe that liberty is the direction of history. We believe that human fulfillment and excellence come in the responsible exercise of liberty. And we believe that freedom— the freedom we prize—is not for us alone, it is the right and the capacity of all mankind. . . . With all the tests and all the challenges of our age, this is, above all, the age of liberty. Each of you at this Endowment is fully engaged in the great cause of liberty.

Some scholars argue that promotion of values should not be a national interest on a par with other basic ones—defense of homeland, economic well-being, and favorable world order. However, promotion of freedom and democracy has been a part of American foreign policy since the country's founding; it has been elevated by recent presidents to such a level that it is cited regularly as an objective of military interventions abroad. The real issue is not whether human rights and promotion of values constitute important national interests of the United States—they do—but whether they rise to the level of vital interests in the absence of a compelling case for action under one or more of the other basic interests. Liberia, for example, was not a vital world-order interest in 2003, and the president was correct in refusing to be drawn into a large deployment of troops. But in view of the heavy pressure exerted by many private organizations, members of Congress, and governments of other countries to deal with Liberia's humanitarian crisis, the president felt justified in raising the issue to the near-vital level, as his father had done eleven years earlier in Somalia, and President Clinton had done in East Timor in deploying a modest U.S. force to assist the United Nations in restoring order in 1999.

MILITARY INTERVENTIONS AND PROMOTION OF VALUES

Between 1989 and 2003 the United States used military force on ten occasions to intervene in another country: Panama, 1989; Kuwait, 1991; Somalia, 1992; Haiti, 1994; Bosnia, 1995; Kosovo, 1999; East Timor, 1999;

Afghanistan, 2001; Iraq, 2003; and Liberia, 2003. Figure 7 is my assessment of how policy makers viewed the importance of the "promotion-of-values" interest when they decided on these military interventions between 1989 and 2003. The cases are discussed below.

In four of the cases cited—Somalia, Haiti, East Timor, Liberia—promotion of values, specifically humanitarian factors, was a principal reason that the United States sent military forces to help stabilize a political situation that had produced a humanitarian disaster. In Somalia, a substantial force was sent in 1993 to ensure delivery of international food shipments to starving people in rural areas. However, when eighteen U.S. soldiers were ambushed and killed in Mogadishu, President Clinton, under congressional pressure, withdrew the force. In Haiti, a U.S. intervention was imposed to oust a military dictator, install a previously elected president, combat starvation, and prevent massive Haitian immigration to the United States. Washington then handed peacekeeping operations to a UN force. In East Timor and in Liberia, the United Nations with U.S. and allied support took the lead in organizing peacekeeping operations to stop the widespread violence resulting from civil war. In both cases U.S. troops were withdrawn after a few weeks. In all of these instances the president acted with UN authorization and in cooperation with allies. These crises rose to the level of a vital U.S. promotion-of-values interest because of the humanitarian issues and because it became

FIGURE 7
PROMOTION OF VALUES AND THE USE OF FORCE

Basic Interest	Intensity of Interest			
	Survival	Vital	Major	Peripheral
Defense of Homeland				
Economic Well-Being				
Favorable World Order				
PROMOTION OF VALUES		**Somalia** **Haiti** **E. Timor** **Liberia**	**Bosnia** **Kosovo** **Afghanistan** **Iraq**	**Panama** **Kuwait**

clear that other nations would not act without participation by the United States.

In four other cases—Bosnia, Kosovo, Afghanistan, Iraq—a vital U.S. world-order interest was at stake, and promotion of values was a secondary consideration. In Bosnia and Kosovo, ethnic cleansing by Serb forces had resulted in the massacre of many civilians and the forced evacuation of tens of thousands. Photos of atrocities were shown on TV across the Western world, and European governments pleaded for American participation in imposing a political solution. Clinton cited humanitarian considerations as a major reason for U.S. military involvement in both Bosnia and Kosovo, but his major motivation was to deal with the security threat that Serbia posed in southeastern Europe, an area considered vital to U.S. relations with NATO. The president sent twenty thousand troops to Bosnia in 1995–96, with UN approval, as part of a larger European force, and order was soon restored. In Kosovo, Clinton was unable to obtain UN backing for an intervention because Russia threatened to veto the resolution. His administration then organized a NATO force and used U.S. Air Force and Navy aircraft to persuade Slobodan Milosevic, Serbia's brutal leader, to halt his ethnic cleansing in Kosovo. After seventy-seven days of constant bombing—in which no Americans were killed because pilots were ordered to fly above the range of antiaircraft missiles—Milosevic withdrew. The Kosovo intervention was controversial because it set a precedent for "preemptive intervention" in other states that posed a threat to U.S. interests.

In two additional cases—Afghanistan and Iraq—humanitarian considerations were important in mobilizing U.S. opinion for war, but in neither of them was promotion of values more than a secondary consideration. The overriding U.S. interest for the invasion of Afghanistan was defense of homeland, because the Taliban government provided sanctuary to Al Qaeda leaders who had planned the September 11 attacks. The primary factor driving the Bush administration toward preemptive war in Iraq was a vital world-order interest, to get rid of a dangerous threat to Middle East peace and establish a favorable political climate there by helping to establish a democratic government. Economic well-being was a major, perhaps a vital, interest in this case. While Afghanistan and Iraq were vital world-order interests, President Bush justified these wars also on promotion-of-values grounds, to liberate the Afghani and Iraqi people from oppression and give them the opportunity to build a free society.

Finally, in two cases, Panama and Kuwait, promotion of values was at best a peripheral consideration. The vital interest in both cases was safeguarding regional order: in Kuwait by countering an Iraqi invasion and occupation of the oil-rich country; in Panama it was the ouster of a military despot, Manuel Noriega, who threatened U.S. interests in the canal and was heavily involved in drug trafficking to the United States. Although former President George Bush claimed in 1990 that U.S. intervention would promote democratic government in Kuwait, it was unrealistic to think that Kuwait's autocratic rulers would relinquish their power to the people following the withdrawal of Iraqi troops.

In sum, promotion of values is usually a supporting, not a controlling, factor in presidential decisions to intervene militarily in another country. However, because the American public reacts emotionally to television clips of genocide and starvation in Africa, ethnic cleansing in the Balkans, and government brutality in Afghanistan, Iraq, and Southeast Asia, it is probably inevitable that presidents and members of Congress justify most military actions in humanitarian terms, even though their primary reason for favoring force lies in another direction. It would be incorrect, however, to downgrade promotion-of-values considerations from our discussion of basic national interests.

THE CASE OF LIBERIA

The Bush administration was deeply divided in 2003 on whether to send peacekeeping troops to Liberia, then suffering from a humanitarian disaster brought on by a prolonged and vicious civil war. The president had visited that continent in June and pledged that the United States would assist Liberia when its dictator, Charles Taylor, chose to resign and go into exile. Secretary of State Powell favored a limited military intervention, on humanitarian grounds, and discussed the matter with the UN Secretary General, Kofi Annan. However, Secretary of Defense Rumsfeld and the military opposed U.S. troop involvement, viewing it as a diversion from the crucial effort to pacify Iraq. The *New York Times* reported that the

Pentagon had concluded that the United States had no vital interest in Liberia and that "the last African intervention, in Somalia, ended in a debacle."[4] The president eventually agreed to deploy only two hundred Marines into Monrovia to assist a West African regional organization, with UN help, to maintain order while another two thousand troops, mostly Marines, remained offshore on three warships in case of need.

The Liberia episode showed that the Bush administration was reluctant to use troops for a strictly humanitarian—promotion-of-values— purpose unless there were also strategic interests at stake. Ronald Reagan's dispatch of Marines to Beirut, Lebanon, in 1982 and George H. Bush's deployment of peacekeepers to Somalia in 1992 were for essentially humanitarian reasons. Both ended in failure because Congress and the public were not prepared to accept military casualties to support only humanitarian objectives. However, George W. Bush had good political reasons for showing support for Africa in 2003; critics argued that he was interested only in fighting terrorism, not in combating humanitarian crises in Africa brought on by repressive governments and the AIDS epidemic. Liberia underlined the reality that in matching national interests to foreign policy decisions, promotion of values by itself rarely justifies the use of military force in a coercive way, although presidential rhetoric may suggest otherwise. It is frequently a contributing factor, however, as in Iraq when one or more other interests are at the vital level and it therefore becomes intolerable to ignore dangerous trends. For example, the absence of a security threat from Liberia contrasted sharply with the menace that North Korea's nuclear weapons program posed. Promotion of values played no part in U.S. policy toward North Korea.

When President Bush was considering whether to send troops to Liberia, a flurry of op-ed commentaries appeared in major American newspapers urging him to act for essentially humanitarian reasons. Two prominent proponents of intervention were Fareed Zakaria, editor of *Newsweek*, and Chester Crocker, former Assistant Secretary of State for Africa and leading expert on African affairs. Zakaria's August 12 column in the *Washington Post* was titled "Take the Lead in Africa." Crocker's appeared in the *New York Times* under the heading "A War America Can Afford to Stop." Crocker's argument was especially pertinent to a discussion of America's promotion of values worldwide: "Liberia is a specific example of a broader challenge posed by failed states everywhere, which we are (slowly) grasping are the incubators of almost every hostile challenge to American interests and values around the globe. And if Washington wants other countries to help us in sharing burdens that fall on its shoulders in the future, it is essential that it play a lead role in Liberia today. Finally, this is about stopping, relatively quickly, a humanitarian disaster at reasonable cost."[5] Crocker's theme was the one that eventually persuaded President Bush to send a small intervention force to Liberia, despite the misgivings of the Department of Defense.

THE CASE OF PALESTINE

The long struggle between Israelis and Palestinians for control over the land of Palestine offers a revealing case regarding competing values among U.S. national interests. The United States has traditionally espoused self-determination for oppressed peoples and also believed since 1945 that European Jews who escaped the Nazi Holocaust should have a homeland where they could establish a sovereign Jewish state. The logical place seemed to be Palestine, because the Jewish historical homeland had been there until the Jews were driven out by the Romans nearly two thousand years ago. The dilemma that all U.S. presidents, beginning with Harry Truman, faced was how to reconcile this moral obligation to the Jewish people with an equally persuasive value held by Americans that the inhabitants of a country should not be forcibly evacuated from their homeland and resettled elsewhere. The reality for President Truman in 1947 was that Great Britain, which had held a League of Nations Mandate in Palestine after the Ottoman Empire collapsed in 1918, decided that it could no longer maintain security there and would withdraw its forces in 1948. That decision opened a power vacuum in Palestine, which the fledgling United Nations sought to resolve by agreeing on a partition of the land between Jews and Palestinians. The major Arab states—Egypt, Syria, and Jordan—rejected the UN plan because it enabled Jews to set up a state on territory long inhabited primarily by Arabs. Thousands of

Jewish militants who had come from Europe organized armed militias to seize control of the land and present the Arabs and the United Nations with a fait accompli. These armed militias defeated the combined forces of Egypt, Syria, and Jordan in 1948 and declared the independent state of Israel. Jerusalem was now divided between Jews and Palestinians. In the process, tens of thousands of the latter were forced to flee their homes and settle in refugee camps in the Gaza Strip, then controlled by Egypt, and in the West Bank, administered by Jordan. President Truman quickly granted diplomatic recognition to Israel, an action that Arabs viewed as a gross injustice. He had to choose between one moral need—to provide a homeland for European Jews—and the equally compelling need to prevent the forced expulsion of thousands of Palestinians from their homes, a form of ethnic cleansing. Truman decided to support a Jewish homeland, and he partially compensated the Palestinians by providing economic aid through the UN refugee agency, which distributed food in the refugee camps.

For fifty-five years the issue of displaced Palestinians has been one of the most vexing problems in American foreign policy. Successive presidents provided large levels of military and economic support to Israel in its struggle to persuade Arab countries to accept the reality of a Jewish state in the Near East. In 1967 Israel took control of the West Bank, Gaza Strip, the Sinai territory, and the Golan Heights after a short war with the Arab states. But the United States refused to recognize Israel's right to annex these lands, calling them "occupied territories" subject to UN supervision. Jordan subsequently gave up its claim to speak for the Palestinian people. Yasser Arafat, as leader of the PLO, was dedicated to establishing a Palestinian homeland in areas occupied by Israel. In 2000 President Clinton tried unsuccessfully at Camp David, Maryland, to broker a negotiated settlement that guaranteed Israel's demand for secure borders and diplomatic recognition by the Arab states, and he also accepted the PA's demand for a viable and internationally recognized state with its capital in East Jerusalem. Failure of these negotiations led to Palestinian violence against Israeli settlements in the West Bank and Gaza and to a hardening of Israel's position. It also led to the election in Israel, in February 2001, of a hard-line prime minister, former general Ariel

Sharon. Sharon broke off contact with the PA's leadership and adopted strong repressive measures against the Palestinians.

At the end of 2003 President Bush had three options for dealing with the dangerous escalation of violence in Palestine: continue to support Sharon's hard-line policy of imposing a peace through military occupation; withdraw from involvement in negotiations and let the violence run its course; use U.S. influence to impose a political settlement, employing economic and political pressure on both sides. Of the three options, the only realistic one, in my view, was the third: to use U.S. and international influence to impose a settlement on the Israelis and Palestinians. A settlement would likely resemble the one that Bill Clinton tried to broker in 2000. This would give Palestinians a viable but demilitarized state to be established in 2005, including more than 90 percent of territory seized by Israel in 1967. This included the Arab sector of Jerusalem, which would be the capital of a sovereign state of Palestine. Palestinians also needed to agree to a permanent peace with Israel, guaranteed by international treaty. For its part, Israel would receive full diplomatic recognition from Arab countries, specifically Egypt, Jordan, Saudi Arabia, and Syria. Palestinians would be obliged to give up their claim of a right to return to their former homes in Israel, while Israel would agree to accept a limited number of returnees as exceptions.

Europeans ask why the United States does not force the two sides to accept the "road map to peace," as both are dependent on Washington for economic aid and, in the case of Israel, a large part of its military equipment. The problem for any U.S. president is that he finds it politically difficult to challenge Israel's influential lobby in Washington, which masterfully ensures that Congress supports large aid programs. For example, when the Republican majority leader in the House of Representatives, Tom DeLay, visited Israel in the summer of 2003, he declared that President Bush should give full support to Sharon's tough policies in dealing with Palestinian terrorism. The influence of the American Israel Political Affairs Committee (AIPAC) is especially potent during presidential election years.

More moderate views were being voiced and reported by the *New York Times* and the *Washington Post,* however. An example was an op-ed commentary in the *Times,* August 28, 2003, titled "The Price of Not Keeping the Peace," with the caption "Withholding U.S. aid is the best cure for the Mideast." The writer, Arthur Hertzberg, identified as a visiting professor at New York University and author of *The Fate of Zionism,* argued that the best way to stop the killings in Israel and the Palestinian territories was for Washington to impose "punitive economic measures" on both sides. Cutting off the Palestinians' foreign sources of subsidy, he wrote, would deprive radical elements like Hamas of their financial appeal to the poverty-stricken Palestinians. As for Israel, Hertzberg's remedy was startling: "The United States finances about $4 billion a year, on average, of Israel's national budget. The continuing effort to defend, support and increase settlements in the West Bank and Gaza costs at least $1 billion a year." His solution: "An American government that was resolved to stop expansion of the settlements would not need to keep sending the secretary of state to Jerusalem to repeat that we really mean what we say. We could prove it by deducting the total cost of the settlements each year from the United States' annual allocation to Israel." Hertzberg added: "The mainstream in Israel and in the Jewish Diaspora will be grateful to America for saving Israel from itself." He also urged the U.S. government to impose strong economic sanctions on the Palestinians until the terrorism stopped.

Another very ambitious proposal for U.S. action was offered by a former U.S. ambassador to Israel in the Clinton administration, Martin Indyk. Writing in the *New York Times,* he argued that Bush's road map for peace was the best formula to achieve a lasting peace between Israel and the Palestinians. But he also wanted the United States to propose an international protectorate to "put the Palestinian territories in trust and supervise the establishment of a Palestinian state with democratic political institutions." Indyk argued that the United States should oversee the implementation of this trusteeship under the UN's authority and also commit U.S. troops as peacekeepers to ensure that both sides carried out its terms. In order for the plan to be effective, he wrote, a trusteeship for Palestine would require "an American-led force to fight terrorists alongside the Palestinian security forces."[6] Indyk seemed to want President Bush to place U.S. troops in the West Bank and Gaza Strip in order to take over the job of stopping Palestinian terrorists, thereby relieving Israel of the huge burden of doing so alone.

The crisis in Palestine highlighted the difficulty that U.S. policy makers encounter when they attempt to balance the traditional way of identifying national interests—defense of homeland, economic well-being, and world order—with the special, perhaps unique, American attachment to promoting freedom, justice, and democracy as part of its foreign policy. The U.S. dilemma in Palestine highlights how a president deals with balancing two contending political and moral values: the right of Israelis to live in peace in a secure Jewish homeland, and the right of Palestinians to have a viable and secure homeland with compensation for the loss of homes in Israel. Dealing with this vexing question may cause the United States and European governments eventually to send peacekeepers to this volatile area to monitor the separation of the two hostile populations until they are able to accommodate the division of Palestine.

GEORGE BUSH'S COMMITMENT TO PROMOTING FREEDOM ABROAD

President Bush's address in November 2003 to the National Endowment for Democracy (see above) on the need for promoting freedom was the clearest statement that any president had ever made about the importance of "promotion of values" as a basic interest of the United States. It was striking to many in Washington and abroad for its sweeping commitment to use U.S. power and influence to enhance the cause of freedom and democracy in countries where it did not exist. It put on notice authoritarian governments in the Middle East, some of which had been on friendly terms with Washington for many years during the Cold War, that his administration would no longer refrain from pressuring their governments about reform and opening the way for participation by opposition parties and dissident groups.[7]

Despite criticism from some skeptics that Mr. Bush was indulging in idealistic rhetoric to bolster questionable policies in Iraq, others applauded his forthright enunciation of U.S. principles. The *Washington Post* commented editorially: "Some critics cast President Bush's speech on democracy in the Middle East Thursday as merely another effort to repackage his troubled and costly mission in Iraq. But the president deserves more credit than that. Not only has he been talking about a political transformation of Arab countries since before the war, but he's right to conclude that such a project is vital to victory in the war on terrorism."[8] The *New York Times* also applauded the president's initiative: "America, with its reverence for law and freedom and its awesome economic power and cultural influence, is well equipped to help democrats around the world. To succeed in this vitally important endeavor, the Bush administration will have to learn to put the same kind of energy and resources into the diplomatic and educational sides of foreign policy as it has devoted to unilateral military action."[9]

The president's promotion of democratic government and human rights in the Middle East took a powerful blow in May 2004 when it was revealed through photographs published in the media that American military and civilian guards at the Abu Ghraib prison complex outside Baghdad had engaged in outrageous behavior against Iraqi prisoners as a means of extracting information. Some of the guards' actions included torture. President Bush immediately denounced the actions, saying they were contrary to Americans' deeply held values. The White House also announced that he had privately criticized Secretary of Defense Rumsfeld for not exercising firmer control over the treatment of prisoners in Iraq. Outrage was expressed throughout Europe and the Middle East; some charged that the United States was hypocritical for permitting the behavior of its troops to mock the president's espousal of America's high moral values. The *New York Times* called for Rumsfeld's resignation, and the *Washington Post* chastised him for changing the rules on interrogation of prisoners: "Beginning more than two years ago Mr. Rumsfeld decided to overturn decades of previous practice by the U.S. military in its handling of detainees in foreign countries. His Pentagon ruled that the United States would no longer be bound by the Geneva Conventions." The paper observed that "abuses that have done so much harm to the U.S. mission in Iraq might have been prevented had Mr. Rumsfeld been responsive to earlier reports of violations. Instead, he publicly dismissed or minimized such accounts." As a result, the paper concluded, Rumsfeld's actions had "undermined the American military's observance of basic human rights and damaged this country's ability to prevail in the war on terrorism."[10]

President Bush's approval rating regarding the war in Iraq showed a sharp drop in the opinion polls in May 2004, with a majority of the public for the first time responding that the war was not worth the mounting cost. A Senate committee hearing on a report by the U.S. general in charge of investigating the Abu Ghraib case revealed a complete breakdown of military discipline and suggested that higher-ranking officers might eventually be held accountable. For the president, who six months earlier had touted the promotion of American values as a major U.S. objective in the Middle East, the repercussions abroad to the prisoner abuse scandal represented a major assault on his foreign policy and management of the war. Although not directly related to the prisoner scandal, the resignation of CIA Director George Tenet indicated that the Bush national security team was under serious strain just six months before the November presidential election.

CHAPTER 9

THE MOUNTING COSTS OF HEGEMONIC POWER

The rising costs of an American foreign policy based on hegemony came into clearer focus for Congress and the American public during the latter part of 2003. The Bush administration, after refusing for months to advise Congress of the anticipated costs of the occupation and reconstruction in Iraq and Afghanistan, presented Congress with a request for an $87 billion FY 2004 supplemental defense appropriation, of which $20 billion was for rebuilding Iraq's economy. Congress had appropriated $79 billion in April to cover the FY 2003 costs of the invasion and initial months of occupation. The Pentagon had expected the pacification of Iraq to be quick and had planned to withdraw many of the U.S. forces by September, to be replaced, it was hoped, by troops from other countries. The $87 billion budget request surprised lawmakers and caused some to warn that the federal deficit for FY 2004 might approach $500 billion, a staggering deficit in an election year. It was also a reversal of the balanced budgets that had been projected before Bush's 2001 tax reduction bill was enacted by Congress. Democratic leaders demanded that the president rescind part of the tax cuts but conceded that he would eventually get most of the funds he sought because lawmakers were not inclined to "shortchange the troops." Some questioned why U.S. taxpayers should pay for rebuilding hospitals, schools, and electrical power facilities in Iraq when there was no extra money in the federal budget for similar projects at home.

Many Democrats accused the Pentagon of grossly underestimating the magnitude of the postwar reconstruction of Iraq and of exaggerating revenues that would accrue from the export of Iraq's petroleum. Senator Edward Kennedy, a leading Democrat, went so far as to charge that the president had perpetrated a "fraud" on the public by taking the country to war on the basis of faulty intelligence. He told the Senate: "The tragedy is that our troops are paying with their lives because the administration failed to prepare a plan to win the peace."[1] Senator John Kerry, a Democratic candidate for president in early 2004, expressed doubts about whether he should have voted in 2002 to support the use of troops in Iraq, in light of the poor intelligence that he was given by the White House regarding WMD. Later, after he had won most of the Democratic Party primaries, Kerry said he would still have voted for the war but taken more time before launching it in order to build international support. *New York Times* columnist Thomas Friedman, observing that American taxpayers would have to pay the bills for Iraq's reconstruction, wrote: "Bush is deeply morally unserious when he tells Americans that we can succeed in this marathon and still have radical tax cuts for the rich and a soaring deficit, and the only people who will have to sacrifice are reservists and soldiers."[2]

FOREIGN CRISES AND THE GROWTH OF HEGEMONIC INFLUENCE

The war in Iraq was only the most recent instance of Congress and the public being influenced by a foreign crisis to give a president the authority, and budgets, to assert U.S. leadership and commit the country to a global role that led inexorably to American hegemony. The first episode was the Japanese attack on Pearl Harbor, which produced a massive rearmament of the United States, eventual victory over both Germany and Japan, and the postwar occupation of both countries. The second case was President Truman's request to Congress in 1947 for a large economic assistance program to save war-ravaged Europe from a takeover by

Soviet-supported communist parties and pressure groups. The cost of the four-year European Recovery Program, the Marshall Plan, was $13 billion (somewhat over $100 billion in 2003 dollars). Strong opposition arose in Congress, especially from isolationists who called it a giant giveaway program. But the legislation eventually passed, and the Marshall Plan proved to be a remarkable success in rebuilding the economies of Western Europe and enabling the countries to form a common market that brought unprecedented prosperity to Western Europe. The Marshall Plan, followed by the North Atlantic Alliance in 1949, enabled the United States to exercise hegemonic influence in Western Europe for forty years and eventually to force the Soviet Union to abandon the Cold War. A third crisis that caused a large increase in defense spending resulted from North Korea's invasion of South Korea in 1950. The Truman administration was totally unprepared militarily for war in Asia, but the president decided nevertheless to organize a coalition and send thousands of troops to defend South Korea. He believed that Moscow was behind the attack and might be prepared to exert new pressure on Europe, specifically in Berlin. Truman obtained from Congress a large increase in defense spending and an expansion of the armed forces, both of which Congress had cut substantially after World War II. President Eisenhower did not increase defense spending in the 1950s, but he allocated a larger share of the budget to the Air Force for strategic forces (bombers) and to a major buildup of the nation's nuclear weapons capability. He reduced the size of the Army so severely that its chief of staff, Gen. Maxwell Taylor, resigned. Eisenhower substantially increased spending for military and economic assistance to many Third World countries that were willing to support his anticommunist policies in Asia, the Middle East, and Africa.

A fourth crisis, in Southeast Asia in the 1960s, produced another expansion of defense spending, mostly for the Army with its new emphasis on special forces and for counterinsurgency operations. This expansion was precipitated by North Vietnam's massive support of an armed insurgency in South Vietnam designed to topple a pro-American government and unite the entire country under Hanoi's communist rule. The Kennedy and Johnson administrations, aware that the Soviet Union and China were providing large shipments of arms and other matériel to North Vietnam's war effort, were convinced that they intended to extend communist domination southward into Thailand, Malaysia, and Indonesia, which would have been a major strategic blow to the United States. Remarkably, the financial cost of the Vietnam War was not matched by either an increase in federal taxes or a reduction in domestic spending. The result was rampant inflation beginning in 1969, which continued even after U.S. forces were withdrawn from Vietnam. The human costs (casualties) of the intervention became so painful to the American public by 1968 that President Johnson, faced with massive protests across the United States, began a gradual withdrawal of U.S. forces, which President Nixon finally completed in 1973. One result of the failed Vietnam War was the public's demand that defense spending be cut and the CIA be severely constrained in its operations. In addition, foreign aid was reduced, and the military draft was ended. A further result of America's failure in Southeast Asia was a sharp decline in its hegemonic influence, so effectively employed in the 1950s and 1960s. This caused European and Asian allies to worry that the United States might return to a form of detachment from world responsibilities, even isolationism—which could encourage the Soviet Union to assert its growing military and political power in Europe and the Middle East.

A fifth instance of a resurgence in American power occurred after Ronald Reagan became president in 1981. His election resulted in part from the public's outrage over the imprisonment of American diplomatic personnel by Islamic extremists in Iran and President Carter's inability to deal with this challenge. The public was frustrated with Carter's tentative response to an additional crisis that was precipitated by Moscow's decision in December 1979 to invade Afghanistan to install a pro-Soviet regime and establish Soviet military bases. Reagan persuaded Congress to approve major increases in the defense and intelligence budgets and the expansion of U.S. forces in Europe and the Middle East. Critics charged that Reagan was intent on "spending the Soviet Union into bankruptcy"; if so, his strategy was largely successful. U.S. budget deficits increased substantially during Reagan's first term, but the public approved of his tough policies toward what he called "the evil empire." It reelected him by a wide margin in 1984. Reagan and his successor, George H. W. Bush, then succeeded in their aim to end the Cold War largely on America's terms. They had help from a new Soviet leader, Mikhail Gorbachev, who recognized that his country had exhausted itself after forty years of Cold War and needed to restructure its economy and relax its political control as well. However, by the time Reagan left office in 1989, the U.S. economy was in serious need of repair. By 1990, with the Cold War over, President George H. W. Bush was able to curtail defense spending and reduce the size of the armed forces. In 1991, after the Soviet Union imploded, America emerged as the world's sole superpower and, potentially, as a hegemonic power.

ECONOMIC AND HUMAN COSTS OF HEGEMONY

The cost of America's rise to superpower status after World War II is reflected in the growth of its defense budgets over fifty years, from 1945 to 1995. In terms of percentage of gross domestic product (GDP) allocated to defense, the figure dropped from a wartime high of 37.5 in 1945 to only 3.5 by 1948, reflecting the public's complacency regarding national security after World War II. Beginning with the start of the Cold War in Europe, however, the percentage of GDP devoted to defense gradually rose from 4.8 in 1949 to 7.4 in 1951 as a result of the Korean War, reaching 14.3 in 1953. Following the end of that conflict, defense budgets leveled off to roughly 10 percent of GDP during the remainder of the 1950s, reflecting President Eisenhower's détente policy toward the Soviet Union in 1955. Although actual defense spending gradually increased over the next thirty years, the percentage of GDP devoted to the Defense Department gradually declined as the U.S. economy expanded. The Vietnam War showed a spike in the percentage devoted to defense, from 7.4 in 1965 to 9.4 in 1968, the year that President Johnson decided to deescalate the war. During the 1970s, after the United States withdrew from Vietnam and entered what President Carter called a period of "malaise," defense budgets as a percentage of GDP dropped to less than 4 by 1980. During the Reagan years, when the Cold War reached its climax, defense spending spiked again to 6.2 percent in 1986 and then declined to 4.4 percent by 1993, as the country returned to a time of complacency following the end of the Cold War and victory in the 1991 Gulf War. The huge expansion of the nation's economy in the 1990s resulted in a reduction of GDP devoted to defense, to only 3.0 percent by 2000, even though spending in dollar terms remained relatively constant during that decade.[3]

In terms of actual military spending after World War II, the figures generally reflect rises in its percentage of GDP during periods of international crises. Between 1947 and 1949, for example, defense spending nearly tripled as the Cold War commenced, from $52.4 to $144 billion. The Korean War caused another major expansion in military spending, from $141.2 billion in 1950 to $442.3 billion in 1953. Again in the 1960s, as a result of the Vietnam War, military spending jumped, from $364.4 billion in 1964 to $449.3 billion in 1968. In the 1980s, during the Reagan years, military spending grew from $295.8 billion in 1979 to $427.9 billion in 1987, declining over the next eight years to $321.6 billion in 1995. It should be noted that in the last two years of the Carter administration the defense budget rose substantially, to $317.4 billion, in response to the Soviet invasion of Afghanistan.[4]

The human costs of America's rise to superpower status were reflected in the military casualties sustained in the wars it fought during the post–World War II period. The first of these, the Korean War from 1950 to 1953, resulted in 33,741 battle deaths and 103,284 wounded. The Vietnam War cost the United States 47,410 battle deaths and 153,303 wounded. In addition, there were 10,769 other in-theater deaths. The 1991 Persian Gulf War, which lasted only a month, resulted in only 147 battle deaths and 467 wounded, with an additional 382 deaths in theater. These casualties contrasted sharply with the levels sustained during World War II, when the United States suffered 291,557 battle deaths and an additional 671,846 wounded. (Some 114,000 deaths occurred from non-battle-related causes.) The United States also sustained military casualties during smaller interventions, as in Lebanon in 1983, when it lost 241 Marines during a suicide bombing of their barracks outside Beirut. Other uses of military forces in Grenada (1983), Panama (1989), Somalia (1993), Haiti (1994), and Bosnia (1996) resulted in small numbers of U.S. casualties. There were no battle deaths of U.S. forces in the Kosovo war (1999). This record led skeptics to suggest that America was willing to fight only casualty-free interventions, or what one observer labeled "immaculate interventions." In sum, America had fought large, costly wars in East Asia in the 1950s and 1960s to prevent the spread of Sino-Soviet influence during the Cold War. In the 1990s it intervened in less costly conflicts in Africa, the Middle East, and Europe to stabilize failed states and prevent local dictators from spreading their influence into areas of strategic interest to the United States.

The end of the Cold War and the new cooperative relations with Russia and China had two important effects on U.S. foreign policy. First, after emerging from forty years of intense competition with the Soviet Union, the United States could afford to divert part of its huge national security budget into restructuring America's economy and making it more competitive with new economic powers such as Japan, Germany, and South Korea. They had surged ahead in key manufacturing areas during the 1980s while the United States was focused on expanding its military power and forcing Moscow to end the Cold War on favorable terms for the West. Second, the lifting of the Soviet military threat to Western Europe meant that after forty years of Cold War, France and other countries found it safe to challenge America's hegemonic policies. As American forces were reduced in Germany, South Korea, and Japan, and withdrawn completely from the Philippines, the French government was emboldened to raise objections to U.S. policies with regard to Russia, NATO, and the Middle East, among others. France's challenge to Clinton's policies at the end of the 1990s found support in other countries, notably Belgium and Germany, where the Kohl government faced growing public opposition to some U.S. policies. The French public had been inspired by President Charles de Gaulle's vision in the 1960s to lead a European power bloc that could operate independently of the United States and deal as an equal with Moscow and Washington. By the end of the 1990s many Europeans questioned the need for an American-led NATO, which they saw as the vehicle by which the United States continued to exert its hegemonic power over European affairs. A frustrated French foreign minister in 1999 expressed what many Europeans felt when he called the United States a "hyperpower."

During the 2000 presidential election campaign, the Republican nominee, George W. Bush, commented that the United States had been involved too deeply around the world, especially in "nation building," and pledged to scale back U.S. participation in many such projects. During his first six months in office President Bush adopted a more nationalistic attitude in foreign policy than Clinton had. He alienated Europeans by his refusal to seek ratification of the Kyoto Treaty on Global Warming and by his announcement that the United States would withdraw from a 1972 ABM treaty with the Soviet Union. He also reversed Clinton's approach to dealing with North Korea, despite the support that policy had received from European and Asian allies. But his administration averted a crisis with China over the capture of a U.S. spy plane off China's coast, a potentially serious confrontation that was negotiated successfully by Secretary of State Colin Powell. Although the new president had been alerted by the Clinton administration that Al Qaeda terrorists were active against U.S. installations overseas and in the United States, the president chose not to issue a general warning to the public. Instead, he focused heavily during his first months in office on persuading a reluctant Congress to pass a massive $1.3 trillion tax cut, which he hoped would help pull the country out of the recession it had recently entered. Foreign policy and homeland defense were not the highest priority for Bush during his first eight months in office.

The 9/11 terrorist attacks fundamentally changed the administration's view not only of the dangers to national security but also of the priority accorded to federal spending versus balanced budgets. Gone was Mr. Bush's emphasis on fiscal responsibility, which Republicans had long championed as part of their political ideology. Gone also were many of Bush's domestic priorities. The decision to go to war in Afghanistan coincided with the first installment on the president's plans for major increases in the defense and intelligence budgets. As a result, military budgets increased from $307.8 billion in 2001 to $379.9 billion in FY 2004. When the $87 billion in supplemental funding for the wars in Iraq and Afghanistan was added, the total military spending for 2004 was nearly $470 billion. The Department of Homeland Security, created in 2002, required a budget that reached $30 billion in 2004. Many government agencies were transferred to the new department, among them the Coast Guard, Border Police, Customs Service, Immigration Service, Transportation Security Administration, and Federal Emergency Management Agency. The president also obtained a major increase in funding for the Central Intelligence Agency to strengthen intelligence collection and carry out quasi-military operations in Afghanistan. Congress expanded the authority and funding of the Justice Department and the FBI to help them apprehend and detain potential terrorists. In sum, the war in Afghanistan was a new test of America's will and capability to defend its national interests against a new enemy, the Al Qaeda terrorist network.

During the sixty years that elapsed between the Japanese attack on Pearl Harbor and Al Qaeda's attack on the World Trade Center, the U.S. government showed a fierce determination not to be intimidated by the Soviet Union, China, or Iraq's Saddam Hussein. The United States may not consciously have set out to establish an American hegemony in the world, but its economic and military power seemed to propel it in that direction. If Washington appeared in the 2000s to be exercising an increasingly coercive hegemonic influence worldwide, this was more a *consequence of its power* than a prime objective of its foreign policy. The enormous increase in America's ability to project its power worldwide was a major contributing factor.

WAR IN IRAQ: THE FINANCIAL COSTS

The president's decision to launch a preemptive war to oust Saddam Hussein threw earlier budgetary calculations into the dustbin. As the Pentagon began its buildup of forces in neighboring Kuwait, Qatar, and Bahrain in mid-2002, it was already acknowledged that the FY 2003 defense budget would require a supplemental appropriation to pay for the mobilization and, potentially, for war. Civilian officials at the Defense Department, among them Secretary Rumsfeld and his deputy, Paul Wolfowitz, predicted in early 2003 that the Iraq campaign would be a short one, that the cost would be less than $100 billion, and that most of the troops could leave Iraq by September. The Army doubted these estimates, based on its experience in Bosnia, Kosovo, and Afghanistan. When pressed by a congressional committee for his personal views, the Army chief of staff Gen. Eric Shinseki estimated that occupying Iraq after the ouster of its regime could require several hundred thousand troops and last three to four years. Within days the four-star general was publicly rebuked by Deputy Secretary Wolfowitz, who called his estimate wildly off the mark.

In April 2003 Congress approved a supplemental defense budget of \$79 billion to cover the costs of the war and occupation through September 2003, but many members expressed skepticism about how long U.S. forces would in fact remain. Rumsfeld's civilian staff had assured Congress before the war that reconstruction in Iraq would be relatively fast and that its oil exports would pay for most of those costs beyond 2003. The administration also expected that the European allies and the United Nations would contribute funds and troops once Saddam Hussein's regime was removed and security restored. The public and Congress were thus led to believe that the overthrow of Saddam's dictatorship would be relatively easy, the occupation short, and the cost to U.S. taxpayers manageable.

Only the first of these predictions proved to be correct—the ouster of the Iraqi regime was in fact rapid. James Fallows, in a scathing analysis of the false assumptions and miscalculations that the Defense Department made about Iraq, later wrote in *The Atlantic,* "All the government working groups concluded that occupying Iraq would be far more difficult than defeating it. Wolfowitz either didn't notice this evidence or chose to disbelieve it." Fallows asked: "How could the Administration have thought that it was safe to proceed in blithe indifference to the warnings of nearly everyone with operational experience in modern military occupation?" He observed that the president must have known that war in Iraq would affect his reelection in 2004 and that the political risk was "enormous and obvious." Fallows's conclusion was that administration officials had convinced themselves that the war was necessary and that a "successful occupation would not require any more forethought than they gave it."[5] The reality of the Pentagon's miscalculation of the war's costs and duration emerged into full view in September 2003 as the Iraq insurgency expanded and U.S. troops were required to remain. The situation drew reproach from the media and congressional Democrats, as well as some Republicans. *Newsweek* captured the frustration in an article headlined "The Unbuilding of Iraq," with a headnote: "Perfect Storm: Wrongheaded assumptions. Ideological blinders. Weak intelligence, missteps, poor coordination and bad luck. How Team Bush's reconstruction efforts went off the rails from day one."[6] *Business Week* featured a story on September 22, "The High Cost of War," with this caption: "The billions needed for Iraq could exact a toll on the still-fragile economy—and on Bush's political fortunes." The *Wall Street Journal* weighed in with a report on September 9 titled "Iraq Costs Fuel Anti-Pentagon Backlash: As Rosy Projections Wilt, Top Military Leaders Face Harsh Questions on Capitol Hill." The paper's columnist, Alan Murray, penned a commentary in the same issue: "Bush's Talk about Spending Discipline Is So Much Hot Air."

The administration's miscalculation on Iraq resulted from four factors that were predictable but had not been appreciated by hawks in the Office of the Secretary of Defense (OSD), or in Vice President Cheney's office. They had lobbied in the summer of 2002 to refocus U.S. strategy from Afghanistan to what they viewed as the larger danger posed by Saddam Hussein's continuing quest for WMD. Their miscalculations were the unwillingness of key U.S. allies, especially Turkey, to support an invasion of Iraq without a new UN resolution; the decisions of Russia and Germany to join France in blocking a U.S.-sponsored resolution for war; the opposition of major Arab states, except Jordan, at least to endorse the U.S.-British decision to use force against Iraq; and the fierceness with which Saddam's Baath Party loyalists and foreign fighters resisted U.S. and British occupation forces following the capture of Baghdad. The administration's blunder on Iraq was reminiscent of the Lyndon Johnson administration's misjudgments on Vietnam before the president decided in the summer of 1965 to send nearly two hundred thousand troops there with an expectation that enemy insurgents would melt away in the face of American power and resolve. An added factor in 2003 was growing discontent in the military, especially in the Army, over the fact that Secretary Rumsfeld and his top officials refused to authorize a sufficiently large ground force to fight the war and then adequately occupy Iraq. Their argument was that ground troops had been stretched to the limit by numerous deployments abroad and that the Army could not sustain a large occupation force in Iraq unless Congress increased its size. Gen. Wesley Clark, retired NATO commander and a Democratic candidate for president in 2004, argued that too few troops were available for both the invasion and occupation of Iraq and that the force should be enlarged. He also faulted the administration for miscalculating the costs of the war in

Iraq and for launching it in haste before the antiterrorist campaign in Afghanistan was finished.

President Bush's budget request in September 2003 for an additional $87 billion to cover the FY 2004 costs of occupation in Iraq and Afghanistan and the Pentagon's failure to find any WMD in Iraq triggered a vigorous debate in Washington about the wisdom of the Iraq war. The issue was how the occupation should be paid for—by the Iraqis, the United Nations, or the U.S. taxpayer. A *Wall Street Journal*/NBC poll conducted in September found that 56 percent of the public thought Bush should cancel the upper-income tax cuts that he had championed in the 2001 tax legislation, 12 percent favored increased government borrowing and a larger budget deficit, 7 percent were willing to drop plans for a Medicare drug benefit, and 6 percent would reduce spending on other domestic programs. Democrats argued that Bush's plan to spend $20 billion for reconstruction in Iraq contrasted sharply with the administration's refusal to spend on similar projects in the United States. One Chicago congressman proposed that for every dollar the president spent on hospital reconstruction in Iraq, he should spend an equal amount on health care in his congressional district. In a *Wall Street Journal* column, Albert Hunt observed that "Republicans are scared stiff about the $87 billion reconstruction measure following the nearly $79 billion already approved." He suggested that Gen. Wesley Clark's entry into the presidential race lent weight to the Democrats' argument that planning for postwar Iraq had been totally inadequate.[7] Adding to the apprehension about the war's cost, a team of specialists from the World Bank and the United Nations that visited Iraq concluded that its reconstruction costs over four years would be $55 billion. Their report raised doubts about whether a U.S.-supported "donors conference" in Madrid scheduled for late October would even approach that goal. The reality was that other countries were not prepared to contribute toward Iraq's reconstruction unless the United Nations gave its approval. Belatedly, the Bush administration decided that it must end the U.S. occupation in June 2004 and seek a UN resolution to support a new sovereign Iraqi government, even if the security situation was not stabilized.

The cost of rebuilding Iraq was certain to be a political issue in the 2004 presidential election, even though Congress finally approved, with

Democratic Party support, the president's request for the additional $87 billion. However, Bush would now have to decide whether to let the federal deficit rise to an unprecedented level or adjust the 2001 tax law to postpone or rescind some tax reductions. If he decided to add the $87 billion cost of Iraq's occupation to the deficit, he ran the risk that fiscally conservative Republicans in Congress would not support what they considered fiscal irresponsibility. In October the Congressional Budget Office released figures showing that although the FY 2003 federal budget deficit had been put at $374 billion, this would rise sharply to $480 billion in FY 2004 even without new spending for the Iraq war. *Washington Post* columnist David Broder warned of unrestrained government spending in a commentary entitled "Fiscal Doomsday in the Offing." He wrote: "Some members of Congress of both parties have argued for months, if not years, that the lack of spending restraint, coupled with the penchant for ever-larger tax cuts, cannot be allowed to go on. Their cautions have gone unheeded."[8]

INTERNATIONAL COSTS

After the attacks of September 11 Americans asked in bewilderment, "Why do Muslims hate us?" Weekly magazines, journals, and TV talk shows were filled with explanations by experts on the motivation of the nineteen Arab hijackers who had rammed the planes into the World Trade Center and the Pentagon. Americans were stunned to see photos of thousands of Muslims dancing with joy in the streets of Cairo and Baghdad. At the same time, there was an outpouring of sympathy from the peoples in Europe and Asia (non-Muslim countries) for the families of victims. Most Europeans supported President Bush's decision to strike at Afghanistan to counter Al Qaeda terrorists who were harbored there. But two years later Americans found that the United States was denounced by many of the same people and governments because of President Bush's unilateral and preemptive war against Iraq, which they believed to be illegal because it was not approved by the United Nations. Foreign criticism irritated Americans and caused many to wonder, "Why doesn't the world support us?"

Criticism of U.S. policies and American culture was not new among Europeans. Leftists across Europe had protested American arrogance and pursuit of hegemonic power for decades before the invasion of Iraq. But this earlier criticism had been constrained by two key considerations: European governments were hesitant to challenge U.S. policies during the Cold War because they understood that Europe's security depended on a large American military presence and the president's willingness to defend them; a second factor was the importance of strong U.S. economic leadership in the post–World War II decades, which produced unprecedented prosperity in Europe as well as in Japan and South Korea. Europeans and Asians applauded the end of the Cold War but were apprehensive about Washington's new role as the world's only superpower. Some had complained earlier about what they considered to be President Clinton's excessive exercise of hegemonic influence during the Kosovo intervention and on the enlargement of NATO.

With President Bush's decision to invade Iraq without UN authorization, international public opinion turned sharply against the United States; many Europeans and most Arabs refused to support the war. Only in Great Britain did a majority of the public initially approve of a governmental decision to join the United States in Iraq. The Spanish government joined the coalition and sent a small number of troops, but Spanish public opinion strongly opposed the war. The same was true in Italy, whose government also agreed to join the coalition. Poland was a fourth large European country that sent troops, but its public too did not strongly support the move. France, Germany, Belgium, and Russia strongly opposed the war and provided no help.

A widely publicized opinion poll in June 2003 conducted by the Pew Research Center illustrated the depth of anti-American opinion that had grown in many countries as a result of the U.S. decision to attack Iraq. The research group conducted fifteen thousand interviews in twenty countries in the spring and found that support for the United States had dropped precipitously. In Germany, France, Italy, and Spain, less than 50 percent of their publics held a favorable opinion of the United States, with Spain among the lowest, with only 38 percent. Even more significant, public support for NATO also had dropped to less than 50 percent, with most continental Europeans believing that Europe should develop its own military capability, one separate from that of the United States. Only in Britain was opinion of the United States favorable, at 70 percent. The most dramatic drop was in Turkey, a key U.S. ally for fifty years. Whereas in 2000 the Pew organization had found that 75 percent of Turkey's public had a favorable view of America, by the spring of 2003 this figure had reversed—an astonishing 83 percent of respondents now held a negative view. These findings suggested that the high percentage of public opposition to the United States was a major reason that Turkey's government refused to allow American forces to use its territory in 2003 to open a second front in the invasion of Iraq, an action that seriously affected the subsequent occupation of Iraq. Andrew Kohut, the Pew Center's director, said of the findings: "The war [Iraq] has widened the rift between Americans and Western Europeans, softened support for the war on terrorism, and significantly weakened global public support for the pillars of the post World War II era—the U.N. and the North Atlantic Alliance."[9]

The *New York Times* ran a story October 1 on a report issued by a White House–appointed advisory group that had interviewed thousands of educated people in Muslim countries on the reasons for the anti-American sentiment in their communities. The front-page headline read, "Bush-Appointed Panel Finds U.S. Image Is in Peril." The paper earlier had carried a story from Jakarta regarding this panel's discussion with prominent Indonesian moderates, among them Yenni Annube Wahid, the Harvard-trained daughter of Indonesia's former prime minister. She asserted that the problem was American policy, not its public relations: "There is no point in saying this is a problem of communication, blah, blah, blah. The perception in the Muslim world is that the problem is the policy toward the Israeli-Palestinian conflict and Iraq."[10] As the world's largest Muslim country, Indonesia has a moderate, democratic government, located thousands of miles from the conflicts in Iraq and Palestine. Still, even members of its American-educated elite think that American policy toward Muslims in the Middle East is unjust and should be opposed.

In March 2004 a dramatic demonstration of foreign public opposition to the U.S. war in Iraq unfolded in Spain just days before it held national elections. Terrorist bombings of several commuter trains in and near Madrid killed nearly two hundred people and injured many more. The incident shocked the public. A terrorist group linked to Al Qaeda declared that the bombing was a protest against Spain's participation in the war and occupation of Iraq. Until then the Socialist Party had lagged in opinion polls behind the conservative government, headed by Prime Minister Jose Maria Asnar, one of George Bush's staunchest allies in the war against Iraq. The train bombing directly affected the outcome of the elections, causing the defeat of Asnar's party. The election then brought to power Jose Luis Rodrigues Zapatero, a Socialist who had campaigned strongly against Spain's participation in the war and had pledged to withdraw Spanish troops.

He soon announced that he would quickly withdraw the one thousand Spanish forces from Iraq and reorient Madrid's policy toward that espoused by France. This stunning reversal in Spain's foreign policy had profound implications for George Bush's policy. First, it removed from the allied coalition a valuable ally, one of only a few major European governments that had given Bush full support for the war in Iraq. Second, it encouraged terrorists elsewhere in Europe to believe they might unseat other governments, for example, in Italy, which supported the war. Bush was also concerned that Australia's Conservative government, headed by Prime Minister John Howard, might lose an election in October 2004 and be replaced by a leftist party that pledged to withdraw Australia's contingent from Iraq. (The Conservatives won the election, and Australia remained part of the coalition.) Finally, the Bush reelection campaign was concerned that emboldened terrorists would try to influence the November 2 American elections by launching a dramatic attack on the United States. Unlike in Spain, Italy, and Australia, however, the opposition party's nominee, Senator Kerry, did not favor a withdrawal from Iraq, even though he was prepared to put a time limit on the U.S. presence. For Secretary of Defense Rumsfeld, who in 2003 had criticized the attitude of "Old Europe" as characterized by the policies of France and Germany, the withdrawal of Spain from the coalition underlined the reality that Old Europe was expanding.

DOMESTIC POLITICAL COSTS

Presidents seeking reelection normally pay less attention to world opinion when deciding foreign policy issues than they do to polls and media comments indicating the preferences of American voters. George W. Bush was no exception. Accordingly, his speech to the United Nations on September 23, 2003, was more of a defense of his policy on Iraq than a recognition that he might need to make concessions to UN Security Council members on the issues of administering postwar Iraq and persuading them to send peacekeeping troops and financial support to Iraq for its reconstruction. The goal of France and some council members was the early transfer of sovereignty from the occupation authority—U.S. and Britain—to an Iraqi provisional government. The president insisted that Iraq needed first to agree on a new constitution so that elections could be held, a new government established, and sovereignty then turned over to a functioning democratic state. Otherwise, Bush argued, Iraq might sink into civil war and perhaps a new dictatorship. Congress generally supported the administration's view. By refusing to accept France's position that the United Nations should have the primary role in shepherding Iraq toward democratic government, the president paid a price in terms of European and American support. A *New York Times*/CBS News poll conducted during late September 2003 found that his approval rating for handling foreign policy had dropped since the major fighting ended in the spring. On one question—"Do you have confidence in George W. Bush's ability to deal wisely with an international crisis, or are you uneasy about his approach?"—only 45 percent expressed confidence, compared with 66 percent in April. However, on another question—"Do you think the policies of the Bush administration have made the United States safer from terrorism?"—60 percent approved of his policies.[11]

Five months after the fall of Baghdad and of Iraq's "liberation," as the Bush administration called it, the political costs at home of this exercise of hegemonic power were visible. The administration's stated reasons for going to war and its expectations for an early withdrawal had been greatly exaggerated. Faulty intelligence on Iraq's WMD was partly at fault. But another factor was the Pentagon's gross miscalculation of the costs and duration of the occupation. Prior to the war, the president, the vice president, the secretaries of state and defense, and the national security adviser all made a strong case to the American public that Saddam Hussein possessed WMD and would likely possess nuclear weapons within a short time. Vice President Cheney had also cited a close link, since discredited, between Al Qaeda and Saddam Hussein's government. At the end of 2003, after five months of exhaustive search in Iraq, a CIA-appointed weapons team headed by Dr. David Kay reported that, although Iraq had had the means to produce WMD, no prohibited weapons were located.

Another obvious and costly miscalculation by Pentagon planners was the widespread looting and disruption of energy infrastructure that occurred after Saddam Hussein's fall, plus the continuing widespread resistance to the occupation in Baghdad and in the so-called Sunni Triangle. Most U.S. military forces were not trained for urban warfare and did not have the numbers to guard Iraqi banks, hospitals, power plants, and other nonmilitary facilities, which looters and terrorists attacked on a regular basis. These incidents were prominently reported in the U.S. media. Democrats now reminded the public that President Bush had declared on the deck of an aircraft carrier off San Diego on May 1 that major fighting in Iraq was over and that U.S. forces had won a great victory. An additional miscalculation by the Pentagon's civilian leadership, one that would affect Mr. Bush's reelection chances if not quickly resolved, was its prediction in April that most combat troops would be withdrawn from Iraq by September 2003 and be replaced by forces from other countries. When these declined to send troops, a dangerous security situation arose in Baghdad and other cities and expanded in 2004. As a result, the tours of duty for many troops were extended to a full year from the expected six months, an expedient that caused grumbling in the ranks. Additional reserve and National Guard units were called up, and the Pentagon's plan for replacing many U.S. units with foreign troops in 2004 was abandoned. The occupation force, consisting of 80 percent American and 20 percent British, including small contingents from other countries, numbered about 145,000 in October 2003. In the spring of 2004 the Pentagon decided to increase the number of U.S. troops remaining in Iraq through 2004 to 138,000. The change was made in order to deal with the continuing insurgency, the withdrawal of Spanish forces, and reductions made by other coalition members.

The Bush administration's failure to meet public expectations regarding the length and cost of invading and rebuilding Iraq led to disillusionment by many regarding the wisdom of going to war. Some talked of a "quagmire," reminiscent of references to the Vietnam War during the election of 1968. The comparison with Vietnam was not accurate, however, because the U.S. force in Iraq was far smaller than the half million in Vietnam, and the commitment in Iraq was not open-ended, as it had seemed to be in the Vietnam conflict. Also, the Bush administration had won the war against Saddam Hussein's regime, whereas in Vietnam President Johnson failed to defeat North Vietnam's forces or persuade its government to negotiate an end to the war. Still, the failure to find WMD in Iraq in 2003, the growing cost of its occupation, and Mr. Bush's inability to persuade other countries to send troops to replace Americans cast a shadow over his hope that he could put the Iraq war behind him before starting his campaign for reelection in 2004.

Vice President Cheney in October 2003 sought to counter the arguments of UN Secretary General Kofi Annan to the General Assembly that the U.S. invasion of Iraq had been against the provisions of the UN Charter and, therefore, was in breach of international law. Annan had also denounced the so-called doctrine of preemptive war. In an address to the Heritage Foundation, Cheney argued that UN procedures for dealing with crises like Iraq resulted in "doing nothing" in the face of danger, and that the United States reserved the right to strike at potential enemies even if other nations did not agree. He said the president "will not permit gathering threats to become certain tragedies," adding that "weakness and drift and vacillation in the face of danger invite attacks." He called the United Nations a "toothless organization" for preventing wars and said that Washington would take unilateral action whenever it determined that its national security was endangered."[12] Cheney's view reflected the sentiments of American conservatives and many others who held a poor opinion of the United Nations and its ability to deal effectively with threats to peace.

THE RISK OF STRATEGIC OVERREACH

All great powers in history have had their rise to the top and, after a time, gone into decline, in some cases to their demise. In *The Rise and Fall of the Great Powers,* Paul Kennedy commented on the prospects for the

United States, as it was emerging from the Cold War as the undisputed superpower. Kennedy used the phrase "imperial overstretch" to describe the crisis a great power encounters when it can no longer sustain the costs of its imperial commitments. "Although the United States is at present still in a class of its own economically and perhaps even militarily," he observed, "it cannot avoid confronting the two great tests which challenged the longevity of every major power that occupied the number one position in world affairs." He said these were "the nation's perceived defense requirements and the means it possesses to maintain those commitments" and asked whether the United States could preserve its technological and economic superiority from "relative erosion" in the face of shifting patterns of global production. The United States was the inheritor of "a vast array of strategical commitments," which were accumulated over many decades, Kennedy wrote, concluding: "In consequence, the United States now runs the risk, so familiar to historians of the rise and fall of previous Great Powers, of what might roughly be called 'imperial overstretch,' that is to say, decision-makers in Washington must face the awkward and enduring fact that the sum total of the United States' global interests and obligations is nowadays far larger than the country's power to defend them all simultaneously."[13] Although Kennedy's view of the United States may have seemed plausible to some in 1987, it was not true in 2003. Not only had U.S. forces induced regime changes in Central Asia and the Middle East, but President Bush's ability to persuade Congress to appropriate large funding for the reconstruction of Iraq and Afghanistan was a reaffirmation of America's ability and willingness to use its power to reshape international politics to further its national interests. Indeed, an argument could be made that in 2003 America had not yet reached the zenith of its power, that its ability to exercise hegemonic influence in the world had actually increased since the 1980s.

Nevertheless, the disappointing U.S. experience in Iraq had the potential effect of causing the United States to limit the exercise of its power in other parts of the world, including Europe. Also, the projected federal budget deficit for FY 2004, estimated at nearly half a trillion dollars, was the largest ever since World War II. These mounting costs of hegemonic power caused Governor Howard Dean, a Democratic presidential candidate, to echo Paul Kennedy's caution about strategic overstretch: "I think what the president is doing is setting the stage for the failure of America. If you look at what's happened to other great countries, they get in trouble when they can't manage their money . . . and they get in trouble when they overstretch their military capabilities."[14]

When I published *America Overcommitted: U.S. National Interests in the 1980s,* the Cold War was not yet over and the Reagan administration had run up large budget deficits in order to expand U.S. military power and force the Soviet Union to negotiate an end to the Cold War. My view in 1984 was that in order to pay for its continuing and costly confrontation with Moscow, Washington needed to reduce military and economic costs in East Asia. In 2004, with the Soviet Union gone and no new power presenting a serious threat to the United States or its allies, there was renewed reason to be concerned about the danger of strategic overreach. New commitments had been made and bases built in Central Asia in 2002, and many U.S. troops were operating in Afghanistan and several Persian Gulf states. The goal that George Bush had outlined in his national strategy in 2002 regarding promotion of freedom in the world was being implemented, and his assertion of a right to use preemptive force to confront dangerous regimes had been demonstrated. Still, the question remained whether Congress and the American people would accept the continuing huge price that Bush's hegemonic policies entailed in future years. Ideological conservatives argued that America was economically so powerful that it could easily afford its worldwide hegemonic role. Pragmatic conservatives and most liberals did not agree, believing instead that America needed the help of allies and friends if it hoped to prevail in building Iraq into a peaceful, functioning democracy and bringing freedom to other Arab countries. When George Bush decided in June 2004 that it was time to compromise with America's allies and friends in order to share the burden of rebuilding Iraq, he implicitly conceded that America could not achieve that goal alone. In effect, the U.S. president was admitting that America's hegemonic power was not unlimited.

CHAPTER 10

COLLABORATIVE OR UNILATERAL INTERNATIONALISM

A t the end of the Cold War America faced a fundamental choice about the country's long-term goals as a superpower. With unparalleled economic, military, and political power, should the country exercise an essentially unilateral, hegemonic world role similar to that of ancient Athens and Imperial Rome? Or should it follow a policy of organizing and leading a collective hegemony that emphasizes collaboration with allies to ensure a favorable world order? For the United States, the objective of both unilateral and collaborative hegemony is to build a peaceful international security environment that thwarts the ambitions of aggressive states that threaten their neighbors and regional security. Such challenges occurred during the 1990s in the Persian Gulf (1991), Somalia (1993), Bosnia (1995), Serbia (1999), and more recently in Afghanistan (2001) and Iraq (2003). A third choice, neo-isolationism, made an appearance in the 1990s. It would have the United States withdraw from most collective security commitments and overseas bases acquired during the Cold War and pursue instead an aloof, protectionist policy toward the rest of the world. Although the three choices were discussed during the presidential primary campaigns in 2004, the neo-isolationist option did not generate sufficient support to change the internationalist positions of either the Republican or Democratic party.

169

During the Cold War Washington followed a relatively consistent and generally collaborative foreign policy in pursuing its international security (world order) objectives. In essence, they were to contain the military power of the Soviet Union and China and prevent communist parties in noncommunist countries, especially in Europe, from achieving political power through a coup d'état or the ballot box. Although the Republican Party had toyed with the idea after World War II of returning to its prewar isolationist and protectionist outlook, Dwight Eisenhower brought Republicans into accord with the internationalist outlook of the Democrats when he became president in 1953. The first postwar Democratic president, Harry Truman, was greatly aided in the task of shepherding his internationalist policy through Congress by the efforts of moderate Republicans, notably Senator Arthur Vandenberg, who strongly supported both the Marshall Plan and ratification of the North Atlantic Treaty. Eisenhower continued these policies, but he placed greater emphasis than had Truman on building military power to confront the Soviet Union's belligerence in Europe and the Middle East, and that of China in East Asia. Both presidents practiced collaborative hegemony with allies in Europe and Asia.

In the 1960s, however, the Vietnam War, as pursued by Lyndon Johnson, produced a serious backlash in Europe and Canada against U.S. policy and led to a deep split within the Democratic Party over his interventionist policies. A powerful leftist faction favored the immediate withdrawal of U.S. forces from Vietnam and a reduction of troops elsewhere. In 1972 this faction gained the ascendancy and selected Senator George McGovern, an opponent of Johnson's interventionist policies, as the party's nominee for president. Richard Nixon won reelection, however, and completed the withdrawal of U.S. troops from Vietnam. He also restored good relations with European allies, which had been severely strained over the war.

The 1970s marked a retrenchment of U.S. military power and influence following the humiliating withdrawal of all Americans from Vietnam in 1975. Jimmy Carter's efforts in the late 1970s to use diplomacy instead of military power to persuade others to accept U.S. leadership had mixed results, especially among Europeans who were skeptical of his emphasis on human rights in foreign policy. Carter's inability to resolve the

Iran Hostage Crisis contributed to his defeat in 1980 by Ronald Reagan, who pledged to expand U.S. military power and then force Moscow to abandon the Cold War. Reagan was at first distrusted by many Europeans for his harsh rhetoric against the Soviet Union and was accused of pursuing a unilateralist foreign policy. But Reagan's success in ending the Cold War and enabling Eastern European countries to escape from Soviet domination was applauded across the continent.

In the 1990s, with the Cold War ended and the Soviet empire in ruins, leadership in both the Republican and Democratic parties faced mounting pressure from dissenters in their ranks who insisted on moving away from free trade policies and military commitments, long favored by party leaders, and concentrating instead on building a better society at home. For Democratic protesters, that meant cutting defense spending and diverting the money to new social programs. For Republican dissidents, it meant bringing troops home from abroad, strengthening defenses in North America, and using the savings to cut the federal budget and taxes. In this political environment, billionare businessman Ross Perot launched a vigorous third-party campaign in 1992 to protest NAFTA and similar trade policies, as well as the high cost of U.S. bases and alliances abroad. His Independent Party won an astonishing 19 percent of the votes in the 1992 presidential election. The Republicans had a problem persuading conservative columnist and TV commentator Pat Buchanan to remain within the party after he launched a vigorous campaign in 1992 to force its convention to adopt a neo-isolationist, protectionist platform resembling the isolationist America First movement of the 1940s. Buchanan favored withdrawing American troops from Europe and Asia and abandoning free trade policies followed by the Republican Party since the 1950s. Neither Perot's nor Buchanan's protests altered the foreign policy stances of the major parties, but they contributed to the election victory of Bill Clinton over the incumbent president, George H. W. Bush, in 1992.

CLINTON'S TESTING OF COLLABORATIVE INTERNATIONALISM

After the collapse of the Soviet empire in 1991, Bill Clinton in the 1990s and George W. Bush in the 2000s had to decide this key question: *What kind* of internationalist policy should their administrations follow in order to sustain American hegemony in a new unipolar world? Another question was: How would Americans respond to the *costs* of using U.S. forces abroad, as in Bosnia and Kosovo (Clinton) and in Afghanistan and Iraq (Bush) if America's allies were not willing to participate? In that case, would the generally collaborative policies of the Cold War years be replaced by a more unilateralist attitude toward the allies?

Clinton straddled that issue during his first term by deferring to Europeans on matters dealing with European security, as in Bosnia and Kosovo, while according them less attention on issues in the Middle East, specifically the Israeli-Palestinian controversy, and in Asia. He frequently acted without close consultation in his dealings with a new Russian president, Boris Yeltsin, and incurred the complaint of some Europeans, especially in France, that he did not take sufficient account of their views. Although generally well regarded in Europe, Clinton was seen as a reluctant partner in 1995 for being slow to respond when European leaders sought U.S. military help in stopping ethnic warfare in Bosnia. He persuaded the allies to expand NATO membership into Eastern Europe, to include Poland, Hungary, and the Czech Republic, even though they feared this action might antagonize Moscow. In sum, during his first five years in the White House, Clinton tried to promote collaborative internationalism with the allies.

During his last three years in office, however, Clinton moved to a more unilateralist mode of operations, causing some Europeans, notably French, to complain that he and Secretary of State Madeleine Albright did not consult them in conducting the war in Kosovo (Serbia), where NATO had intervened to force the withdrawal of Serbia's troops that were engaged in the expulsion of ethnic Albanians. They also disagreed with the administration's policy in Iraq, where the United States and Britain had been enforcing a UN-mandated no-fly zone as part of the sanctions imposed on Saddam Hussein's regime after the Gulf War. France and Germany wanted the sanctions rescinded. Regarding the Israeli-Palestinian peace process, Clinton excluded the Europeans and the United Nations because of Israel's objections. This U.S. acquiescence to Israel's demands frustrated many European governments.

Clinton's reasons for adopting a more unilateralist policy during the

Kosovo war resulted from the widening disparity in arms capability between America and Europe, except for Britain. Problems over burden sharing in Bosnia and Kosovo also became a major issue. News that NATO countries, including Canada, had sharply reduced their defense budgets during the 1990s while the United States maintained its level of spending was another source of frustration for Clinton.

The United States and its allies had different views regarding the value of the United Nations in handling serious international disputes. Whenever the Soviet Union had vetoed Security Council resolutions proposed by the Western powers, this action had played into the hands of conservatives and neo-isolationists who were never reconciled to the internationalist view adopted by the Republican Party after World War II. Anti-UN sentiment had grown during the 1970s and 1980s when the General Assembly passed frequent resolutions by overwhelming majorities to condemn Israel for its occupation of Palestinian territories. Many Americans were outraged when the world body voted against the United States on the question of returning control of the Panama Canal Zone and canal to Panama. Washington was forthcoming with financial support, however, until the 1990s when it withheld part of its annual UN assessment because of congressional dissatisfaction over the large size of the U.S. contribution as well as alleged gross mismanagement of the organization's finances. Europeans and Canadians, on the other hand, gave the United Nations more support after the Soviet Union's collapse because they believed the Security Council was a forum where the allies could exert some influence over U.S. policy in a period when it was the sole superpower and less interested in the views of the allies. Many Europeans were concerned that the United States was behaving like a coercive superpower instead of collaborating with its allies. France now assumed the leadership of an informal coalition, supported by Russia and Germany, whose purpose was to restrain the growing power of the United States.

By 1998 the idea of collaborative internationalism was giving way in Washington to a view that even though Europe's strategic importance was declining, NATO might still be useful in assisting the United States in establishing a stable world order in the Middle East, a vast area where Al Qaeda terrorists had attacked U.S. military installations and bombed two American embassies in East Africa. Most NATO countries, however, strongly favored diplomacy over military force in dealing with security issues outside Europe. Clinton had by now come to the view that dangerous regimes in the Middle East and Central Asia could not be dealt with effectively through diplomacy alone and that a willingness to use force was necessary to achieve satisfactory results.

The reality was that only the United States had decisive military power to intervene in dangerous situations, whereas France, Germany, Italy, and others lagged behind and had a limited capability for military interventions. Only Britain maintained a military that matched the United States in technical capability. A fully collaborative policy was therefore difficult for the Clinton administration to follow when it decided in 1998 to confront the Al Qaeda terrorist organization. Clinton responded militarily by bombings in Afghanistan and Tanzania after the terrorist attacks on U.S. embassies, and he increased bombing on Iraqi military installations after Saddam Hussein forced the withdrawal of UN arms inspectors. Neither NATO nor the UN Security Council was consulted on these actions. By the time Clinton left office in 2001, the United States had already moved away from a policy of collaborative internationalism and was relying on American arms and the support of Great Britain, whose vital interests paralleled those of the United States.

BUSH'S UNILATERAL INTERNATIONALISM

It was but a short step from Clinton's and Albright's increasingly restrictive approach to dealing with international security issues to George W. Bush's early pattern of largely ignoring the NATO allies and the United Nations. His early decisions against negotiations with North Korea, non-ratification of the Kyoto Treaty on Global Warming, and cancellation of the 1971 ABM treaty with Russia shocked European and Canadian opinion leaders and caused their governments to worry about where the NATO alliance was going with this new, untested American president. Their attitude was reminiscent of the early 1980s when Europeans thought the same of Ronald Reagan, whom many viewed simply as a Hollywood cowboy. Events on 9/11 brought the European allies to America's support, but their support was tentative because at the beginning of 2002

George Bush signaled to the world in his State of the Union address that he intended to force radical changes in international relations. Another issue that turned European opinion against the feared U.S. unilateralist policies was Bush's decision in June to support Israel's hard-line policies in dealings with Palestinian terrorists. Europeans had long been more sympathetic than Americans to the Palestinians' quest for a sovereign state as their homeland, and they were less restrained than Americans in criticizing Israel's brutal military operations in the occupied territories.

Bush's unilateral internationalism came into sharp focus in February–March 2003, when France, Germany, Russia, China, Mexico, and Chile, among others, declined to support a UN Security Council resolution authorizing the United States and Britain to use force against Iraq. When France threatened to veto the resolution, the president, along with the leaders of Britain, Spain, Poland, and Australia, decided to proceed without UN approval. Even Canada, America's closest neighbor and largest trading partner, refused to provide any assistance in Iraq without the UN's blessing, which it knew was unlikely so long as France was opposed. The result was that the war and occupation of Iraq was primarily a U.S.-British operation, with small military contributions from Australia, Spain, Poland, the Netherlands, Denmark, Italy, and others. UN Secretary General Annan sent a team of reconstruction experts to Iraq in the summer, but it was withdrawn in August after twenty-two personnel were killed in a suicide bombing of the UN headquarters in Baghdad. A dangerous security situation, bordering on an insurgency, emerged in Baghdad and discouraged other international aid organizations from sending people to Iraq.

Several favorable events occurred in December 2003 that led the White House to hope the president could weather the public's growing unease about his Iraq policy. The major story was the capture of Saddam Hussein by U.S. troops after many months of searching. He was apprehended in a humiliating situation in a dugout beneath a rural house in central Iraq. Many Arabs in neighboring countries were stunned that the flamboyant dictator had permitted himself to be taken alive and without a fight. Bush's approval ratings jumped the following week. In another case, the Libyan dictator, Muammar Gaddafy, suddenly bowed to years of U.S. and British pressure and agreed to halt his secret program to produce WMD and allow international inspections of his industrial facilities. He also invited U.S. and British companies to upgrade Libya's industry and its export of oil. Libya honored its commitment, and six months later, in June 2004, the United States and Libya reestablished diplomatic relations after a lapse of twenty-four years. Bush supporters claimed that the president's tough policies on terrorism and the U.S. invasion of Iraq had produced the breakthrough with Gadaffy, under whom Libya had been labeled by several administrations as a supporter of international terrorism.

A second piece of good news for the Bush administration was an offer in November 2003 by Iran's hard-line government to accept IAEA inspections and unlimited access of its nuclear facilities. Iran's Revolutionary Islamic regime had previously denied that it was building a nuclear weapons plant, but it was persuaded by the joint efforts of Britain, France, and Germany, supported by Washington, to suspend this program in return for the West's lifting its economic sanctions. In June 2004, however, the IAEA reported that Iran had not complied with the agreement. Iran claimed that the Europeans and Americans had not carried out their promises and asserted the right to become a nuclear power if it so decided.

A third positive event in late 2003 was an announcement that the leaders of India and Pakistan had agreed to begin talks on dividing the disputed northern province of Kashmir, an explosive political issue that had brought these nuclear powers to the verge of war in 2002. Bush administration supporters claimed, with justification, that U.S. diplomacy had played a role and that the ouster of the Taliban government in Afghanistan and the establishment of good U.S.-Pakistan relations had been key factors in persuading India and Pakistan to negotiate.

MOUNTING THE POLITICAL COSTS OF WAR

Despite these positive developments at the end of 2003, the costs of Bush's hegemonic foreign policy came into sharper focus for the public and Congress in late 2003 and early 2004. Much soul searching prevailed in Washington regarding the effectiveness of the Coalition Authority's efforts to control security in Iraq in the face of a mounting insurgency, pressed by pro-Saddam militants and foreign fighters who allegedly had ties to Al Qaeda. Without security in the cities, it was difficult to repair Iraq's infrastructure, including its large oil industry, on which the country's future economic well-being depended. Mounting casualties among U.S. troops and shocking photos in the media contributed to a growing public suspicion that the Pentagon's handling of the postwar situation might be failing. In November the White House concluded that the U.S.-led occupation needed to end soon in order to remove Americans as the principal target of the terrorists. June 30, 2004, was chosen as the time for the coalition to end its occupation and turn over the job of governing Iraq to an interim government until national elections could be held, it was hoped, in January 2005. A provisional constitution was promulgated in the spring and an interim Iraqi cabinet was selected by the UN's representative and the U.S. Administrator, Paul Bremer. It took office on June 28. The future status of coalition forces remained ambiguous, however, and critics charged that the White House was turning over power to Iraqis in order to remove the war as a U.S. election issue in 2004. The granting of sovereignty had the beneficial effect, however, of clearing the way for the United Nations to return to Iraq and supervise the holding of elections and writing of a new constitution. The UN Security Council had unanimously approved this plan in April 2004.

The financial costs of the occupation in 2004 were running far higher than the Pentagon had predicted. Defeating the Iraqi insurgency was taking far longer, requiring more troops, and producing more casualties than the public had been led to expect. By spring the president's public approval rating dropped below 50 percent for the first time, and in June it stood at 44 percent in several opinion polls. His handling of the war was at 50 percent, a significant drop from December 2003. A contributing factor was the Abu Ghraib prisoner abuse scandal, which broke in the media early in 2004 and reflected poorly on the Pentagon's administration of the occupation. Whereas in December 2003 many political experts had been predicting that Bush was probably unbeatable in 2004, six months later they were concluding that this would be an extremely close election. Senator Kerry had voted for the Senate's war resolution in October 2002, but he now criticized Bush for grossly mismanaging postwar policy.

Spain's decision to withdraw its thousand-man contingent from Iraq was a damaging blow to the Coalition Authority's hopes of obtaining European support for reconstruction in Iraq. The stark reality was that Al Qaeda had cleverly exploited widespread antiwar sentiment in Spain, which now cost George Bush and Tony Blair the support of an important ally in the war against Saddam Hussein.

The mounting insurgency caused the Pentagon to rethink its plans to reduce the number of U.S. forces in Iraq to about 115,000. In April it announced that it would increase troop strength to 137,000 by calling up additional National Guard units and extending the tours of duty for others. Secretary Rumsfeld announced in the summer that some 12,000 troops would be withdrawn from South Korea and that 4,500 of them would be sent to Iraq to augment U.S. forces there. He also announced that seventy thousand would be withdrawn from Europe, most of them from bases in Germany. These decisions resulted from two unforeseen military realities: the insurgency was more widespread and damaging than anticipated, and the hoped-for commitment of additional troops from NATO and other countries had not occurred. In fact, at a NATO summit meeting in Istanbul in June, France and Germany reiterated that they would not send any troops to Iraq, although they were willing to train Iraqi police and army units outside the country. French President Jacques Chirac declared that NATO as an organization should not be involved in Iraq. Spain refused to reconsider its decision to withdraw troops; instead it joined France and Germany in an emerging European bloc that opposed Anglo-American policy in Iraq. Bush was able to persuade other coalition members, including Italy, Poland, Denmark, the Netherlands, and Australia to keep their forces in Iraq for the time being, even though public opinion in each country was somewhat opposed. With the insurgency expanding and the interim Iraqi government taking on administrative responsibility, the Bush administration concluded that it had little choice but to send additional American troops to prevent a potential civil war and assist the government to get control of the country. This was especially important in the Sunni areas that had strongly supported Saddam Hussein's Baathist regime. The financial cost of keeping 137,000 troops in Iraq through 2005, however, was projected by the Congressional Budget Office to be at least as high as in 2004. Even though the

UN had unanimously approved the transfer of authority from the Coalition Authority to an interim Iraqi government in June, no European country was willing to contribute substantial financial assistance to rebuild Iraq. Even oil-rich Arab states were reluctant. With the U.S. military carrying the major burden of providing security and U.S. agencies paying most of the bills for Iraq's reconstruction, the war's cost became a key issue in the 2004 election campaign.

Another cost was America's loss of public support abroad, especially among Europeans. As opinion turned against the U.S. policy and strong criticism of the United States dominated Europe's media, some Democrats seized on this sentiment to criticize the Bush administration for severely damaging relations with America's longtime allies and friends. Tony Blair's political difficulties in Britain were cited by U.S. war critics to show that even Britain might turn against "Bush's war." In June a *Washington Post*/ABC News poll of U.S. opinion found that Bush and Kerry were running about even on this question: "Whom do you trust to do a better job of handling the U.S. campaign against terrorism, Bush or Kerry?" On another question—"All in all, considering the costs to the United States versus the benefits to the U.S., do you think the war with Iraq was worth fighting, or not?"—52 percent answered no and 47 percent said yes, a reversal from six months earlier.[1] A *Wall Street Journal*/NBC poll published a week later reported that 56 percent of the public thought it was right for the United States to have gone to war, down from 69 percent a year earlier. Moreover, Bush's approval rating in the *WSJ* poll had dropped from 56 percent in mid-2003 to 45 percent in June 2004. Clearly, the public was impatient over the length and cost of the war and its casualties, which in June reached 860 American troops dead and thousands more wounded.

WAS THE IRAQ WAR A "BRIDGE TOO FAR?"

By summer 2004 a major issue before the American people was the one that historian Paul Kennedy had anticipated in his *The Rise and Fall of the Great Powers:* Had the United States "overstretched" in its drive for world hegemony by invading Iraq and attempting to impose a Western-style democracy on its people? In light of the high price Americans were now asked to pay for the intervention, President Bush argued that freedom and democracy were the desire of people in all the Arab countries, not just Iraq, and that U.S. forces would remain in Iraq as long as was necessary to help the interim government hold elections and bring terrorism under control. But at what price? John Kerry, now the Democratic Party's nominee for president, did not at first disagree with Bush that it was necessary to remove Saddam Hussein from power. But he argued that the administration had misled the American public on the reasons for going to war and had grossly mismanaged the occupation. He also criticized Bush for faulty management of relations with America's allies, which had resulted, he said, in many of them refusing to support the war and rebuild Iraq. In a July op-ed column in the *Washington Post,* Kerry wrote that the United States should offer the allies economic incentives to encourage them to join the reconstruction effort: "Our goal should be an alliance commitment to deploy a major portion of the peacekeeping force that will be needed in Iraq for a long time to come." Kerry said that "Iraq must be separated from our politics" and concluded that "with the right kind of leadership from us, NATO can be mobilized to help stabilize Iraq and the region. And if NATO comes, others will too."[2] Kerry thus showed a degree of bipartisan support for the administration's goal of building a peaceful, democratic, and friendly Iraq in the Middle East. But he also displayed, in the view of many, a good deal of wishful thinking about the allies' willingness to share the burden in Iraq.

Several earlier Democratic contenders for the party's nomination, whom Kerry defeated in the primaries, were sharply antiwar in their views. The most prominent was the outspoken former governor of Vermont, Howard Dean, who strongly attacked Bush for the decision to go to war and for bungling the occupation of Iraq. By calling for the early withdrawal of American troops, Dean tapped into the deep concerns of a vocal minority of Democrats who wanted the party to blast Bush for taking the country into an unnecessary war and "lying" about WMD. Dean was the early front-runner among Democrats for the nomination, but he failed to attract enough support in the primaries to prevent Kerry's emergence as the party favorite. Kerry had supported the 2002 Senate vote to authorize Bush to launch a war against Iraq, but many Democrats did not agree with his position. It remained an open question whether he would be able to unite the party behind him in the presidential race.

Bush and Vice President Cheney had argued forcefully in early 2003 that ousting Saddam Hussein's regime was a vital national interest, for two major reasons: he already possessed WMD and was in the process of acquiring nuclear ones as well; Saddam had links to Osama bin Laden's terrorist organization and intended to supply it with WMD for use against the United States. Following nine months of intensive searches in Iraq after the war ended, neither a UN inspection team nor a CIA-appointed American team of weapons experts found any significant evidence to show that Saddam had rebuilt his WMD capability during the 1990s. Regarding links between Saddam and Al Qaeda, the bipartisan 9/11 Commission, which investigated the intelligence breakdown that resulted in the disaster, failed to find any conclusive evidence that Saddam Hussein had conspired with it in the events of September 11.[3] When neither reason for the war was substantiated, the administration then emphasized the crimes that Saddam Hussein had committed against his own people and in Kuwait, asserting that Iraq and the world were better places without the hated tyrant. Another unstated reason for ousting Saddam's regime was to facilitate an Israeli-Palestinian peace settlement by removing the principal military threat to Israel in the Middle East. In 1981 Israel had bombed Iraq's nuclear weapons plant because it had evidence that Saddam would use these weapons to threaten it. Under pressure from Washington, Israel remained out of the 1991 Gulf War but was dissatisfied that Saddam's regime had not been ousted at that time. By overthrowing Saddam in 2003, Bush believed that he had removed a major impediment to persuading Ariel Sharon to withdraw his troops from the West Bank and Gaza and to accept a peace deal that guaranteed Israel's borders and created a Palestinian state. In May 2004 Sharon persuaded his cabinet to dismantle Israeli settlements and withdraw troops from Gaza by 2005. He continued, however, to build a protective barrier in the West Bank to prevent Palestinian terrorists from entering Israel.

UNSTATED STRATEGIC REASONS FOR WAR

Were there larger, unstated, strategic reasons that caused President Bush and Prime Minister Blair to conclude in 2002 that Iraq's regime must be ousted by force in 2003? A reasonable case can be made, I believe, that Bush's controversial decision for war was based on his assessment that vital interests were at stake, but were not explained to the public. This left his stated reasons for launching the war open to sharp criticism when no clear evidence was found to support them.

One unstated reason for confronting Iraq may be summarized as follows. The United States faced a serious credibility test immediately after 9/11 among leaders in many countries, friendly and otherwise, over its willingness to use military force if this resulted in large numbers of military casualties and incurred high financial costs. Afghanistan did not result in serious costs to the United States, so there remained reasons to doubt America's willingness to fight a major war to defend its vital interests. Following the withdrawal of U.S. troops from Lebanon (1984) and Somalia (1993) due to large casualties, the perception grew among hostile governments and terrorist groups that America was a "paper tiger." Even allies began to wonder whether the United States had the "staying power" to fight a protracted and costly global war against Al Qaeda terrorists. Leaders of nations like Iraq, Iran, Libya, and North Korea remembered that the American public had demanded the withdrawal of U.S. troops from Vietnam when casualties became high and victory was not in sight. After Al Qaeda's massive bombings at two U.S. embassies in East Africa and U.S. Air Force facilities in Saudi Arabia, plus a devastating attack on the USS *Cole* in Yemen, President Clinton's response seemed to many observers to be too mild, as was Jimmy Carter's to Iran's kidnapping of American diplomats in 1979.

The American-led military defeat of Saddam Hussein's armies in the 1991 Gulf War led President George H. W. Bush to remark that America had finally "put Vietnam behind us." But the continuing terrorist attacks in the 1990s led leaders in Iraq, Iran, Syria, and Afghanistan to conclude that the United States, for all its military power, would not fight a costly war against international terrorists because the American public would accept only cost-free wars, as in Haiti, Bosnia, and Kosovo. George W. Bush thus faced a major test of wills, first with the Taliban regime in Afghanistan, which protected Osama bin Laden's installations, and thereafter with Iraq and Iran, which hoped to drive the United States out of the Persian Gulf. A case can be made that had Bush appeared indecisive about using massive force, even a war of choice, to confront growing dangers to U.S. economic and world-order interests in the Middle East, Al Qaeda would eventually have found a new home in Iraq, Yemen, or Pakistan (if President Musharraf were ousted from power or assassinated).

Another strategic consideration that likely played a role in the U.S.-British decision to invade Iraq was their calculation that Osama bin Laden's prime objective was the overthrow of Saudi Arabia's monarchy and its replacement by a radical Islamic regime. Osama, an exiled Saudi dissident, made no secret of this aim, and he recruited many other Saudis into the Al Qaeda organization for that purpose. In 2003 the United States withdrew all its military forces from the kingdom in order to defuse Al Qaeda's claim that "American infidels," in cooperation with a corrupt monarchy, had damaged Saudi Arabia's culture and defiled its Muslim shrines. George Bush and Tony Blair feared that the Saudi monarchy might not move quickly or aggressively enough against Al Qaeda to save itself. Were that to occur, the three largest Persian Gulf oil-producing states, which hold the world's largest known reserves, would be controlled by anti-Western regimes. Although these countries would still need to sell their oil, the prices they could charge by manipulating world markets would be a dangerous (vital) threat to the economic well-being of the United States, Europe, and Japan. By removing Saddam Hussein's hostile regime, the United States and Britain would rid the Middle East of its most threatening tyrant and ensure that one of the key Persian Gulf oil states remained in friendly hands should Al Qaeda succeed in Saudi Arabia. The threat of a devastating blow to the U.S. economy, larger than the one that resulted from an Arab oil embargo in 1973, is a vital national interest that no American president could ignore and remain in office. However, neither George Bush nor any other president would find it politically prudent to tell the American people that they needed to go to war to protect America's high standard of living.[4]

LEGITIMATE USES OF PREEMPTIVE MILITARY FORCE

The intervention in Iraq and the resulting split in the Atlantic Alliance poses a fundamental question regarding the use of American military power in the twenty-first century. Under what circumstances does an external threat to U.S. security become so dangerous that the president is justified in using military force, even if his action is opposed by major allies and the United Nations? It is clear that the president has authority and the responsibility to use whatever means are available, including the unilateral use of force, to prevent an attack on the U.S. homeland. President Kennedy's plan in 1962 to launch a preemptive strike against Soviet missile installations in Cuba demonstrated this. President Bush's decision to invade Afghanistan following the 9/11 attacks was another example. Similarly, few would argue that a dangerous threat to an important ally—for example, Germany, Japan, or Britain during the Cold War—would have required the president to use force to defend them, even though the United States itself was not threatened.

But the more difficult question is: should Washington respond with preemptive military action to serious international threats that do *not* involve either U.S. territory or that of an ally? This situation occurred in Somalia, Haiti, Bosnia, and Kosovo, and in each case the U.S.-led interventions were collective, preemptive actions not involving an ally. In all of them the United States had the approval of either the United Nations for its action (Somalia, Haiti, Bosnia), or NATO (Kosovo). The Clinton administration hailed these interventions as evidence of its collaborative foreign policy. Opponents of George Bush's preemptive invasion of Iraq argue that it was an unnecessary use of force because that country had been largely disarmed by UN arms inspectors during the 1990s and did not pose an imminent threat to its neighbors or the United States. Still, Saddam Hussein had made war on Iran and Kuwait earlier and had tried for years to acquire nuclear as well as chemical and biological weapons. Iraq was also a major supporter of terrorism against Israel. In sum, Iraq posed a real threat to its neighbors in the Middle East.

A crucial issue for the Bush administration in 2002 was whether these circumstances qualified Iraq as a dangerous threat to vital U.S. interests, justifying the use of large military forces without the support of many allies and the Security Council. In my view, they did. This was true also in 1990 when George H. W. Bush decided that Iraq's invasion of Kuwait was so dangerous to America's strategic interests in the entire Middle East that he had to lead a major attack against Iraq. He was strongly supported by British Prime Minister Margaret Thatcher and other European allies. However, in 1990 this threat was not sufficiently dangerous to persuade most Democratic senators to vote for the war. In 2002 George W. Bush persuaded most Democratic senators to vote yes, including John Kerry and John Edwards, who ran for president and vice president in 2004.

Even if one concluded, as Bill Clinton did in 1998, that Saddam Hussein posed a dangerous world-order threat to U.S. interests and should be removed, the difficult question remained: How should Washington organize an international coalition to accomplish that objective? If it could not, should the United States proceed alone? Some in the Bush administration argued in 2002 that NATO, not the United Nations, should be the vehicle for invading Iraq because it included Britain, which was already committed to using force, as well as other NATO members who were willing to join a coalition. The problem was that key NATO allies—France, Germany, Belgium, Canada, and Turkey—wanted the United Nations to approve the use of force. President Bush therefore faced the decision in March 2003 whether to launch a preemptive war without UN or NATO authorization but with support from Britain, Spain, Poland, and Australia, among others. I believe he was justified in doing so after he obtained the authorization of Congress in 2002. In the final analysis, it is the president's responsibility to defend America's vital interests even when most other countries do not agree with his actions. Bush acted after concluding that removing Saddam Hussein would preserve America's strategic presence in the Persian Gulf and rid the region of a dangerous dictator. In that judgment he was correct.

The high price that Bush paid at home could not be adequately gauged until after the November 2004 elections. A key factor in the public's assessment was whether the president was justified to launch the war based on what many believed were exaggerated intelligence estimates that Iraq possessed WMD. In July 2004 the Senate Select Committee on Intelligence, after a lengthy investigation of the CIA's handling of information about the WMD danger posed by the Iraqi regime, unanimously concluded that there had been no WMD in Iraq and no relationship between its government and the 9/11 attacks. Vice President Cheney had continued to make that claim as late as the spring of 2004. Senator Pat Roberts, Republican chairman of the Intelligence Committee, was asked at a press conference whether Congress would have supported a war resolution in 2002 had it been aware of this information. He responded, "I don't know," adding that he probably would have voted for war on humanitarian grounds, as he had on Bosnia. The ranking Democrat on the same committee, Senator Jay Rockefeller, was more emphatic: "We in the Congress would not have authorized that war, in 75 votes, if we knew what we know now." However, he acknowledged that the measure might have passed with fewer votes. As a result of the war, Rockefeller said, "the U.S. standing in the world has never been lower."[5]

An important lesson to be learned from America's war in Iraq is this: When democratic governments like those in Britain and America decide to make war on a country where the direct danger is not clear, it is prudent to obtain the consent of key allies and, if possible, the United Nations, and not proceed immediately to war on the assumption that others will eventually be persuaded of the correctness of the decision. Such an assumption proved wrong for the Johnson administration in the Vietnam War, and it was increasingly the case with Iraq. The fallout in Britain from the duration and the mounting costs of the occupation of Iraq became so marked in mid-2004 that Tony Blair was in danger of losing the leadership of his Labour Party. George Bush also saw his approval ratings plunge. By the end of the summer, however, Bush had regained a small lead over Kerry in the polls and Blair's leadership also had strengthened. In November American voters would have a chance to decide whether the country was in better hands with the incumbent president, or whether the war's large costs made it desirable to change leadership and follow a more collaborative internationalism in foreign policy.

CHAPTER 11

LIMITS TO THE EXERCISE OF HEGEMONIC POWER

2004 was the first election opportunity that Americans had to express a preference for President Bush's policy based on the unilateral exercise of American power, or one that Senator John Kerry emphasized, collective action in support of U.S. world-order interests. The political campaign that commenced that summer highlighted a major challenge that George Bush faced in commencing hostilities against Iraq, in spite of opposition from key allies and the UN Security Council. Kerry threw down the gauntlet to the president in a speech at his party's convention in Boston: "I know what we have to do in Iraq," he declared. "We need a president who has the credibility to bring our allies to our side and share the burden, reduce the risk to American taxpayers, and reduce the risk to American soldiers. That's the right way to get the job done and bring our troops home. . . . That won't happen until we have a president who restores America's respect and leadership—so we don't have to go it alone in the world." Kerry assured his audience that he would "never hesitate to use force when it is required."[1] The *Washington Post* called the speech disappointing: "Mr. Kerry could have spoken the difficult truth that U.S. troops will be needed in Iraq for a long time. He could have reaffirmed his commitment to completing the task of helping build democracy. Instead, he chose words that seemed designed to give the impression that he could engineer a quick and pain-

187

less exit."[2] In June Kerry had asserted in a speech in Baltimore that the United States needed allies to share the burden in Iraq, arguing that it was essential that "the president get real support—not resolutions, not words—but real support of sufficient personnel, troops, and money, to assist in the training of security forces, in order to be able to guarantee a rapid, real transition, and most importantly to be able to provide adequate security on the ground."[3] A casual observer might be forgiven for wondering how a president John Kerry would have persuaded NATO allies such as France, Germany, Belgium, and Canada to contribute troops and funding for the occupation and rebuilding of Iraq when they were convinced that the war was a mistake and that the security situation there was getting worse.

President Bush staunchly defended his decision for war. In a major foreign policy address at Oak Ridge, Tennessee, he argued that it was necessary to oust Saddam Hussein's regime even though no WMD were found: "Today, because America has acted and because America has led, the forces of terror and tyranny have suffered defeat after defeat, and America and the world are safer." Responding to Democratic critics such as Senator Edward Kennedy, who had attacked him for taking the country to war on false pretenses, Mr. Bush argued that his decision was correct. "We removed a declared enemy of America . . . who had the capability of producing weapons of mass murder and could have passed that capability to terrorists bent on acquiring them. In the world after September the 11th, that was a risk we could not afford to take."[4] A casual observer could also be forgiven for wondering what had happened to the administration's forceful argument in 2002 that it was necessary to overthrow Saddam Hussein's regime because it already had WMD and intended to use them against the United States.

From their foreign policy statements made during the campaign, it appeared that, despite differences on Iraq, both George Bush and John Kerry had concluded that the United States should continue to exercise a world hegemonic leadership role because of its overwhelming economic, political, and military power. Where they differed was on *how* the United States should use its power and the importance of gaining support from key allies and the United Nations before launching military actions abroad. Like Bush, Kerry favored free trade, the stationing of U.S. forces abroad, and alliances with friendly countries in order to protect vital American interests. However, Kerry and Bush had different ideas on how extensively they would consult with the European allies in making decisions about using U.S. military forces against another country. They also disagreed on how to deal with North Korea's nuclear weapons program. They agreed, however, on the need for a robust American world role, placing them at odds with a third-party candidate, the antiestablishment maverick Ralph Nader, who represented the small Reform Party. Nader was opposed to both Republican and Democratic stands on free trade and U.S. military bases abroad. Like Howard Dean earlier, he favored the immediate withdrawal of U.S. troops from Iraq.

REDEPLOYMENT OF U.S. TROOPS FROM GERMANY AND SOUTH KOREA

President Bush's decision, announced in Cincinnati on August 16, to withdraw up to seventy thousand U.S. troops from Europe and East Asia represented a major shift in U.S. post–Cold War policy and suggested that his administration might be downgrading the importance of Europe in America's global defense posture. Although the plan was negotiated with their governments, public unease resulted in Germany and in South Korea, where major cuts were planned. However, most Americans thought the troop reductions were correct and agreed with the president's statement in Cincinnati: "For decades America's armed forces abroad have essentially remained where the wars of the last century ended, in Europe and Asia." The previous strategy, he said, was designed to protect the Europeans from Soviet aggression, a "threat that no longer exists."[5] The Pentagon announced that reductions would be made primarily in Germany, where some seventy-one thousand military personnel were stationed in 2004, plus one hundred thousand dependents and support staff. In South Korea, where thirty-eight thousand troops were based, about fourteen thousand were to be withdrawn, with some four thousand redeployed to Iraq, leaving a force of twenty-four thousand to reassure South Korea and Japan of America's continuing commitments to their security. Some forty thousand American troops, including two army divisions, would be removed from Germany over six years, while the Pentagon planned to station smaller, more mobile brigade-sized forces, in several Eastern European NATO countries closer to the Middle East.

Bush's announcement prompted Kerry to assert, in an August 18 speech to the same veterans' group in Cincinnati, that "withdrawing troops from Europe will further undermine already strained relations with long-time NATO allies." He deplored troop cuts in South Korea "at the very time we are negotiating with North Korea—a country that really has nuclear weapons. This is really the wrong signal to send at the wrong time."[6] However, editorial opinion in major newspapers supported the president's move, and Kerry quietly dropped his criticism. Coming at a time when the administration was criticized by both Democratic and Republican members of Congress for failing to deploy large enough forces to Iraq to provide security there, the redeployment of troops from Europe and Asia to augment the force in Iraq tended to defuse pressure from Congress to enlarge the overall size of the Army, a move that the administration resisted.

Reducing U.S. troop strength in Europe had the effect of reminding Europeans of their own responsibilities for providing defense. At a time when the United States was increasing its already huge defense budget, European governments, including Britain, were reducing theirs. Germany, for example, had cut its army to the point where the Schroeder government would not have been able to send a contingent of respectable size to Iraq even had his government reversed its policy and joined the U.S.-led coalition. The U.S. redeployment of troops from Europe and Asia was considered by most Americans to be overdue. The Pentagon argued that it would save U.S. taxpayers money and make U.S. forces more mobile in a new kind of war with Al Qaeda. The move also put allies and friends on notice that the U.S. security umbrella does not come free of charge.

9/11 COMMISSION'S PRESCRIPTION FOR HOMELAND DEFENSE

An important event in the national debate during the summer of 2004 was the publication of the final report of the National Commission on

Terrorist Attacks upon the United States, better known as the 9/11 Commission. The document was unanimously endorsed by a bipartisan group of five prominent Republicans and five prominent Democrats, and it immediately became a best-seller across the country. Most of the report dealt in detail with the history of the Al Qaeda organization, its daring attacks on U.S. diplomatic and military installations abroad during the 1990s, and what it characterized as a shocking lack of coordination in the U.S. intelligence community that led to its failure to detect the plot to use passenger planes to attack New York and Washington, D.C. The last three chapters contained the commission's recommendations as to what should be done to reorganize the U.S. intelligence community to prevent additional Al Qaeda attacks. They were titled "Foresight—And Hindsight"; "What to Do? A Global Strategy"; and "How to Do It? A Different Way of Organizing the Government." The most prominent recommendation was for the appointment of a national intelligence director (NID) within the White House with authority to supervise fifteen different intelligence agencies, approve their budgets, and exercise major influence on the appointment of their top officials.

The commission's chairman and vice chairman, Thomas H. Kean and Lee H. Hamilton, respectively, said in subsequent television interviews that they intended to bring pressure on the executive and legislative branches of government to move immediately to implement its recommendations. Some of these could be accomplished by executive order by the president, but others, including budget authority, reorganization of intelligence agencies, and creation of a National Counterterrorism Center, required legislation. The leaders of the Senate and House of Representatives exhibited little inclination to start hearings or contemplate new legislation before the November elections. However, wide public support for the commission, intense lobbying by families of September 11 victims, and extensive coverage by the media persuaded congressional leaders to hold public hearings immediately and to plan on scheduling a vote before November. This huge public interest in the issue during the election year persuaded a reluctant Congress to act.

Among the many merits of the 9/11 Commission's report, according to observers, was its reluctance to place blame for the 2001 disaster on either President Clinton or President Bush. It criticized Clinton for a lack of a forceful response after the 1998 bombings of two U.S. embassies in East Africa but noted that his decisions had been made "under extremely difficult domestic political circumstances," among them that his political opponents "were seeking the President's impeachment."⁷ The report also concluded that the public was not sufficiently aroused before September 2001 to enable either president to take sustained action against Al Qaeda. A more direct intervention against its sanctuary in Afghanistan before 9/11, it noted, "must have seemed . . . to be disproportionate to the threat." The commission was also restrained in its criticism of the CIA for lack of coordination with other intelligence agencies: "Before 9-11 no agency had more responsibility—or did more—to attack al Qaeda, working day and night, than the CIA. But there were limits to what the CIA was able to achieve in its energetic, worldwide efforts to disrupt terrorist activities or use proxies to try to capture or kill Bin Laden and his lieutenants."⁸ In effect, it concluded that the CIA had not been in a position before 9/11 to urge a more robust policy against targets in Afghanistan.⁹

The media generally praised the commission's report. The *Washington Post* commented editorially that "most important is the commission's unwavering insistence—coming at a time when America's commitment is starting to waver—on the fundamental importance of countering Islamist terrorism in the coming generation." The paper thought that the quality of the commission's work and the strength of its evaluation of the bureaucratic problems "should serve as a catalyst for a tremendously important discussion: Is America prepared to commit itself to this war for the long term, and how must society be organized to do so?"¹⁰ David Brooks, a columnist for the *New York Times,* praised the report for emphasizing that the United States was not engaged in a war on terrorism but instead is in the midst of an ideological conflict with a "hostile belief system that can't be reasoned with but can only be destroyed or utterly isolated."¹¹

Another columnist, David Ignatius, observed in a review of the commission report for the *Washington Post* Book World: "If the 9-11 report had been written as a novel, nobody would believe it." He thought "the idea was so far-fetched"—that a group of Islamic fanatics, whom the CIA knew about, had entered the country and used planes to kill three thousand people, an event that "knocked the United States so far off balance that, nearly three years later, it still hasn't recovered." Ignatius was surprised, however, that the commission had not adequately addressed the Israeli-Palestinian issue, which he said had contributed to the willingness of the hijackers to become martyrs. "What drove Atta, the middle-class son of an Egyptian attorney, to turn himself into a human missile?" The reviewer thought it odd "in a report that aims to be comprehensive, to find almost no mention of the Arab-Israeli conflict as a source of tension in the Middle East—and no urging of a revived American role in peace negotiations."[12]

THE LIMITS OF HEGEMONY: THE INTERNATIONAL DIMENSION

By the summer of 2004, few Americans doubted that the United States had suffered a serious decline in influence and prestige around the world resulting from its invasion and occupation of Iraq. European public opinion and the view of many governments was that the war was a grave mistake and that Bush's decision to ignore key allies and the United Nations had been a huge blunder, if not illegal. Anti-Americanism had risen sharply across the Middle East as a result of the war. The *Washington Post* reported that two Zogby polls, conducted in six Arab countries in June, had found that negative opinion toward the United States was almost universal. In Egypt, an important ally, 98 percent of the population had an unfavorable view of the United States. In Morocco it was 88 percent, and in Saudi Arabia it was 94 percent. U.S. policies, rather than American values and culture, were the major issue, according to the poll results. When asked what their first thought was when they heard the word "America," respondents replied: "Unfair foreign policy." A chief reason cited was U.S. support of Israel against the Palestinians. Most of those polled thought the U.S. invasion of Iraq had caused more terrorism and that Iraq was worse off now than it had been under Saddam Hussein.[13]

Anti-U.S. sentiment in Europe was not as deep as in the Middle East countries, but no one doubted the extent of public disillusionment with U.S. policy among Europeans. Opinion polls showed that the Abu Ghraib prison scandal, which became public knowledge in 2004, had a major negative impact on European opinion of the United States, much of it directed at George Bush personally rather than at the American people. U.S. policies in Iraq and on the Israeli-Palestinian conflict, plus the arrogance that Europeans sensed in U.S. leadership, affected negatively the policies of key NATO governments, including those of France, Germany, Belgium, Spain, and Canada. Even in Britain, one of the few major European countries to join the coalition in Iraq, the war was deeply controversial.

While Republicans and Democrats accepted the reality that Bush administration policies had contributed to the decline in America's image, they differed on the implications for future foreign policy. Kerry deplored the sharp drop in U.S. prestige that he attributed to Bush's unilateral policies. Bush argued that whenever the United States uses force, some allies will not agree, in which case a president will have to decide what is needed to protect U.S. security and not be dissuaded by reluctant allies or world opinion. Iraq was such a case, he asserted. Moderate voices on this issue tended to be drowned out by partisan campaign rhetoric, however. For example, the views of two key members of the Senate Foreign Relations Committee, Republican Richard Lugar and Democrat Joseph Biden, did not receive the wide public attention they deserved. Along with many of their colleagues, Lugar and Biden believed that ousting Saddam Hussein's regime was necessary, but they were critical of Bush for his handling of the occupation and for not doing more to mitigate the opposition of France, Germany, and Russia before the invasion was launched. The withdrawal of Spain and the Philippines from the coalition in 2004 contributed to the moderates' view that the White House could have done a better job of diplomacy in explaining U.S. policy and listening to the views of allies.

The remarkable negative shift in foreign opinion in just three years after the 9/11 attacks raised a fundamental question about Washington's ability to persuade other countries to accept U.S. leadership at a time of increased international danger. Despite the Bush administration's expectations in 2002 that many countries, including non-European ones, would join in providing security and rebuilding Iraq along democratic lines, by mid-2004 those hopes had turned to deep frustration. The governments of Pakistan, India, South Korea, and others showed great reluctance to send peacekeepers to Iraq, and several coalition members indicated their intention to withdraw their troops by the end of 2004. Lack of security was cited by Kofi Annan as the reason for UN reluctance to return personnel to Iraq after the bombing of its headquarters in Baghdad in 2003.

In sum, America had lost its ability to persuade other governments to accept its leadership in the rebuilding and pacification of Iraq, a clear signal that its hegemonic power had declined. Did this portend a permanent decline? This was an unanswerable question in 2004.

LIMITS TO HEGEMONY: DOMESTIC POLITICAL CONSIDERATIONS

In a democracy like the United States, the ultimate decision on whether the government continues to pursue a high degree of hegemonic influence rests with the voters. They must decide whether the price for conducting such a foreign policy is too high, or manageable, and select a president and members of Congress who reflect their views. In the months before the 2004 elections, the answer was unclear. The rising costs of keeping 137,000 U.S. troops in Iraq well into 2005 caused dissatisfaction among those in Congress who wanted to spend more money on domestic programs. The fast-rising cost of health care was a major issue cited in opinion polls as needing more government attention. Another pressing issue was bolstering energy resources at a time when the price of gasoline and heating oil was increasing steadily due to uncertain world oil supplies and America's huge need of imported oil to satisfy the growing needs of millions of motorists. The economic problem was highlighted when the government announced that the federal budget deficit for fiscal 2004 was $419 billion, the highest on record. Democrats blamed George Bush's 2001 tax cuts, while Republicans claimed the cuts were necessary to cope with the recession and stimulate future economic growth. However, job growth in July and August was far below expectations, and this news resulted in the stock markets dropping significantly.

An added factor weighing on public opinion was mounting U.S. casualties in Iraq. By September the number of dead from the war and occupation of Iraq surpassed one thousand, and the wounded exceeded seven thousand. Although the figures were far less than at the height of the Vietnam War, the large toll in dead and wounded was nevertheless high, and Americans wanted to know when the fighting would stop and the troops would return home. This was a particularly sensitive issue for the White House because it had hoped that relinquishing authority to the Iraqi transitional government in June would reduce U.S. casualties and also encourage Iraqis to do more fighting. In the short term, this move had done neither.

Regardless of who eventually won the 2004 presidential election, neither George Bush nor John Kerry would be able to pursue the degree of hegemonic foreign policy practiced by Bill Clinton in the late 1990s, or Bush early in the 2000s. The limited duration and few casualties that resulted from Clinton's interventions in Bosnia, Kovoso, and Haiti insulated his administration from serious public criticism of his interventionist policies, even though congressional critics questioned why the United States had paid most of the bills for those operations. The large costs, both human and financial, of Bush's interventions in Afghanistan and Iraq and the Pentagon's inability to end the insurgencies in either country in 2004 encouraged Kerry, critics in Congress, and the media to denounce Bush's unilateral policies. *Washington Post* columnist Jim Hoagland underscored this point in a June 24 commentary, "The Toll of 'No More Iraqs.'" He predicted that the threshold for preventive wars had been raised significantly by the Iraq war and that "widespread disillusionment will also seriously undercut idealistic rationales for deploying U.S. forces overseas, including for humanitarian interventions." That judgment may have been premature. Even when the number of U.S. deaths in Iraq reached one thousand there was no groundswell of support for the view that the war had been a mistake and that American troops should be withdrawn. Instead, there was recognition that withdrawing before a democratic Iraqi government was functioning would be a great blunder.

Nevertheless, the price of America's exercise of hegemonic power in Iraq would make it more difficult for either a president Bush or a president Kerry to muster the needed public support to carry out Bush's ambitious goal of fostering democracy in all the countries of the Middle East. This growing reality was illustrated by the publication during the summer of 2004 of two books that challenged the basis of Bush's war on terrorism and his intervention in Iraq. One of them, *Imperial Hubris: Why the West Is Losing the War on Terror*, was a frontal attack on the Bush administration for its misunderstanding of the threat posed by Osama bin Laden and Al Qaeda, and for its policies for dealing with the danger. The anonymous author was identified simply as "a senior U.S. intelligence official with nearly two decades of experience in national security issues related to Afghanistan and South Asia." Media sources identified him as a career CIA intelligence analyst who had been permitted by the agency to publish his sharp criticism of government policy on terrorism if his name was withheld. The book strongly criticized Bush's decision to downgrade the war against Al Qaeda and instead launch the invasion of Iraq. In the opinion of "Anonymous," the U.S. government, under both presidents Clinton and George W. Bush, completely misunderstood the nature of the threat posed by Osama bin Laden's organization and therefore was losing the war on terrorism. It will continue to do so, he argued, until Washington changes its policies to meet the long-term threat posed by Al Qaeda to the entire non-Muslim world.[14]

A second book critical of U.S. policy in both the Clinton and Bush administrations was authored by Patrick Buchanan, a conservative Republican pundit who had been a third-party candidate for president in 1996. Titled *Where the Right Went Wrong: How Neoconservatives Subverted the Reagan Revolution and Hijacked the Bush Presidency*, the book elaborated Buchanan's quarrel with Bush for abandoning the Republican Party's conservative roots and embracing a globalist missionary role that was bankrupting the United States. Buchanan, who had been labeled a neo-isolationist by critics during the 1990s, claims to be a nationalist who believes U.S. foreign policy must be based on a prudent view of national interests, not on the romantic idealism of neoconservatives who want to remake the world in America's image. It was a theme that resonated with many conservatives and some liberals who deplored the influence that neoconservatives had on George Bush to launch a war in Iraq.[15]

HEGEMONIC POWER AND AMERICAN DEMOCRACY

America's pursuit of the role of hegemonic superpower raises other important questions for its citizens to ponder. First, is the U.S. government, with its system of limited powers and checks and balances, capable *and willing* to sustain a consistent world leadership role over the coming decades? Second, is America willing to be a *collaborative* partner in exercising its power, or does it instead intend to pursue a more nationalist, *unilateralist* means of asserting its national interests? Third, are Americans more willing, or less, to support strong presidents who sometimes defy domestic and world opinion to take large foreign policy risks in the belief that they are defending vital U.S. interests? Presidents Lyndon Johnson and Richard Nixon paid large political prices for continuing a war in Southeast Asia that Americans decided was too costly in lives and treasure. After the Vietnam experience America turned inward for nearly ten years and questioned whether it wanted to continue pursuing a hegemonic leadership role, until Ronald Reagan persuaded a majority to try again in the 1980s.

Divided government, in which the president is of one party and Congress is controlled by the opposition, is not an ideal way for a superpower to conduct foreign policy. That situation existed in both the Nixon and Reagan administrations. Political gridlock, which occurred in 2001 because the country was evenly divided between Republicans and Democrats, is also a hindrance to the conduct of a consistent foreign policy. In mid-2004 the electorate again appeared to be evenly divided between Republicans and Democrats, opening the possibility that the November election might result in four more years of gridlock over social legislation; judicial appointments; and, probably, foreign policy. Because of the costs of war in Afghanistan and Iraq, the public might choose a president and Congress who preferred to concentrate on dealing with the problems of "Middle America" instead of the Middle East.

America in the twenty-first century is unlike Britain in the nineteenth when London presided over a worldwide empire with remarkable consistency in policy. At that time Britain was led by a relatively small group of leaders who decided the country's national interests and pursued the policies necessary to advance them. They were not concerned about other countries' internal politics but rather with international behavior. The British public was not involved in deciding the large issues of foreign policy until early in the twentieth century. In present-day America, by contrast, foreign policy is influenced by a mass media and huge numbers of interest groups that demand to be heard by the president and Congress, often playing them against each other.

This raises a central question about whether the United States, as its democratic system is constituted, is capable of sustaining into the twenty-first century the hegemonic role played in Bill Clinton's second administration and by George W. Bush after 2001. The Iraq war brought this issue into clearer focus for the public during 2004. If elected president, John Kerry would no doubt pursue a policy far more restrained than Bush's and more collaborative with the European allies, particularly France and Germany.

REORIENTING U.S. STRATEGIC POLICY FROM EUROPE TO EAST ASIA

The new long-term war against Islamic-sponsored terrorism resembles the West's forty-year Cold War struggle against the spread of Soviet-sponsored communism. That reality is forcing the U.S. government to rethink its strategic goals as the world's only superpower. Alliances concluded during the early period of the Cold War to contain Soviet power are not adequate for the new challenges of the twenty-first century. Islamic extremists who use sophisticated methods of terrorism to change the foreign policies of nation-states pose a new kind of global danger. Unlike with the Soviet threat, the menace posed by Osama bin Laden and the Al Qaeda network may not be containable and will require, as the 9/11 Commission suggested, eradication by force. President Bush's decision to eliminate Saddam Hussein's regime caused a major breach in the Atlantic Alliance, forcing its members to decide whether or not they would support his view of the threat in the Middle East. Some did, but many key members—France, Germany, Belgium, Canada, and Turkey—did not. Spain joined them in opposition in 2004.

The probability now looms that this split in NATO is a fundamental, not a temporary, parting of the ways. The crisis results from significant differences in the way many European states view their interests in the twenty-first century, which are not the same as those they held during the Cold War years. This change is exacerbated by the recent movement toward a more tightly knit EU in which foreign and defense policy is a major issue among its members. I believe it is more likely than not that the EU will increasingly pursue an independent foreign policy, different from and frequently opposed to that preferred by Washington. Iraq is only the most dramatic example of this trend. The reality is that NATO is no longer an organization that shares America's vision of how to create a stable world order. European countries today are less willing than is America to challenge forcefully Islamic extremists abroad, in part because of preoccupation with Muslim immigrants at home. Another factor is that, after enduring an entire century of devastating continental wars and fear of another during the Cold War, most Europeans are exhausted emotionally and simply do not have the will to engage in conflicts outside Europe. In fact, pacifism among young people is growing in most West European countries.[16]

As a result of these realities, Europe and America are, after sixty years of fighting fascism and communism, now parting company on the issue of sharing responsibility for defending a new world order against the threat of extremist Islamic fundamentalism. Even though NATO agreed in 2002 to take on a major security responsibility in Afghanistan, its financial aid and troop support for that effort was still seriously deficient in 2004. Similarly, despite U.S. and British success in persuading the UN Security Council in 2004 to play a role in implementing Iraqi national elections in 2005, French objections made it difficult for NATO to launch a large police-training program to provide security for them. In fact, most Europeans did not see any need for their governments to send troops or spend money on Middle East security programs. Even Britain bowed to this sentiment when the Blair government announced in July significant reductions in its armed forces and defense budget. Britain too may eventually be persuaded to move away from its close strategic relationship with the United States and adopt policies that are closer to the emerging EU policies favored by France, Germany, and Spain.

Henry Kissinger, one of America's best known Atlanticists, acknowledged in July 2004 that Europe may no longer be a reliable strategic partner of the United States. In a remarkable commentary in the *Washington Post*, the former secretary of state and noted historian observed that "Europe finds itself suspended between institutions not yet sufficiently cohesive for a strategic foreign policy and nations sufficiently advanced on the road toward European unification to have lost their historic conviction about a national foreign policy." Paradoxically, Kissinger observed, "the structural estrangement of America from Europe is taking place as the center of gravity of international politics is shifting to Asia." Kissinger proposed that America should rethink its strategic policy and focus attention on the emerging powers of Asia, specifically China, Japan, India, and Russia. "Though they reject what they consider hegemonic aspects of U.S. policy, they do so on a case-by-case basis via traditional diplomacy." To them, "Iraq is not a litmus test of American moral fitness to lead but of American endurance in pursuit of strategic insights."[17]

In 2004 the United States faced a fundamental dilemma in its future relations with the world: Should it try to find a new, modified strategic understanding with the major countries in the EU or hold the transatlantic alliance in abeyance for the time being while forging a new strategic relationship with the four major Asian powers cited by Kissinger—China, Japan, India, and Russia? The objective of this new relationship would be to maintain regional peace in East Asia while fighting Al Qaeda terrorists in countries such as Indonesia, the Philippines, Malaysia, and Thailand, where Islamic extremists provide them support. A precedent for this great power Asian security cooperation is the five-power effort sponsored by the Bush administration to persuade North Korea to abandon its nuclear weapons program. Eventually the new security grouping could include Great Britain, Australia, and South Korea, all of which have modern military forces to contribute to agreed-upon peace-enforcing missions.

The United States will be obliged to pay a significant price for participation in an Asian security arrangement. A major concession would surely be that Washington would need to modify its propensity to act as the paramount power in East Asia, pursuing its own interests without adequate regard for the interests of its partners. President Bush demonstrated his willingness to accept such restraint by his collaborative approach to North Korea. A similar effort to persuade Taiwan to abandon its goal of national independence would be a test of America's willingness to work with others to find a diplomatic solution to a dangerous regional problem. A third challenge is how to deny Al Qaeda training facilities in the remote areas of Indonesia, Malaysia, and the southern Philippines. All these are dangers that require collective efforts by regional powers.

Because of America's costly occupation of Iraq in 2004, John Kerry attracted wide support for his view that the country should not engage in large-scale military operations abroad without the support of major allies and, ideally, the United Nations. Opinion polls conducted in September found that although a majority of the public supported Bush in the war on terrorism, a slight majority disapproved of his handling of the Iraq war. Democratic Party leaders hoped that the November election would focus on the economy and loss of jobs during Bush's tenure, but the war appeared to be a major issue for many voters. This raised the possibility that if reelected, George Bush might decide to modify the hegemonic superpower posture he outlined in his National Security Strategy document of 2002 (see chapter 4). However, no matter whether Bush or Kerry won the election, the war on Al Qaeda terrorism would remain the highest priority in U.S. foreign policy.

EPILOGUE

The presidential election on November 2, 2004, resulted in a clear victory for President George Bush over Senator John Kerry, both in the electoral count and in the popular vote. Unlike the delayed result in the 2000 presidential race, the key state of Ohio gave the president a sufficiently large majority to persuade Kerry to concede the election on November 3.

Pundits speculated about why the Iraq war was not the primary issue for most voters and why Bush's unilateralist internationalism did not resonate to his disadvantage in key state contests. During the closing weeks of the campaign Kerry had strongly criticized Bush for misleading the country about WMD as a reason for launching the preemptive war on Iraq and for his "incompetence" in handling Iraq's internal security after major combat ended in April 2003. Three influential newspapers—the *Washington Post,* the *New York Times,* and the *Economist*—had cited the lack of progress in dealing with Iraq's insurgency as a major reason for their decisions to endorse John Kerry. Nevertheless, Bush's leadership qualities were cited by many voters as a factor in their support for him over Kerry.

The reaction in Europe, according to the *New York Times,* was one of "shock"; much of the population "simply couldn't conceive that people would want to keep Mr. Bush in power." The *Wall Street Journal* reported that Bush's victory would embolden "those who want to build a new international structure that doesn't rest primarily on Europe's alliance with the U.S." It cited a statement by French foreign minister Michel Barnier after Bush's victory: "Our world needs several powers. They [the U.S.] are the first. We are in the process of gathering the pieces and the will to become another power."[1] The *Financial Times,* in a report from Brussels, cited a statement by President Jacques Chirac that it had become "evident that Europe today has more need than ever to reinforce its unity and dynamism." Chirac subsequently met with German chancellor Gerhard Schroeder and Spanish prime minister Jose Luis Zapatero, all strongly opposed to U.S. and British intervention in Iraq, to discuss their future policies.[2]

What changes, if any, might Europe and the world expect in foreign policy from George Bush's second administration? Washington pundits speculated on a range of possibilities, some of it wishful thinking by former Clinton officials who thought the president should adopt a bipartisanship approach in order to heal the rift with European allies. However, the most authoritative view on what to expect from the new administration was expressed by President Bush himself in a wide-ranging press conference on November 4. Regarding the war in Iraq, Bush insisted that "every civilized country also has a stake in the outcome of this war. Whatever our past disagreements, we share a common enemy. . . . I'll continue to reach out to our friends and allies, our partners in the E.U. and NATO, to promote development and progress, to defeat the terrorists, and to encourage freedom and democracy as alternatives to tyranny and terror." In response to the question, "Do you believe that America has an image problem in the world?" the president said: "Listen, I've made some very hard decisions—decisions to protect ourselves, decisions to spread peace and freedom. And I understand that in certain capitals and certain countries those decisions were not popular." With regard to Iraq, the president observed: "And of course the Iraq issue is one that people disagreed with. And I don't need to rehash my case. But I—I did so—I made the decision I made in order to protect our country, first and foremost. I will continue to do that, as the president. But as I do so, I will reach out to others and explain why I make the decisions I make."[3]

The president affirmed that his foremost concern was to defend the national interests of the United States, as defined by him. While pledging to "reach out to others," Mr. Bush did not promise to consult them before making final decisions, but only to *explain why I make the decisions I make*" (emphasis added). If that is his approach to allies and friends, President Bush will no doubt encounter as much difficulty in getting support in Europe and the Middle East in his second administration as he did in his first.

In response to a question about his plans to facilitate the peace process between Israel and the Palestinian Authority, the president referred to his June 24, 2002, Rose Garden pledge (see chapter 2), stating: "I think it's very important for our friends, the Israelis, to have a peaceful Palestinian state living on their border. And it's very important for the Palestinian people to have a peaceful, hopeful future. That's why I articulated a two-state vision in that Rose Garden speech. I meant it when I said it and I mean it now." The illness of Palestinian leader Yasser Arafat and his urgent evacuation to a hospital in Paris, where he subsequently died, raised hopes in Europe and the Middle East that President Bush would feel emboldened to make a new effort to bring the Israeli government and a new Palestinian leadership together to agree on an overall peace accord that met the fundamental needs of both sides. A settlement of the vexing Israel-Palestinian crisis would presumably help the president to find support among friendly Arab countries and others in Europe to help with the long-term task of reconstruction in Iraq.

On the controversial question of promoting freedom and democracy abroad, the president was assertive about its continuing importance in his foreign policy: "There is a certain attitude in the world by some that says, you know, it's a waste of time to try to promote free societies in parts of the world. I've heard that criticism. I remember I went to London to talk about our vision of spreading freedom throughout the greater Middle East. And I fully understand that that might rankle some and be viewed as folly. I just strongly disagree with those who do not see the wisdom of trying to promote free societies around the world." The president reaffirmed his strong belief in America's "promotion-of-values" interest (see chapter 4), by stating: "You cannot lead this world and our country to a better tomorrow unless you see a better—unless you have a vision of a better tomorrow. And I've got one based upon a great faith that people do want to be free and live in democracy."

What, then, are the country and the world likely to find in George Bush's foreign policy in a second term that is different from the first? Will there be more unilateral decision making in Washington? Will the use of preemptive military action become more, or less, likely as part of the president's national strategy into 2009?

It may reasonably be argued that George Bush, having won a clear election victory, will now conclude that he has a mandate to continue the hegemonic policies he pursued in the first term, to reshape the world to fit a vision of peace and freedom based on a *Pax Americana* that could entail the frequent use of military power to bolster an assertive foreign policy. But, it can also be argued persuasively, I believe, that the costs of pursuing the robust hegemonic foreign policies that characterized the first Bush administration will weigh heavily on decision makers in his second term. They are already deeply concerned that America's economic strength is being eroded by "imperial overreach" in its huge security obligations abroad.[4]

President Bush will, in my view, continue the grand stategy and policies outlined in his September 2002 National Security Strategy document (see chapter 4). But he will probably adopt a less confrontational approach to dealing with allies and friends. European leaders, many of whom hoped for his defeat in the November 2 election, will wait to see what measures he may take to mend political fences. His pressure on Israel and the Palestinians to make peace would go a long way toward gaining European and Arab support for his policy in Iraq. On the fundamental question of the future of NATO, however, I believe it is unlikely that the breach that opened in March 2003 between France and Germany on one side, and Britain and the United States on the other, over intervention in Iraq can be healed in the foreseeable future. A growing divergence of national interests exists between large continental states like France, Germany, and Spain, and those of the United States and Britain regarding Middle East policy and a range of economic and environmental issues. Other states, such as Italy and Poland, have so far supported President Bush on his policies in the Persian Gulf, but public support in those countries is eroding. Even Tony Blair has had difficulty keeping the support of his own Labour Party.

America was fortunate in November 2004 that John Kerry chose not to contest the outcome of the close election in Ohio and, in a fine display of statesmanship, conceded the victory to George Bush. Despite the rancor of the campaign and disillusionment of many Americans over the election's outcome, the country is stronger and more confident about the future than it was during George Bush's first term. It may therefore be time for a less strident tone in foreign policy and for greater emphasis on the domestic needs of the country during the next years. Barring additional terrorist attacks on the United States, George Bush may have less incentive in his second term to use military force to promote America's hegemonic influence in the world.[5]

NOTES

CHAPTER 1

1. For an account of the U.S. drive for empire in the late nineteenth century, see Ivan Musicant, *Empire by Default* (New York: Henry Holt, 1998).

2. Andrew Bacevich, *American Empire: The Realities and Consequences of U.S. Diplomacy* (New York: Harvard University Press, 2003). See chapter 1, "The Myth of the Reluctant Superpower."

3. The postwar transition in U.S. foreign policy is described in Stanley Hoffmann, *Primacy or World Order* (New York: McGraw-Hill, 1980). See part 3, "An American Policy for World Order."

4. Adam Watson, *The Limits of Independence: Relations between States in the Modern World* (London: Routledge, 1997), 137–38.

5. Paul Kennedy, *The Rise and Fall of the Great Powers* (New York: Random House, 1987). See "The United States: The Problem of Number One in Relative Decline," 514.

6. Joseph S. Nye, Jr., *Bound to Lead: The Changing Nature of American Power* (New York: Basic Books, 1990), 38–40.

7. Ronald Steele, *Pax Americana* (New York: Viking, 1967), vii.

8. William J. Fulbright, *The Arrogance of Power* (New York: Vintage Books, 1966), 15.

9. Donald E. Nuechterlein, *America Overcommitted: U.S. National Interests in the 1980s* (Lexington: University Press of Kentucky, 1985).

10. Zbigniew Brzezinski, *The Choice: Global Domination or Global Leadership* (New York: Basic Books, 2004).

11. *The National Interest*, Winter 2003–2004, 10.

12. Bacevich, *American Empire*, 6.

13. Chalmers Johnson, *The Sorrows of Empire: Militarism, Secrecy, and the End of the Republic* (New York: Henry Holt, 2004).

14. Inis L. Claude, Jr., *States and the Global System* (New York: St. Martin's, 1988), 99–100.

15. Niall Ferguson, *Colossus: The Price of America's Empire* (New York: Penguin Press, 2004), 8, 29.

CHAPTER 2

1. Bob Woodward, *Bush at War* (New York: Simon & Schuster, 2002), 144.
2. Bob Woodward, *Plan of Attack* (New York: Simon & Schuster, 2004), 87–88.
3. Woodward, *Bush at War*, 197, 222.
4. Ibid., 325.
5. Woodward, *Plan of Attack*, 1–3.

CHAPTER 3

1. Richard A. Clarke, *Against All Enemies: Inside America's War on Terror* (New York: Free Press, 2004), 32.
2. Ibid., 265.
3. Available at www.whitehouse.gov/news/releases/2002/06/20020001-3.html.
4. Woodward, *Bush at War*, 343–44.
5. Woodward, *Plan of Attack*, 150–51.
6. "Cheney Says Peril of a Nuclear Iraq Justifies Attack: Sees Big Risk in Inaction," *New York Times*, August 27, 2002, A1.
7. "Rumsfeld Says Allies Will Support U.S. on Iraq," *New York Times*, August 28, 2002, A1.
8. Available at www.whitehouse.gov/news/releases/2002/09/20020912-1.html.
9. *New York Times*, October 11, 2002, A14.
10. *New York Times*, October 12, 2002, A10.
11. Despite the urgings of Senator Levin and several other Democrats, an amendment to oblige the president to return to Congress for another vote to authorize war was voted down.
12. *New York Times*, October 12, 2002, A1.

CHAPTER 4

1. A comprehensive analysis of the National Security Strategy document may be found in Robert Jervis, "Understanding the Bush Doctrine," *Political Science Quarterly* 118, no. 3 (2003).
2. These and subsequent quotations are excerpted from a presidential docu-

ment, *The National Security Strategy of the United States of America* (Washington, D.C.: The White House, September 22, 2002).

3. Joseph S. Nye, Jr., *The Paradox of American Power: The World's Only Superpower Can't Go It Alone* (Oxford: Oxford University Press, 2002). See chapter 5, "Redefining the National Interest."

4. See Donald Nuechterlein, *America Recommitted: A Superpower Assesses Its Role in a Turbulent World,* 2nd ed. (Lexington: University Press of Kentucky, 2000), chap. 1, "Defining U.S. National Interests: An Analytical Framework."

5. See chapter 11 for a discussion of this policy course.

6. Woodward, *Plan of Attack,* 254.

7. *New York Times,* January 29, 2003, A12.

8. These and the following quotations are from Powell's address to the UN Security Council, reported by the *New York Times,* February 6, 2003, A16.

9. In May 2004 a high-level U.S. arms inspection team, which had spent months in Iraq searching for WMD, reported that no WMD were present there. Secretary Powell publicly retracted that part of his UN presentation, saying that his citation of Iraq's stockpiles of WMD had been based on faulty intelligence provided by both U.S. and foreign intelligence services. See also chapter 11.

10. "Scowcroft Lambasts Core Bush Foreign Policies," *Financial Times,* October 14, 2004, 4.

11. Ivo Daalder and James Lindsay, *America Unbound: The Bush Revolution in Foreign Policy* (Washington, D.C.: Brookings Institution, 2003), 195. See chapter 8, "The Bush Strategy."

CHAPTER 5

1. *New York Times,* July 25, 2003, A1.

2. The report of the bipartisan 9/11 Commission is discussed in chapter 11.

3. In 2004 Congress urgently drafted legislation to create a national intelligence director (NID), who would have broad authority over all the intelligence agencies. See chapter 11.

4. "America Needs More Spies," *The Economist,* July 12, 2003, 30.

5. Robert Gates, *From the Shadows* (New York: Simon & Schuster, 1996), 554–55.

CHAPTER 6

1. Thomas L. Friedman, *The Lexus and the Olive Tree: Understanding Globalization* (New York: Farrar, Straus, and Giroux, 1999), 93.

2. "Manufacturing Job Losses Continue, Lawmakers Stirred to Find Answers," *Washington Post,* August 2, 2003, A8.

3. "Trade with China Is Heating Up as a Business and Political Issue," *Wall Street Journal,* July 30, 2003, A1.

4. "Facing Up to the China Challenge," *Washington Post,* August 1, 2003, E1.

5. This dilemma in U.S. priorities was highlighted in a widely discussed book by Peter G. Peterson, *Running on Empty: How the Democratic and Republican Parties Are Bankrupting Our Future and What Americans Can Do About It* (New York: Farrar, Straus, and Giroux, 2004).

CHAPTER 7

1. The final report of the bipartisan 9/11 Commission, issued in July 2004, is discussed more fully in chapter 11.

2. *Washington Post,* August 7, 2003, A21.

3. "Bush Urges Commitment to Transform Mideast," *Washington Post,* November 7, 2003, A1. His speech is discussed more fully in chapter 8.

4. For additional discussion on the problems of occupation in Iraq, see chapter 11.

5. In March 2004 Spain had a change of government and decided to withdraw its troops.

CHAPTER 8

1. Charles A. Beard, *President Roosevelt and the Coming of the War* (New Haven, Conn.: Yale University Press, 1948).

2. *The National Security Strategy of the United States,* 2002, 3.

3. "Transforming the Middle East," *Washington Post,* August 7, 2003, A21.

4. "U.S. Resists Entreaties to Send Peacekeepers to Liberia," *New York Times,* July 22, 2003, A3.

5. *New York Times,* August 1, 2003, A23.

6. "Let the Fight Begin," *New York Times,* August 21, 2003, A25.

7. Samuel P. Huntington dealt with the large issue of promoting Western values in the Middle East in his influential 1996 study *The Clash of Civilizations and the Remaking of World Order* (New York: Simon & Schuster, 1996). See "Islam and the West," 209–218.

8. "A Democracy Policy," *Washington Post,* November 8, 2003, A26.

9. "A Global Democracy Policy," *New York Times,* November 8, 2003, A26.

10. "Mr. Rumsfeld's Reponsibility," *Washington Post,* May 6, 2004, A24.

CHAPTER 9

1. "Kennedy Lashes Out on Iraq, Angering G.O.P. Colleagues," *New York Times,* September 27, 2003, A7.

2. "2 Servings of Reality, Please," *New York Times,* September 28, 2003.

3. See Office of Management and Budget, *Historical Tables of the Federal Government: Fiscal Year 2005 (2004)* (Washington, D.C.), 45–52.

4. *U.S. Military Spending, 1946–2004* (Washington, D.C.: Center for Defense Information, 2004).

5. "Blind into Baghdad," *The Atlantic,* January–February 2004, 62, 74. See also "Catastrophic Success: The Strategy to Secure Iraq Did Not Foresee a 2nd War," *New York Times,* October 19, 2004, A1.

6. "The Unbuilding of Iraq," *Newsweek,* October 6, 2003, 34–37.

7. "Bush, Iraq, Tax and Clark," *Wall Street Journal,* September 25, 2003, A19.

8. *Washington Post,* October 5, 2003, B7.

9. "World's View of U.S. Sours after Iraq War, Poll Finds," *New York Times,* June 4, 2003, A19.

10. "U.S. Asks Muslims Why It Is Unloved. Indonesians Reply," *New York Times,* September 27, 2003, A10.

11. *New York Times,* October 3, 2003, A23.

12. "Cheney Goes on Offensive Over Iraq: Unyielding Speech Is Designed to Regain Support," *Washington Post,* October 10, 2003, A1.

13. Kennedy, *The Rise and Fall of the Great Powers,* 514–15.

14. *New York Times,* October 9, 2003, A26.

CHAPTER 10

1. "Bush Loses Advantage in War on Terrorism," *Washington Post,* June 22, 2004, A1.

2. "A Realistic Path in Iraq," *Washington Post,* July 4, 2004, B7.

3. For a fuller discussion of the 9/11 Commission's report, see chapter 11.

4. It is noteworthy that in September 2004 a secret CIA National Intelligence Estimate, prepared in 2003 before the invasion of Iraq, became public in Washington. It warned of the likelihood of instability in postwar Iraq and the large costs that could be incurred by U.S. forces during the occupation. The *New York Times* quoted "a senior administration official" who likened President Bush's decision to invade Iraq to having risky surgery even when doctors warn of serious side effects. The *Times* quoted the official as observing: "We couldn't live with the status quo because, as a result of the status quo in the Middle East, we were dying and we saw the evidence of that on Sept. 11." ("Prewar Assessment on Iraq Saw Chance of Strong Divisions," *New York Times,* September 28, 2004, A1, A11.)

5. "Panel Condemns Iraq Prewar Intelligence," *Washington Post,* July 10, 2004, A1.

CHAPTER 11

1. "Kerry's Acceptance: We Have It in Our Power to Change the World Again," *New York Times,* July 30, P6.

2. "Missed Opportunity," *Washington Post,* July 30, A18.

3. "Kerry Urges More Effort on Iraq Aid," *Washington Post,* June 29, 2004, A18.

4. "Bush Forcefully Defends War, Citing Safety of U.S. and World," *New York Times,* July 13, 2004, A1.

5. "Bush Tells Veterans of Plan to Redeploy G.I.'s Worldwide," *New York Times,* August 17, 2004, A6.

6. "Bush Troop Realignment Plan Is Decried," *New York Times,* August 19, 2004, A6.

7. *The 9/11 Commission Report* (New York: W. W. Norton, 2004), 348.

8. Ibid., 349.

9. Some observers did not agree that the 9/11 Commission had done a good job on placing responsibility. Writing in *Harper's* (October 2004), Benjamin DeMott strongly criticized the commission for not holding anyone to account, including either president, for the disaster. See his "Whitewash as Public Service: How the 9/11 Commission Report Defrauds the Nation."

10. "The 9/11 Panel's Report," *Washington Post,* July 23, 2004.

11. "Report Defines Our Predicament," *New York Times,* August 1, 2004.

12. "The Book on Terror," *Washington Post,* Book World, August 1, 2004, 5.

13. "Poll Shows Growing Arab Rancor at U.S.," *Washington Post,* July 28, 2004, A26.

14. *Imperial Hubris: Why the West Is Losing the War on Terror* (Washington, D.C.: Brassey's, 2004).

15. Patrick J. Buchanan, *Where the Right Went Wrong: How Neoconservatives Subverted the Reagan Revolution and Hijacked the Bush Presidency* (New York: St. Martin's, 2004).

16. A strong case for the transatlantic alliance was made by Timothy Garton Ash in his 2004 book *Free World: America, Europe, and the Surprising Future of the West* (New York: Random House, 2004).

17. "A Global Order in Flux," *Washington Post,* July 9, 2004, A10.

EPILOGUE

1. "Europe Surveys Its Options after Bush's Victory," *Wall Street Journal,* November 4, 2004, A12.

2. "European Leaders Remain Split over Bush Election and Future Diplomacy," *Financial Times,* November 6, 2004, 4.

3. These excerpts of the president's November 4 press conference are from a transcript as reported by the *New York Times,* November 5, 2004, A16.

4. An insightful look at foreign policy in the second Bush term is contained in John Lewis Gaddis, "Grand Strategy in the Second Term," *Foreign Affairs,* January–February 2005, 2–15.

5. Many observers were encouraged by the president's selection of Dr. Condoleezza Rice as his secretary of state in the new administration.

INDEX

ABOUT THE AUTHOR

Donald Nuechterlein's long career includes the U.S. Navy in World War II, the U.S. Foreign Service, academe, and journalism. During his government service he worked in Berlin, Reykjavik, Bangkok, and Washington, D.C. He also served in the Office of the Secretary of Defense (ISA) during the 1960s. He was a founding faculty member of the Federal Executive Institute, where he taught international relations, and a visiting professor at the University of Virginia, George Washington University, Queen's University in Ontario, and the University of Kaiserslautern in Germany. He is the author of eight previous books on U.S. foreign policy, the most recent *America Recommitted: A Superpower Assesses Its Role in a Turbulent World* (2000). Mr. Nuechterlein is a columnist for several Virginia newspapers. He and his wife make their home in Charlottesville.